A MATTER OF
CRIME

A MATTER OF
CRIME

New Stories from
the Masters
of Mystery & Suspense

VOL. 1

Edited by

Matthew J. Bruccoli & Richard Layman

A HARVEST/HBJ BOOK

HARCOURT BRACE JOVANOVICH, PUBLISHERS

SAN DIEGO   NEW YORK   LONDON

"James Ellroy: An Interview," "The Black Dahlia" copyright © 1987 by James Ellroy.
"The Au Pair Girl," copyright © 1987 by Joyce Harrington.
"Bodyguards Shoot Second," copyright © 1987 by Loren D. Estleman.
"Far Eyes," copyright © 1987 by Robert Sampson.
"The Trouble Shooters," copyright © 1987 by Dan Brennan.
"Murder Most Kind," copyright © 1987 by B. M. Gill.
"It's a Hard World," copyright © 1987 by Andrew Vachss.
"Murder," by Enrique Anderson-Imbert, copyright © siglo xxi editores, s. a. de c. v., 1971; translation copyright © 1987 by Sara Heikoff Woehrlen.
"A Flash of Red," copyright © 1987 by Edward D. Hoch.
"Bale Jumpers," copyright © 1987 by Richard B. Harper.
"Deceptions," copyright © 1987 by Marcia Muller.
"To Sleep, Perchance to Dream," copyright © 1987 by J. Birney Dibble.
"China Blue," copyright © 1987 by David Gates.

Editorial correspondence should be directed to the editors at: Bruccoli Clark Layman, Publishers, Inc., 2006 Sumter Street, Columbia, SC 29201.
ISSN 0892-9416
ISBN 0-15-657719-4
Designed by G.B.D. Smith
Printed in the United States of America
First Harvest/HBJ edition 1987
A B C D E F G H I J

Contents

Editors' Note

A Matter of Crime, Volume 1 launches a series of original paperbacks comprising the best of contemporary mystery and suspense fiction.

A Matter of Crime is a product of its own time. No good writer—or editor—ignores literary tradition; few good writers—or editors—are bound by it. While we admire the hardboiled fiction of the past half-century, we resist the inclination to extend past glories into the present. The contemporary writers who command our attention are those who write from the hardboiled tradition, not in imitation of it. Nor are we indifferent to the merits of other schools.

Convincing characters and realistic plots; stories about people with believable motivations, confronted by compelling situations: That is the material of *A Matter of Crime*. We restrict ourselves only to previously unpublished stories (and excerpts from works-in-progress) about crime—whether it be American or foreign, against individuals or against nations.

In Dashiell Hammett's "The Gutting of Couffignal," the Continental Op describes *The Lord of the Sea* by M. P. Shiel: "There were plots and counterplots, kidnappings, murders, prisonbreakings, forgeries and burglaries, diamonds large as hats and floating forts larger than Couffignal. It sounds dizzy here, but in the book it was real as a dime." The proof is in the reading. We trust you will find these stories as real as a dime.

A MATTER OF
CRIME

James Ellroy:
An Interview

In six years and seven novels, James Ellroy has
established himself as one of the most talented
crime writers in America. He is best known for
his three novels about Los Angeles police detective Lloyd Hopkins: *Blood on the Moon, Because
the Night,* and *Suicide Hill. Blood on the Moon*
is being made into a motion picture with James
Woods as Hopkins.

The mixture of procedural realism, psycholog-
ical complexity, and narrative drive that have
characterized Ellroy's work from the beginning
is displayed admirably in his most recent work,
The Black Dahlia, to be published this fall by The
Mysterious Press. Based on an unsolved 1947
murder that occurred in Los Angeles, where Ellroy was raised, *The Black Dahlia* is the story of
a policeman whose dark obsession with a murder
victim he never met controls his life. It is a novel
of uncommon quality.

The following interview was conducted by
phone. Ellroy was in Los Angeles researching his
next novel, which will involve some of the characters from *The Black Dahlia.*

AMOC: Your first novel was published in 1981,
when you were thirty-three. What inspired you, at
the brink of middle age, to begin writing fiction?
Ellroy: I didn't know thirty-three was middle-aged!

Anyway, it was time; I never wanted to do anything but write fiction. What surprised me was that it was crime fiction. I thought I'd write tortured, urban, mainstream fiction. Whatever gave me that fatuous idea, I don't know, since I can't stand reading stuff like that. But I thought that I didn't have the kind of brain that could come up with complex, well-layered plots. But the story that started building in my mind when I was thirty—when I started writing *Brown's Requiem*—was indeed very complex and well-layered, and, surprise of surprises, a first-person private eye book. So I just followed the lead. It was time. I wasn't getting any younger, and I jumped right in.

AMOC: Had you written anything before that time?

Ellroy: I had written nothing.

AMOC: What had you done?

Ellroy: Essentially I was a drunk and a drug addict and had spent the previous fourteen years in Los Angeles—sleeping in parks; sleeping in cheap pads, drug-recovery crash pads, drunk tanks; going to jail; shoplifting; pulling B and E's; and so forth.

AMOC: How much of the material that goes into your books is based on your early experience, and how much is based on new research?

Ellroy: The criminal stuff I know pretty well, mostly from doing county jail time. I wasn't any bad-ass, but I probably spent eight or nine months of my life in the LA county jail system. You stick around there, you listen, and you pick things up: the language, what these men—sleazy low-lifes, most of them—like to do, and so forth. For police procedure, I've talked to a lot of cops; I've read forensic textbooks; I've read a lot of true-crime documentary accounts. Most police work involves just plain logic. You start with a crime, and you start with a supposition. It doesn't take a really spectacular brain to figure out the simplest things to do early in the case. It's when the investigation gets complex that you have to go off into mastermind stuff, which is where most police novels and general detective books end up.

AMOC: Has there been a period before each of your books devoted to research? I know, for example, that right now you're in Los Angeles researching a book that won't be published until 1988. Is that the way you operate?

Ellroy: Well, *Brown's Requiem* has as its base the Club Mecca firebombing, LA, 1957, and I looked into that a little bit; I read the newspaper accounts. For *Clandestine*, which is set in 1951, I set out to do some research, but I got eyestrain from the microfilm, so I dropped it and just started work. The three Hopkins books, zero research. I knew the procedure, they were all set in the present, and essentially there was nothing to do. On *The Black Dahlia*, yes, a lot of research, although I've been conversant with the case, obsessed with the case even, for damn close to thirty years. I did chronologies of all the actual events and read up on it extensively, again on microfilm. My next book—*The Big Nowhere*—I'm researching heavily. I don't particularly like research, though. I get hopped up to write a book, and I want to write a book. Let's do it *now*. But on the historical stuff research is important. So I've been reading about the Red Scare and Hollywood in that era. I've talked to a few policemen out here about it. It wasn't essential to come out here to Los Angeles for that, but I've got the money now, and I figured why half-ass it? If

I can come out here, be-bop around a little bit, talk to some people and learn a few things, then it's well worth it. I'll be having dinner tonight with a man named Nick Beck, who's pretty amazing. He's an AP/UPI boxing stringer who grew up with Jim Jacobs, Mike Tyson's manager. The man is fifty-three or fifty-four, and he knows the low-life history of LA better than anyone I've ever known. He can be important for background. So I am doing the research, but I'm very anxious to start blocking out the book.

AMOC: Lloyd Hopkins, the detective of three of your novels, is a psychologically complex character, a psychotic who has a great deal in common with the people he is pursuing, which is maybe why he's so good at his job. Is Hopkins an unalloyed product of your imagination, or is there a model for him?

Ellroy: As I said in something I wrote for Otto Penzler's *Mysterious News*, Hopkins is my antidote to the world-weary, beer-drinking, woman-yearning, first-person PI hero that I despise. He's definitely not a nice guy; he is almost totally concerned with order. In fact, he has a pathological need to restore order to other people's lives, because there is no order in his own. I wanted to do a real, tough, repressed, right-wing LA cop. One of the things that surprised me is that he's pretty much an up-front psycho in the first two books, but in the third he begins to cave in a little bit, to come to grips with his humanity, and I think that is what his ultimate journey will be.

AMOC: In *Suicide Hill*, the third Hopkins book, he is emotionally drained at the end, and he seems to have gained enough self-awareness that he's afraid of his own obsessions.

Ellroy: Yes.

AMOC: The character's not spent?

Ellroy: No. There will be two more. I was here in LA last summer to work on the *Blood on the Moon* movie project, and I outlined the fourth Hopkins book. But I just signed a three-book contract with The Mysterious Press, and Otto Penzler and I decided that lengthier period books were the things to concentrate on for now. So I put the Hopkins aside, but sooner or later I'll get to it.

AMOC: What are the three books that you're under contract for with Mysterious Press?

Ellroy: My new book, *The Black Dahlia*, will be the first book in a quartet called, for lack of a better title, the "LA Quartet." *The Black Dahlia* is set in 1947–1949; *The Big Nowhere*, 1950. The subsequent books in this series will be set in 1956 and 1959. There'll be some recurring characters. For instance, unscrupulous Deputy DA Ellis Loew, a major character in *The Black Dahlia*, is an even bigger character in *The Big Nowhere*. There's a very minor character in *The Black Dahlia* named Buzz Meeks, a Hollywood fixer, who becomes the hero of *The Big Nowhere*. Dudley Smith, the demonic Irish cop of *Clandestine*, recurs in *The Big Nowhere*. Russ Millard, the fatherly older cop in *The Black Dahlia*, will return as an old man dying of cancer in the last book of the quartet. What I want to do is recreate the Los Angeles of my past, which I am totally obsessed with. The quartet will display LA's changing social and geographical and criminal history over the years from

1947 to 1959, with some recurring characters, but no continuing plot lines, essentially.

AMOC: Do you have anything to say about serial characters in general?

Ellroy: Yeah, I think that they burn out real easy, and I think they're great for establishing a readership, but become a detriment.

AMOC: Has Hopkins taken on those qualities for you?

Ellroy: I'm tired of him, and was infinitely relieved when Otto and I mutually agreed to put him aside for now. It's the reason that I chose only to do five Hopkins books. For one thing, he's too volatile to sustain indefinitely. Readers become enamored of your characters and want them to continue in the same vein. That sells you lots of books, gets you the readership and the money, but it can kill you as a writer. It's a self-limiting process. I don't want to get trapped that way. I want to do books in the first person and in the third person and in different periods. I don't want to get stale.

AMOC: *Blood on the Moon* is being filmed with James Woods as Hopkins. What has been your role with regard to that movie?

Ellroy: The book was optioned about a year and a half ago by James B. Harris, a filmmaker whose movies I respect. He produced a lot of old Stanley Kubrick flicks—*The Killing, Paths of Glory, Lolita*—and wrote and directed a nuclear war thriller called *The Bedford Incident*; and a good movie with James Woods five years ago that got limited release called *Fast Walking*, about a prison guard. Jimmy Harris has a great feel for crime fiction—he loves it. When he got stymied a little bit on the first draft of the script, he flew me out to Los Angeles and we restructured a contrapuntal story—Cop-Killer, Cop-Killer, Cop-Killer—into a strict police procedural. The movie will start shooting March 10th—I don't know the status of the final script. I wrote some scenes, but essentially it's Jimmy's script. What we did was talk and talk and talk and rehash the plot continually, so that the thematic gist of the book remained intact but the plot was reworked extensively.

AMOC: How do you feel about having your character transformed into a film personality, for lack of a better phrase?

Ellroy: A book is a book and a movie is a movie. The movie itself will not be my book, but will create a readership for my book. The paperback will get reissued; I'll gain readers that way. Plus a few bucks. Send me the check, Jimmy. Do it now.

AMOC: The Black Dahlia murder case, which is the subject of your novel that will be published in September, has figured repeatedly in your works, notably in *Clandestine*. The Black Dahlia is also mentioned in *Brown's Requiem* and *Suicide Hill*. What is it about the Black Dahlia that obsesses you so?

Ellroy: I'll give you a little bit of background. In 1958, when I was ten, my mother was murdered. It wasn't a brutal sex killing like The Black Dahlia, but a man picked her up in a bar and strangled her and dumped her in a roadway by a high school. The killer was never found. I went to live with my father then, and became obsessed with crime fiction: the Hardy Boys and Ken Holt; Nero Wolf and Mickey Spillane, and then the *real* stuff. Early in '59 my dad got me a book called *The Badge*, by Jack Webb, a paean to the Los Angeles Police Department that rehashed a lot of great old LA crimes. In it there was a hauntingly written ten-page summary of the Black Dahlia murder case—and I became *obsessed*. It was all the horror of my mother's death, plus a lot more. The Black Dahlia, Elizabeth Short, was tortured for days and then bisected and deposited nude at 39th and Norton in Los Angeles. I'm not a phobic person, and I tend not to have nightmares, probably because I lead such an adventurous fantasy life. But boy, oh boy, I was plagued by Dahlia nightmares for years and years and years. When I was thirteen, I met a kid my own age, and he became my best friend— we've been best friends for twenty-five years now— and he had heard about the Black Dahlia and was obsessed with her, too. So Randy Rice and I used to hash over the case. We'd do endless, endless riffs on it for years and years and years. I knew when I started writing that sooner or later I would write that book. *Clandestine*, which is set in 1951, was originally to have been The Black Dahlia. But it was 1980 when I wrote the book and John Gregory Dunne's novel *True Confessions*, nominally based on the Black Dahlia case, had been published several years before. Not knowing publishing the way I do now, I was afraid that would kibosh my selling a book based on the same case. So I put if off and put it off and put it off and got started on the Hopkins series. I'm glad I did, because the Hopkins books have taught me how to write. I think the book is substantially better and more powerful than it would have been had I undertaken it much earlier.

AMOC: Each of your novels is better than the last. Each one shows a marked increase in your skills as a writer, your ability to develop characters and sustain narrative drive.

Ellroy: That shows I'm doing my job.

AMOC: With *The Black Dahlia* you've reached a very high point. It's a most impressive novel. Have you reached the peak of your powers there?

Ellroy: No, I'm only 39 years old. I try to stay in a world of relative humility, where I see what I'm doing wrong. I don't get cocky; I don't think my shit doesn't stink. What I'm working on right now is scope. I want to write bigger books. I want to write more complex plots; broader reaching books socially. I think *The Black Dahlia*, which is in the first person, was the training ground for me to write an even larger, more densely populated book, but this time third-person, multiviewpoint, which is what *The Big Nowhere* will be.

AMOC: Do you ever see yourself writing about anything other than crime?

Ellroy: I'd love to do a first-person coming-of-age novel, autobiographical, shamelessly, of course, set in the mid-sixties. I would love to do a true-crime book, if the right case comes along and I get access to the police and their investigation.

AMOC: You are known as a tough critic of contemporary writers. Who do you admire and why do you admire them?

Ellroy: I think the best hardboiled writer right now, and the dominant hardboiled writer of the past thirty years, is Joseph Wambaugh. I think single-handedly he transformed the hardboiled hero from the private eye to the cop. I've learned a lot from him. Of course, it is his beat and it's my beat; he's Los Angeles and police, and I'm Los Angeles and police. I think Dutch

Leonard's middle books—*Split Images, City Primeval, Cat Chaser*—are very fine. There are individual novels that I've liked a lot . . . *Red Dragon* by Thomas Harris, *Switch* by William Bayer, *The Death of the Detective* by Mark Smith, *True Confessions* by John Gregory Dunne, a very fine, underrated book, *No Beast So Fierce* by Edward Bunker. Those are some books that I've admired. Of course the great guys, the really great ones: Hammett, Chandler, Ross Macdonald. Ross Macdonald—on an emotional level—for me is the great teacher. The great realist is Dashiell Hammett. I owe Raymond Chandler for illuminating my own home town with style. I think he's overrated, though; primarily he's a stylist.

AMOC: *The Black Dahlia* is going to attract a lot of attention in Hollywood. Do you have any interest in turning screenwriter and reaching that far larger audience?

Ellroy: None. None. Let me reiterate that a little bit. None: Zero, minus zero. I just want to write novels and maybe longer, broader short stories for *A Matter of Crime*. The long Chandler/Hammett short stories obsess me; the Hammett stories especially.

AMOC: Who do you write for? Do you write for some reader or do you write for yourself?

Ellroy: I write for myself. Sometimes I think I write for women I want to impress.

AMOC: You know what Freud said: There are only three reasons men write books: fame, money, and love of beautiful women.

Ellroy: Yeah, Freud was no dummy. I write for myself. You know about Stephen King being asked, "Why do you write these awful, scary books?" And he said, "Why do you assume that I have a choice?"

There's that factor, but most of all I love doing it. I have stories to tell. I don't really think about what they mean, and they don't come into perspective for me until after I have a sizable block of a book finished. But I have to write them for myself more than anything else. I certainly want the fame and the beautiful women. A few bucks wouldn't hurt, too.

The Black Dahlia

JAMES ELLROY

The place: LA. The time: 1946—scant months before the Black Dahlia murder case galvanized public interest as no local crime has before or since. In the chapter reprinted here, Bucky Bleichert and Lee Blanchard, ex-boxer cops and the novel's heroes, have just fought ten hard rounds as part of an LAPD scheme to promote passage of a bond issue that will raise cops' salaries. Bleichert joins Blanchard on the Department's elite Warrants Squad as his reward for the fight.

James Ellroy says: "The triumvirate of Bucky, Lee, and Kay forms the core of the book, the Dahlia driving each of them in different directions. Here are the three in their beginning."

Central Division Warrants was on the sixth floor of City Hall, situated between the L.A.P.D.'s Homicide Bureau and the Criminal Division of the D.A.'s Office—a partitioned-off space with two desks facing each other, two file cabinets spilling folders, and a map of the County of Los Angeles covering the window. There was a pebbled glass door lettered with "Deputy District Attorney Ellis Loew" separating the cubicle from the Warrants boss and D.A. Buron Fitts—his boss—and nothing separating it from the Homicide dicks' bullpen, a huge room with rows of desks and corkboard walls hung with crime reports, wanted posters, and miscellaneous memoranda. The more battered of the two desks in Warrants had a plate reading "Sergeant L. C. Blanchard." The desk facing it had to be mine, and I slumped into the chair picturing "Officer D. W. Bleichert" in wood next to the phone.

I was alone, the only one on the sixth floor. It was just after 7:00 a.m., and I had driven to my first day's duty early in order to savor my plainclothes debut. Captain Harwell had called to say that I was to report to my new assignment on Monday morning, November 17, at 8:00, and that the day would begin with the reading of the felony summary for the previous week, which was mandatory for all L.A.P.D. personnel and Criminal Division D.A.'s. Lee Blanchard and Ellis Loew would be briefing me on the job itself later, and after that it would be the pursuit of fugitive warrantees.

The sixth floor housed the Department's elite divisions: Homicide, Administrative Vice, Robbery and Bunco, along with Central Warrants and the Central Detective Squad. It was the domain of specialist cops, cops with political juice, and up-and-comers, and it was my home now. I was wearing my best sports jacket/slacks combo; my service revolver hung from a brand-new shoulder rig. Every man on the force owed me for the 8 percent pay raise that came with the passage of Proposition 5. My departmental juice was just starting. I felt ready for anything.

Except rehashing the fight. At 7:40 the bullpen started filling up with officers grumbling about hangovers, Monday mornings in general, and Bucky Bleichert, dancemaster turned puncher, the new kid on the block. I stayed out of sight in the cubicle until I heard them filing into the hall. When the pen fell

13

silent, I walked down to a door marked "Detectives' Muster Room." Opening it, I got a standing ovation.

It was applause military style: the forty or so plain-clothesmen standing at parade rest by their chairs, clapping in unison. Looking toward the front of the room, I saw a blackboard with "8 percent!!!" chalked on it. Lee Blanchard was next to the board, standing beside a pale fat man with the air of high brass. I sighted in on Mr. Fire. He grinned; the fat man moved to a lectern and banged on it with his knuckles. The claps trailed off; the men sat down. I found a chair at the back of the room and settled into it; the fat man rapped the lectern a last time.

"Officer Bleichert, the men of Central Dicks, Homicide, Ad Vice, Bunco, et cetera," he said. "You already know Sergeant Blanchard and Mr. Loew, and I'm Captain Jack Tierney. You and Lee are the white men of the hour, so I hope you enjoyed your ovation, because you won't get another one until you retire."

Everyone laughed. Tierney rapped the podium and spoke into an attached mike. "Enough horseshit. This is the felony summary for the week ending November 14, 1946. Pay close attention, it's a doozie.

"First off, three liquor store stick-ups, on the nights of 11/10, 11/12 and 11/13, all within ten blocks on Jefferson in University Division. Two teenaged Caucasians with sawed-offs and the heebie-jeebies, obviously hopheads. The University dicks have got no leads, and the squad boss there wants a Robbery team on it full time. Lieutenant Ruley, see me at 0900 on this, and all you men put out the word to your snitches—hophead-heister is a bad M.O.

"Moving east, we've got freelance prosties work-

ing the restaurant bars in Chinatown. They're serv-
icing their johns in parked cars, low-balling the girls
Mickey Cohen's been running there. Misdemeanor
stuff so far, but Mickey C. doesn't like it and the
chinks don't like it because Mickey's girls use the
hot-sheet flops on Alameda—all chink-owned. Sooner
or later we're looking at grief, so I want the restaurant owners pacified and forty-eight-hour detentions
on every Chinatown whore we can grab. Captain
Harwell's detaching a dozen nightwatch blues for a
sweep later in the week, and I want the Ad Vice
whore files gone through and mug shots and rap sheets
pulled for every independent hooker known to work
Central. I want two men from Central dicks in on
this, with Ad Vice supervising. Lieutenant Pringle,
see me at 0915."

Tierney paused and stretched; I looked around the
room and saw that most of the officers were writing
in notebooks. I was cursing myself for not bringing
one when the captain slammed the lectern with two
flattened palms. "Here's a collar that would please
old Captain Jack no end. I'm talking about the Bunker
Hill house burglaries Sergeants Vogel and Koenig
have been working on. Fritzie, Bill, have you read
the S.I.D. memo on it?"

Two men sitting side by side a few rows up from
me called out, "No, Cap," and "Nossir." I got a
good profile look at the older of them—the spitting
image of fat Johnny Vogel, only fatter.

Tierney said, "I suggest that you read it immediately after this briefing. For the benefit of you men
not directly involved with the investigation, the print
boys found a set of latents at the last break-in, right
near the silverware cupboard. They belonged to a

15

white male named Coleman Walter Maynard, age 31, two sodomy priors. A sure-fire degenerate baby raper.

"County Parole's got no line on him. He was living at a transient hotel on 14th and Bonnie Brae, but he hotfooted around the time the burglaries started. Highland Park's got four sodomy unsolveds, all little boys around eight years old. Maybe it's Maynard and maybe it isn't, but between them and the B and Es we could fix him up with a nice one-way to Q. Fritzie, Bill, what else are you working on?"

Bill Koenig hunched over his notebook; Fritz Vogel cleared his throat and said, "We've been working the downtown hotels. We collared a couple of key thieves and rousted some pickpockets."

Tierney tapped the podium with one heavy knuckle. "Fritzie, were the key thieves Jerry Katzenbach and Mike Purdy?"

Vogel squirmed in his chair. "Yessir."

"Fritzie, did they snitch each other off?"

"Ah . . . yessir."

Tierney rolled his eyes up to heaven. "Let me enlighten those of you not familiar with Jerry and Mike. They're homos, and they live with Jerry's mother in a cozy little love nest in Eagle Rock. They've been bedmates since God was a pup, but every once in a while they have spats and get the urge to chase jailhouse chicken, and one rats the other off. Then the other reciprocates and they both draw a County jolt. They stool on the gangs while they're in stir, pork nancy boys, and get sentence reductions for their snitch duty. This has been going on since Mae West was a virgin. Fritzie, what *else* have you been working on?"

There was a rumble of laughter throughout the room. Bill Koenig started to get up, twisting his head to see who the laughers were. Fritz Vogel pulled him back down by his coat sleeve, then said, "Sir, we've also been doing some work for Mr. Loew. Bringing in witnesses for him."

Tierney's pale face was working toward beet red. "Fritzie, I am the commander of Central Detectives, not Mr. Loew. Sergeant Blanchard and Officer Bleichert work for Mr. Loew, you and Sergeant Koenig do not. So drop what you're doing for Mr. Loew, leave the pickpockets alone, and bring in Coleman Walter Maynard before he rapes any more little boys, would you please? There's a memo on his known associates on the squadroom bulletin board, and I suggest all officers acquaint themselves with it. Maynard's a lamster now, and he might be holing up with one of them."

I saw Lee Blanchard leave the muster room by a side exit. Tierney leafed through some papers on the lectern and said, "Here's one that Chief Green thinks you should know about. Over the past three weeks someone's been tossing chopped-up dead cats into the cemeteries off Santa Monica and Gower. Hollywood Division's taken a half dozen reports on it. According to Lieutenant Davis at 77th Street, that's a calling card of nigger youth gangs. Most of the cats have been dumped on Thursday nights, and the Hollywood roller rink's open to shines on Thursdays, so maybe there's something to that. Ask around, talk to your informants and relay anything pertinent to Sergeant Hollander at Hollywood dicks. Now the homicides. Russ?"

A tall, gray-haired man in an immaculate double-breasted suit took the podium; Captain Jack plopped into the nearest available chair. The tall man carried himself with an authority that was more like a judge or hotshot lawyer than a cop; he reminded me of the smooth Lutheran preacher who palled around with the old man until the Bund went on the subversive list. The officer sitting next to me whispered, "Lieutenant Millard. Number two in Homicide, but the real boss. A real piece of velvet." I nodded and listened to the lieutenant speak in a smooth voice:

" . . . and the coroner ruled the Russo-Nickerson job murder-suicide. The Bureau is handling the hit-and-run on Pico and Figueroa on November 10th, and we located the vehicle, a '39 La Salle sedan, abandoned. It's registered to a male Mexican named Luis Cruz, age 42, of 1349 Alta Loma Vista in South Pasadena. Cruz is a two-time loser with a Folsom jacket—both falls Robbery One. He's long gone, and his wife claims the La Salle was stolen in September. She says it was snatched by Cruz's cousin Armando Villareal, age 39, who's also missing. Harry Sears and I took the initial squeal on this one, and eyeball witnesses said there were two male Mexicans in the car. Have you got anything else, Harry?"

A squat, dishevelled man stood up, turned around and faced the room. He swallowed a few times, then stammered, "C-C-C-Cruz's wife is sc-screwing the c-c-c-cousin. The c-c-c-car was never reported st-stolen, and the neighbors s-say that the wife wants the c-cousin's parole violated so C-C-Cruz won't find out about them."

Harry Sears sat down abruptly. Millard smiled at him and said, "Thanks, partner. Gentlemen, Cruz and Villareal are now state parole absconders and

18

priority fugitives. A.P.B.'s and absconder warrants have been issued. And here's the punch line: Both of these guys are boozehounds, with over a hundred plain drunks between them. Hit and run drunks are a damn menace, so let's get them. Captain?"

Tierney stood up and shouted "Dismissed!" Cops swarmed me, offering glad hands and back slaps and chucks under the chin. I soaked it in until the muster room cleared and Ellis Loew approached, fiddling with the Phi Beta Kappa key dangling from his vest.

"You shouldn't have slugged with him," he said, twirling the key. "You were ahead on all three cards."

I held the D.A.'s stare. "Proposition 5 passed, Mr. Loew."

"Yes, it did. But some patrons of yours lost money. Play it smarter here, Officer. Don't blow this opportunity like you did the fight."

"You ready, canvasback?"

Blanchard's voice saved me. I went with him before I did something to blow it then and there.

We headed south in Blanchard's civilian car, a '40 Ford coupe with a contraband two-way under the dashboard. Lee rambled on about the job while I looked out at the downtown LA street scene.

" . . . mostly we go after priority warrantees, but sometimes we chase down material witnesses for Loew. Not too often—he's usually got Fritzie Vogel running his errands, with Bill Koenig along for muscle. Shitbirds, both of them. Anyway, we get slack periods sometimes, and we're supposed to go by the other station houses and check the squadrooms for their priority stuff—warrants filed in the regional courts. Every L.A.P.D. station has two men working Warrants, but they spend most of their time catching squeals, so we're supposed to help out. Sometimes, like today, you hear something at the felony summary or get something hot off the bulletin board. If it's *really* slow, you can serve papers for the Department 92 shysters. Three bucks a throw, chump change. The real moolah's in repos. I've got delinquent lists from H. J. Caruso Dodge and Yeakel Brothers Olds, all the nigger stiffs the credit agents are too pansy to move on. Any questions, partner?"

I resisted the urge to ask "Why aren't you screwing Kay Lake?" and "While we're on the subject, what's the story on her?"

"Yeah. Why'd you quit fighting and join the Department? And don't tell me it was because your kid sister disappeared and catching criminals gives you a sense of order. I've heard that one twice, and I don't buy it."

Lee kept his eyes on traffic. "You got any sisters? Kid relatives you really care about?"

I shook my head. "My family's dead."

"So's Laurie. I figured it out when I was fifteen. Mom and Dad kept spending money on handbills and detectives, but I knew she was a snuff job. I kept picturing her growing up. Prom queen, straight As, her own family. It used to hurt like a bastard, so I pictured her growing up wrong. You know, like a floozy. It was actually comforting, but it felt like I was shitting on her."

I said, "Look, I'm sorry."

Lee gave me a gentle elbow. "Don't be, because you're right. I quit fighting and joined the cops because Benny Siegel was putting the heat on me. He bought out my contract and scared off my manager, and he promised me a shot at Joe Louis if I took two dives for him. I said 'No' and joined the Department because the Jew Syndicate boys have got a rule against killing cops. I was scared shitless that he'd kill me anyway, so when I heard that the Boulevard-Citizens heisters took some of Benny's money along with the Legion's, I shook down stoolies until I got Bobby De Witt on a platter. I gave Benny first crack at him. His number-two man talked him out of a snuff, so I took the dope to Hollywood dicks. Benny's my pal now. Gives me tips on the ponies all the time. Next question?"

I decided not to push for information on Kay. Checking out the street, I saw that downtown had given way to blocks of small, unkempt houses. The Bugsy Siegel story stayed with me; I was running with it when Lee slowed the car and pulled to the curb.

I blurted, "What the hell?"

Lee said, "This one's for my own personal satisfaction. You remember the baby raper on the felony sheet?"

"Sure."

"Tierney said there's four sodomy unsolveds in Highland Park, right?"

"Right."

"And he mentioned that there was a memo on the rape-o's K.A.'s?"

"Sure. What—"

"Bucky, I read that memo and recognized the name of a fence—Bruno Albanese. He works out of a Mex restaurant in Highland Park. I called Highland Park dicks and got the addresses on the assaults, and two of them were within a half mile of the joint where the fence hangs out. This is his house, and R. & I. says he's got a shitload of unpaid traffic tickets, bench warrants issued. You want a diagram for the rest of it?"

I got out of the car and walked across a weedy front yard strewn with dog turds. Lee caught up with me at the porch and rang the bell; furious barks issued from inside the house.

The door opened, held to the frame by a chain. The barks grew to a crescendo; through the crack I glimpsed a slatternly woman. I shouted, "Police officers!" and Lee wedged his foot into the space between the door jamb and runner. With the chain slackened, I reached up and popped it off. Lee pushed the door open, and the woman ran out onto the porch. I stepped into the house, wondering about the dog. I was eyeballing a seedy living room when a big brown mastiff leaped at me, his jaws wide open. I fumbled for my piece—and the beast started licking my face.

We stood there, the dog's front paws resting on my shoulders like we were doing the Lindy Hop. A big tongue lapped at me, and the woman yelped, "Be nice, Hacksaw! Be nice!"

I grabbed the dog's legs and lowered him to the floor; he promptly turned his attention to my crotch. Lee was talking to the slattern, showing her a mugshot strip. She was shaking her head "No," hands on hips, the picture of an irate citizen. With Hacksaw at my heels, I joined them.

Lee said, "Mrs. Albanese, this man's the senior officer. Would you tell him what you just told me?"

The slattern shook her fists; Hacksaw explored

Lee's crotch. I said, "Where's your husband, lady? We don't have all day."

"I told him and I'll tell you! Bruno's paid his debt to society! He doesn't fraternize with criminals, and I don't know any Coleman what's his name! He's a businessman! His parole officer made him quit hanging out at that Mexican place two weeks ago, and I don't know where he is! Hacksaw, be nice!"

I looked at the real senior officer, now stagger-dancing with a two-hundred-pound dog. "Lady, your husband's a known fence with outstanding traffic warrants. I've got a hot merchandise list in the car, and if you don't tell me where he is, I'll turn your house upside down until I find something dirty. Then I'll arrest *you* for receiving stolen goods. What's it gonna be?"

The slattern beat her fists into her legs; Lee wrestled Hacksaw down to all fours and said, "Some people don't respond to civility. Mrs. Albanese, do you know what Russian roulette is?"

The woman pouted, "I'm not dumb and Bruno's paid his debt to society!" Lee pulled a .38 snubnose out of his back waistband, checked the cylinder and snapped it shut. "There's one bullet in this gun. You feeling lucky, Hacksaw?"

Hacksaw said, "Woof"; the woman said, "You wouldn't dare." Lee put the .38 to the dog's temple and pulled the trigger. The hammer clicked on an empty chamber; the woman gasped and started turning pale; Lee said, "Five to go. Prepare for doggie heaven, Hacker."

Lee squeezed the trigger a second time; I held in belly laughs when the hammer clicked again and

Hacksaw licked his balls, bored over the whole thing. Mrs. Albanese was praying fervently with her eyes shut. Lee said, "Time to meet your maker, doggy"; the woman blurted, "No no no no no! Bruno's tending bar in Silverlake! The Buena Vista on Vendome! Please leave my baby alone!"

Lee showed me the .38's empty cylinder, and we walked back to the car with Hacksaw's happy barks echoing behind us. I laughed all the way to Silverlake.

The Buena Vista was a bar and grill shaped like a Spanish rancho—whitewashed adobe walls and turrets festooned with Christmas lights six weeks before the holiday. The interior was cool, all dark wood. There was a long oak bar just off the entrance foyer, with a man behind it polishing glasses. Lee flashed his shield at him and said, "Bruno Albanese?" The man pointed to the back of the restaurant, lowering his eyes.

The rear of the grill was narrow, with leatherette booths and dim lighting. Wolfish eating noises led us to the last booth—the only one occupied. A thin, swarthy man was hunched over a plate piled high with beans, chili, and huevos rancheros, shoveling the slop in like it was his last meal on earth.

Lee rapped on the table. "Police officers. Are you Bruno Albanese?"

The man looked up and said, "Who, me?"

Lee slid into the booth and pointed to the religious tapestry on the wall. "No, the kid in the manger. Let's make this fast, so I don't have to watch you eat. You've got outstanding warrants, but me and

24

my partner like your dog, so we're not taking you in. Ain't that nice of us?"

Bruno Albanese belched, then said, "You mean you want some skinny?"

Lee said, "Whiz kid," and smoothed the Maynard mugshot strip on the table. "He cornholes little boys. We know he sells to you, and we don't care. Where is he?"

Albanese looked at the strip and burped. "I never seen this guy before. Somebody steered you wrong."

Lee looked at me and sighed. He said, "Some people don't respond to civility," grabbed Bruno Albanese by the scruff of the neck, and smashed his head face first into the plate of goo. Bruno sucked in grease through his mouth, nose, and eyeballs, flapping his arms and banging his legs under the table. Lee held him there, intoning, "Bruno Albanese was a good man. He was a good husband and a good father to his son Hacksaw. He wasn't very cooperative with the police, but who expects perfection? Partner, can you give me a reason to spare this shitbird's life?"

Albanese was making gurgling sounds; blood was leaking into his huevos rancheros. "Have mercy," I said. "Even fences deserve a better last supper."

Lee said, "Well put," and let go of Albanese's head. He came up for air bleeding and gasping, wiping a whole Mexican cookbook off his face. When he got breath he wheezed out, "The Versailles Apartments on Sixth and Saint Andrews, room 803, and please don't give me a rat jacket!"

Lee said, "Bon appetit, Bruno"; I said, "You're

good." We ran out of the restaurant and highballed it code three to 6th and Saint Andrews.

The mail slots in the Versailles lobby listed a Maynard Coleman in Apartment 803. We rode the elevator up to the eighth floor and rang the buzzer; I put my ear to the door and heard nothing. Lee took a ring of skeleton keys from his pocket and worked them into the lock until one hit and the mechanism gave with a sharp click.

We entered a hot, dark little room. Lee flicked on the overhead light, illuminating a Murphy bed covered with stuffed animals—teddy bears, pandas, and tigers. The crib stunk of sweat and some medicinal odor I couldn't place. I wrinkled my nose, and Lee placed it for me. "Vaseline with Cortisone. The homos use it for ass lube. I was gonna turn Maynard over to Captain Jack personally, but now I'm gonna let Vogel and Koenig have him first."

I moved to the bed and examined the animals; they all had ringlets of soft children's hair taped between their legs. Shivering, I looked at Lee. He was pale, his features contorted by facial tics. Our eyes met, and we silently left the room and took the elevator downstairs. On the sidewalk, I said, "What now?"

Lee's voice was shaky. "Find a phone booth and call the D.M.V. Give them Maynard's alias and this address and ask if they've processed any pink slips on it the past month or so. If they have, get a vehicle description and a license number. I'll meet you at the car."

I ran to the corner, found a pay phone and dialed

the D.M.V. Police Information Line. A clerk answered, "Who's requesting?"

"Officer Bleichert, L.A.P.D. badge 1611. Auto purchase information, Maynard Coleman or Coleman Maynard, 643 South Saint Andrews, LA. Probably recent."

"Gotcha—one minute."

I waited, notebook and pen in hand, thinking of the stuffed animals. A good five minutes later, "Officer, it's a positive," jarred me.

"Shoot."

"1938 De Soto sedan, dark green, license B as in boy, V as in Victor, 1–4–3–2. Repeat, B as in boy . . ."

I wrote it down, hung up and ran back to the car. Lee was scrutinizing an LA street atlas, jotting notes. I said, "Got him."

Lee closed the atlas. "He's probably a school prowler. There were elementary schools near the Highland Park jobs, and there's a half dozen of them around here. I radioed the Hollywood and Wilshire desks and told them what we've got. Patrol cars are gonna stop by the schools and put out the skinny on Maynard. What's the D.M.V. got?"

I pointed to my notesheet; Lee grabbed the radio mike and switched on the outgoing dial. Static fired up, then the two-way went dead. Lee said, "Fuck it, let's roll."

We cruised elementary schools in Hollywood and the Wilshire District. Lee drove; I scanned curbs and schoolyards for green De Sotos and loiterers. We stopped once at a gamewell phone, and Lee called

Wilshire and Hollywood stations with the D.M.V. dope, getting assurances that it would be relayed to every radio car, every watch.

During those hours we hardly spoke a word. Lee gripped the wheel with white-knuckled fingers, slow lane crawling. The only time his expression changed was when we pulled over to check out kids at play. Then his eyes clouded and his hands shook, and I thought he would either weep or explode.

But he just kept staring, and the simple act of moving back into traffic seemed to calm him. It was as if he knew exactly how far to let himself go as a man before getting back to strict cop business.

Shortly after 3:00 we headed south on Van Ness— a run by Van Ness Avenue Elementary. We were a block away, going by the Polar Palace, when a green De Soto, BV 1432, passed us in the opposite direction and pulled into the parking lot in front of the rink.

I said, "We've got him. Polar Palace."

Lee hung a U-turn and drew to the curb directly across the street from the lot. Maynard was locking the De Soto, eyeing a group of kids skipping toward the entrance with skates slung over their shoulders. "Come on," I said.

Lee said, "You take him, I might lose my temper. Make sure the kids are out of the way, and if he pulls any hinky moves, kill him."

Solo plainclothes rousts were strictly against the book. "You're crazy. This is a . . . ."

Lee shoved me out the door. "Go get him, goddammit! This is Warrants, not a fucking classroom! Go get him!"

I dodged traffic across Van Ness to the parking

lot, catching sight of Maynard entering the Polar Palace in the middle of a big throng of children. I sprinted to the front door and opened it, telling myself to go smooth and slow.

Cold air stunned me; harsh light reflecting off the ice rink stung my eyes. Shielding them, I looked around and saw papier-mâché fjords and a snack stand shaped like an igloo. There were a few kids twirling on the ice, and a group of them oohing and aahing at a giant taxidermied polar bear standing on its hind legs by a side exit. There was not an adult in the joint. Then it hit me: check the men's room.

A sign pointed me to the basement. I was halfway down the stairs when Maynard started up them, a little stuffed rabbit in his hands. The stench of room 803 came back; just as he was about to pass me, I said, "Police office, you're under arrest," and drew my .38.

The rape-o threw up his hands; the rabbit went flying. I shoved him into the wall, frisked him, and cuffed his hands behind his back. Blood pounded in my head as I pushed him up the stairs; I felt something pummeling my legs. "You leave my daddy alone! Leave my daddy alone!"

The assailant was a little boy in short pants and a sailor's jumper. It took me half a second to make him as the rape-o's kid—their resemblance was bone deep. The boy attached himself to my belt and kept bawling, "Leave my daddy alone"; the father kept bawling for time to say goodbye and get a babysitter; I kept moving, up the stairs and through the Polar Palace, my gun at the rape-o's head, my other hand pushing him forward, the kid dragging behind me, yowling and punching with all his might. A crowd had formed; I shouted "Police officer!" until they separated and gave me a shot at the door. An old geezer opened it for me, blurting, "Hey! ain't you Bucky Bleichert?"

I gasped, "Grab the kid and call for a matron"; the junior tornado was yanked off my back. I saw Lee's Ford in the parking lot, shoved Maynard all the way to it and into the back seat. Lee attached the roof light, hit the siren, and peeled; the rape-o mumbled Jesus mumbo jumbo. I kept wondering why the siren blare couldn't drown out the little boy's shrieks for his daddy.

We dropped Maynard off at the Hall of Justice jail, and Lee phoned Fritz Vogel at Central squadroom, telling him the rape-o was in custody and ready to be interrogated on the Bunker Hill burglaries. Then it was back to City Hall, a call to notify the Highland Park dicks of Maynard's arrest, and a call to Hollywood Juvie to ease my conscience on the kid. The matron I talked to told me that Billy Maynard was there, waiting for his mother, Coleman Maynard's ex-wife, a car hop with six hooking convictions. He was still bawling for his daddy, and I hung up wishing I hadn't called.

Three hours of report writing followed. I wrote the arresting officer's summary longhand; Lee typed it up, omitting mention of our break-in at Coleman Maynard's apartment. Ellis Loew hovered around the cubicle as we worked, muttering "Great collar," and "I'll kill them in court with the kid angle."

We finished our paperwork at 7:00. Lee made a check mark in the air and said, "Chalk another one up for Laurie Blanchard. You hungry, partner?"

I stood up and stretched, food suddenly a great idea. Then I saw Fritz Vogel and Bill Koenig approaching the cubicle. Lee whispered, "Make nice, they've got juice with Loew."

Up close, the two resembled gone-to-seed refugees from the LA Rams' middle line. Vogel was tall and fat, with a huge flat head that grew straight out of his shirt collar and the palest blue eyes I'd ever seen; Koenig was plain huge, topping my six foot three by a couple of inches, his linebacker's body just starting to go soft. He had a broad, flattened nose, jug ears, a crooked jaw, and tiny chipped teeth. He looked stupid; Vogel looked shrewd; they both looked mean.

Koenig giggled. "He confessed. The kiddie porks and the burglaries. Fritzie says we're all gonna get commendations." He stuck out his hand. "Good fight you gave blondie."

I shook the big fist, noticing fresh blood on Koenig's right shirt cuff. I said, "Thanks, Sarge," then extended my hand to Fritz Vogel. He took it for a split second, bored into me with coldly furious eyes and dropped it like it was a hot turd.

Lee slapped my back. "Bucky's aces. Smarts *and* cojones. You talked to Ellis about the confession?"

Vogel said, "He's 'Ellis' to lieutenants and up."

Lee laughed. "I'm a privileged character. Besides, you call him 'Kike' and 'Jewboy' behind his back, so what do you care?"

Vogel flushed; Koenig looked around with his mouth open. When he turned, I saw blood spatters on his shirtfront. Vogel said, "Come on, Billy"; Koenig dutifully followed him back to the squadroom.

"Make nice, huh?"

Lee shrugged. "Shitbirds. If they weren't cops they'd

31

be in Atascadero. Do as I say, not as I do, partner. They're afraid of me, and you're just a rookie here."

I wracked my brain for a snappy reply. Then Harry Sears, looking twice as sloppy as he did in the morning, poked his head in the doorway. "I heard something I thought you should know, Lee." The words were spoken without a trace of a stutter; I smelled liquor on the man's breath.

Lee said, "Shoot."

Sears said, "I was over at County Parole, and the supervisor told me Bobby De Witt just got an 'A' number. He'll be paroled to LA around the middle of January. Just thought you should know."

Sears nodded at me and took off. I looked at Lee, who was twitching like he did up in room 803 of the Versailles. I said, "Partner . . ."; Lee managed a smile. "Let's get ourselves some chow. Kay's making pot roast, and she said I should bring you home."

I tagged along for the woman and was astounded by the pad: a beige deco-streamline house a quarter-mile north of the Sunset Strip. Going in the door, Lee said, "Don't mention De Witt; it'll upset Kay." I nodded and took in a living room straight out of a movie set.

The wainscoting was polished mahogany, the furniture was Danish modern—gleaming blond wood in a half dozen shades. There were wall prints of paintings by hotshot twentieth-century artists, and carpets embroidered with modernistic designs, mist-hung skyscrapers or tall trees in a forest, or the spires of some German Expressionist factory. A dining area adjoined the living room, and the table held fresh flowers and chafing dishes leaking the aroma of good eats. I said, "Not bad on a cop's pay. You taking a few bribes, partner?"

Lee laughed. "My fight stash. Hey babe, you here?"

Kay Lake walked in from the kitchen, wearing a floral dress that matched the tulips on the table. She took my hand and said, "Hello, Dwight"; I felt like a punk kid crashing the junior prom.

"Hello, Kay."

With a squeeze she dropped my hand, ending the longest shake in history. "You and Leland partners. It makes you want to believe in fairy tales, doesn't it?"

I looked around for Lee, and saw that he'd disappeared. "No. I'm the realistic type."

"I'm not."

"I can tell."

"I've had enough reality to last me a lifetime."

"I know."

"Who told you?"

"The *LA Herald Express*."

Kay laughed. "Then you did read my press clippings. Come to any conclusions?"

"Yeah. Fairy tales don't work out."

Kay winked like Lee; I got the feeling that she was the one who taught him. "That's why you have to turn them into reality. Leland! Dinner time!"

Lee reappeared, and we sat down to eat; Kay cracked a bottle of champagne and poured. When our glasses were full, she said, "To fairy tales." We drank, Kay refilled, Lee said, "To Bond Issue B." The second dose of bubbly tickled my nose and made me laugh; I proposed, "To the Bleichert-Blanchard rematch at the Polo Grounds, a bigger gate than Louis and Schmeling."

Lee said, "To the second Blanchard victory"; Kay said, "To a draw and no gore." We drank, and killed the bottle, and Kay fetched another from the kitchen, popping the cork and hitting Lee in the chest. When our goblets were full, I caught my first blast of the juice and blurted, "To us." Lee and Kay looked at me in something like slow motion, and I saw that our free hands were all resting a few inches apart on the tabletop. Kay noticed me notice and winked; Lee said, "That's where I learned how." Our hands moved together and formed a triad, and we toasted "To us," in unison.

Opponents, then partners, then friends. And with the friendship came Kay, never getting between us, but always filling our lives outside the job with style and grace.

That fall of '46, we went everywhere together. When we went to the movies, Kay took the middle seat and grabbed both our hands during the scary parts; when we spent big band Friday evenings at the Malibu Rendezvous, she alternated dances with the two of us and always tossed a coin to see who got the last slow number. Lee never expressed an ounce of jealousy, and Kay's come-on subsided into a low simmer. It was there every time our shoulders brushed, every time a radio jingle or a funny billboard or a word from Lee hit us the same way and our eyes met instantaneously. The quieter it got, the more available I knew Kay was—and the more I wanted her. But I let it all ride, not because it would have destroyed my partnership with Lee, but because it would have upset the perfection of the triad.

After tours of duty, Lee and I would go to the

house and find Kay reading, underlining passages in books with a yellow crayon. She'd cook dinner for the three of us, and sometimes Lee would take off to run Mulholland on his motorcycle. Then we talked.

We always spoke around Lee, as if discussing the brute center of the three of us without him present was a cheat. Kay talked about the six years of college and two master's degrees that Lee had bankrolled with his fight stash and how her work as a substitute teacher was perfect for the "overeducated dilettante" she'd become; I talked about growing up Kraut in Lincoln Heights. We never spoke of my snitching for the Alien Squad or her life with Bobby De Witt. We both sensed the other's general story, but neither of us wanted details. I had the upper hand there: the Ashida brothers and Sam Murakami were long gone and dead, but Bobby De Witt was a month away from LA parole—and I could tell Kay was afraid of his return.

If Lee was frightened, he never showed it past that moment when Harry Sears gave him the word, and it never hindered him during our best hours together—the ones spent working Warrants. That fall I learned what police work really was, and Lee was my teacher.

From mid-November through the New Year we captured a total of eleven hard felons, eighteen traffic warrantees, and three parole and probation absconders. Our rousts of suspicious loiterers got us an additional half-dozen arrests, all of them for narcotics violations. We worked from Ellis Loew's direct orders, the felony sheet, and squadroom scuttlebutt—filtered through Lee's instincts. His techniques were sometimes cautious and roundabout and sometimes brutal, but he was always gentle with children, and when he went strong-arm to get information, it was because it was the only way to grab results.

So we became a "Good guy—Bad guy" interrogation team; Mr. Fire, the black hat; Mr. Ice, the white. Our boxing reputations gave us an added edge of respect on the street, and when Lee rabbit-punched for information and I interceded on the punchee's behalf, it got us what we wanted.

The partnership wasn't perfect. When we worked twenty-four-hour tours, Lee would shake down hop-heads for Benzedrine tablets and swallow handfuls to stay alert; then every Negro roustee became "Sambo," every white man "Shitbird," every Mexican "Pancho." All his rawness came out, destroying his considerable finesse, and twice I had to hold him back for real when he got carried away with his black hat role.

But it was a small price to pay for what I was learning. Under Lee's tutelage I got good fast, and I wasn't the only one who knew it. Even though he'd dropped half a grand on the fight, Ellis Loew warmed to me when Lee and I brought in a string of felons he was drooling to prosecute, and Fritz Vogel, who hated me for snatching Warrants from his son, reluctantly admitted to Loew that I was an ace cop.

And, surprisingly, my local celebrity lingered long enough to do me some extra financial good. Lee was a favored repo man with H. J. Caruso, the auto dealer with the famous radio ads, and when the job was slow, we prowled for delinquent cars in Watts and Compton. When we found one, Lee would kick in the driver's side window and hot wire the sled, and I would stand guard. Then we'd run a two-car convoy to Caruso's lot on Figueroa, and H. J. would slip us a double sawbuck apiece. We gabbed cops and robbers and fight stuff with him, and afterwards he kicked back a good bottle of bourbon that Lee always turned over to Harry Sears to keep us greased with good tips from Homicide.

Sometimes we joined H. J. for the Wednesday night fights at the Olympic. He had a specially constructed ringside booth that kept us protected when the Mexicans in the top tier tossed coins and beer cups full of piss down at the ring, and Jimmy Lennon introduced us during the prefight ceremonies. Benny Siegel stopped by the booth occasionally, and he and Lee would go off to talk. Lee always came back looking slightly scared. The man he'd once defied was the most powerful gangster on the West Coast, known to be vindictive, with a hair-trigger temper. But Lee usually got track tips—and the horses Siegel gave him usually won.

So that fall went. The old man got a pass from the rest home at Christmas, and I brought him to dinner at the house. He had recovered pretty well from his stroke, but he still had no memory of English and rambled on in German. Kay fed him turkey and goose, and Lee listened to his Kraut monologues all night, interjecting "You tell 'em, pop," and "Crazy, man" whenever he paused for breath. When I dropped him back at the home, he gave me the fungoo sign and managed to walk in under his own steam.

On New Year's Eve, we drove down to Balboa Island to catch Stan Kenton's band. We danced in 1947, high on champagne, and Kay flipped coins to see who got last dance and first kiss when midnight hit. Lee won the dance, and I watched them swirl across the floor to "Perfidia," feeling awe for the way they had changed my life. Then it was midnight, the band fired up, and I didn't know how to play it.

Kay took the problem away, kissing me softly on the lips, whispering, "I love you, Dwight." A fat woman grabbed me and blew a noisemaker in my face before I could return the words.

We drove home on Pacific Coast Highway, part of a long stream of horn-honking revelers. When we got to the house, my car wouldn't start, so I made myself a bed on the couch and promptly passed out from too much booze. Sometime toward dawn, I woke up to strange sounds muffling through the walls. I perked my ears to identify them, picking out sobs followed by Kay's voice, softer and lower than I had ever heard it. The sobbing got worse—trailing into whimpers. I pulled the pillow over my head and forced myself back to sleep.

The Au Pair Girl

JOYCE HARRINGTON

Joyce Harrington, executive vice-president of the Mystery Writers of America, is known primarily for her short stories. She won an Edgar in 1973 for her first story, "The Purple Shroud," and has been active in the field since then. Ms. Harrington has also written three novels, all with St. Martin's: *No One Knows My Name* (1981), *Family Reunion* (1982), and *Dreemz of the Night* (scheduled for the fall of 1987).

I never thought, when I came to New York to be an actress, that I'd wind up being a nursemaid. That's what it amounts to, even though Carl and Stacy insist on referring to me as "the au pair girl." To tell you the truth, I had to look it up to find out what it meant, and I'm still not sure. It sounds as if there ought to be two of me, both tiny and dark-haired, one to change the diapers and the other to teach French. I can change the diapers all right. I've had lots of experience at that, babysitting for small change and taking care of each new kid my mother seemed to produce while she was thinking about something else, but I was never very good at French or anything else in school. I guess my mind was too occupied with trying to figure out how to get out of Mudville. And tiny and dark, I'm not. Five foot eleven and a half, you might as well say six foot, and naturally blonde all over. Even my eyebrows.

My hometown's not really called Mudville. I just call it that because it fits, and because I wouldn't want anybody there to know about what's been going on here. I changed my name, too, but I did that when I left home, to something a little more suitable to my new life. And I don't mean my life as an au pair girl. I still intend to see Nadya Nystrom up in lights on Broadway, although between you and me I would gladly settle for off-Broadway or off-off, or even a New Jersey car dealer commercial in sequins and smiles, just to get started.

Stacy says that Nadya Nystrom is a perfect name for an au pair girl. Sometimes she's so insensitive. She tells her snooty friends that she brought me over from a tiny village in Sweden where the only thing I could look forward to was marrying a local boy and getting old before my time. Sounds pretty much like Mudville to me, so I don't argue with her. I even put on a fake Swedish accent whenever any of her friends come over. I figure it's good training in case I ever have to play that sort of role on stage.

Stacy and Carl have had a Major Tragedy in their lives, even though they're rich and young. I don't know exactly how rich they are, but they pay me more than I could make waiting tables, even with tips, and they live in this absolutely gorgeous duplex penthouse apartment with a view of the whole city— the sort of place I'm going to have some day. I live here, too, of course, so I can take care of the baby. Stacy can't take care of her because she's too nervous. Stacy, I mean. Not the baby. Everything, every little thing, upsets her. And how I know how old she is, is because that upsets her most of all. The fact that she'll be thirty in a couple of years. You'd think her life was coming to an end, when I know for a fact that my mother is well over forty and she gets more fun out of a night at the bowling alley than Stacy ever had in a year of whatever it is she does with her time. Carl's already thirty. I came to work here the day after his thirtieth birthday party, and that was the first thing I had to do. Clean up the morning-after mess. I would have walked out on the spot, except the baby was a mess too, and Stacy was flaked out in bed with one of those blue cold-pack masks over her eyes. And anyway, like I said, the pay's good and I have my own room and whenever I have to go to an audition, Stacy gets a babysitter.

She says she likes to think she's helping out a future star. I don't argue with her.

But I was going to tell you about their Major Tragedy. This baby they have now, Alyssa Morgana Winston, is adopted. And the reason she's adopted is that Stacy can't have any more kids. She's had two already, and they both died. Crib death. One right after the other. They were twins, and they both died in the same month, October, almost two years ago. So you can understand how come Stacy's a nervous wreck. Carl told me once that right after it happened he was afraid he was going to lose her, too. You know what I mean. The Big S. Suicide. I think Carl likes me a little.

Well. Now that you know a little of the background, I guess I'd better fill you in on the foreground. The stuff I wouldn't want making the rounds of all the breakfast nooks and back porches of Mudville, U.S.A. Not that I ever intend to go back there, but one never knows, do one?

What I said a little while back, about how I think

Carl likes me a little? That was just a slight misunderstatement. Carl likes me a lot. So much, in fact, that he's been helping me with this scene I have to do for my acting class. It's a scene from *A Streetcar Named Desire*. You know the one, where Stanley and Blanche? and lah-di-dah and so forth. I do a pretty good Southern accent, too. But Carl trying to be mean and sexy is pretty laughable. Not that he's not handsome and all that, but it's such a clean kind of handsome. I don't think his alligator polo shirts know the meaning of the word "sweat." I got the giggles so bad, his feelings were hurt, so of course I had to make it up to him. And one thing led to another, and there we were.

I should say, and there we are. Because that was a week ago, and since then, every night, Josephine, he's in my room. My room is downstairs, along with the kitchen and the laundry and Alyssa Morgana's room and things like that. And Carl's den. The room he calls his "home office" on his income tax return, and how I know that is, he told me. He tells me lots of things. Sometimes he comes to my room just to talk. It's as if he never had anybody to talk to in his whole life. Well, I'll admit it's a little hard to get a word in edgewise with Stacy, the way she goes on. So I listen. I listen to him and I listen to her, and little by little I guess I know more about both of them than they know about each other.

I think it'll come in handy in my acting career. You can never know too much about people if you're going to be a great actress.

So now we're up to yesterday when the weirdest thing happened. I'd just come back from the park with Alyssa Morgana in her pram. That's short for perambulator which is a fancy English way of saying baby carriage. I write things like that down in my notebook because you never know when you're going to need them. Anyway, we got off the elevator which opens right into the apartment and I took Alyssa Morgana into her room to change her diaper. And guess what? There was Stacy, all curled up in Alyssa Morgana's crib, sucking on her thumb.

Well, I'd seen that old movie, *Baby Doll*, where Carroll Baker does that. I just love Tennessee Williams, don't you? He's so weird. So I said, "Hi, there, Baby Doll. Rise and shine."

That's what my mother always said to me whenever I was trying to get a few minutes extra sleep. "Rise and shine." Only she didn't call me Baby Doll. She called me a lot of other things that don't bear repeating, but never anything remotely decent. My mother's mouth could singe the hide off an alligator, but she goes to church and sings hymns as if sweetness and light was all that ever passed her lips.

Stacy rolled over and buried her face in Alyssa Morgana's Cabbage Patch Kid and let out a howl that sounded like *The Night of the Living Dead*. Alyssa Morgana started crying, too, so I really had my hands full.

I put Alyssa Morgana down on her dressing table but I couldn't leave her there because she's old enough to wiggle right off but not old enough to know she'd fall on the floor and break her neck if she did. So I held onto her and changed her and powdered her and tickled her and pretty soon she was laughing.

But Stacy was still howling. In between the shrieks and the moans and the groans, there were words. I started listening. I couldn't help it. She wasn't whispering or trying to keep anything a secret. I started hearing things like "wish I were dead" and "he doesn't care about me" and worst of all "send the baby back where she came from."

Well. Without Alyssa Morgana, I'd be out of a job and a nice place to live. Not to mention that I doubted very much if Carl would take the trouble to visit my room if my room was a dingy two-by-four in a fleabag hotel which is all I could afford if I went back to waitressing, which I never want to do again in all my life.

So I thought about that. And about how tough it was turning out to be to even get started being a great actress. There are only about two million girls from Mudvilles all over the country here in New York trying to be great actresses. The other two million are out in Hollywood. And out of those four million, maybe three—count 'em, three—get to be really big stars. And even that could be an exaggeration.

On the other hand, here was Stacy Winston with no ambition to be anything, miserable and whining like a baby in spite of having everything handed to her. So she wished she were dead. Not a bad idea. So Carl didn't care about her. Well, I'd sort of caught on to that little moment of truth quite some time ago, without any help from her. But send Alyssa Morgana back where she came from? Over my dead body!

Or Stacy's.

Now that was a thought to be thought about. There she was in the crib just asking to be put out of her misery. Not the same crib, let me assure you, in which those poor twin baby boys died of crib death.

Actually, there'd been two cribs, and Carl told me they'd both been donated to one of those ritzy thrift shops on Third Avenue. So, some other babies are sleeping in them now, and Alyssa Morgana's crib is a brand-new one, very modern and expensive looking. From Bloomingdale's. Stacy told me that.

However. It was hard to think about anything, especially how to make Stacy's wish come true, with all that screeching going on. I put Alyssa Morgana into her playpen and gave her a teething biscuit to gnaw on, and went over to the crib for a closer look at Stacy.

She was wearing her dove gray designer sweatsuit, so she must have been doing her physical jerks when the fit came on. She has a real thing about keeping in shape, even though she weighs about ninety-nine pounds fully decked out in one of her five fur coats. In case you're wondering, two of them are mink for everyday use, one's Russian sable for evening wear, one's an outrageous Canadian lynx that I'd kill for if it wasn't too small for me, and then there's the old sheared beaver left over from her college days that she never wears anymore.

My winter coat is a leftover, too. From high school. My mother picked it out. It's orange, green, and purple plaid, and about the only good thing you can say about it is, it's warm and I think it scares muggers.

Stacy's face was red and wet. The shape she was in, not even those five fur coats could make her look like anything but a mess. I said, "Stacy, what's the matter, honey?"

She bawled some more, but the volume was lower. Maybe she was losing her voice.

I said, "Come on, Stacy. Alyssa Morgana needs to take her nap."

You may be wondering why I call her Stacy and not Mrs. Winston like a real servant person should. That's the way she wants it. She told me I shouldn't be made to feel like a servant since I was really an actress, and anyway she was far too democratic to expect people to treat her as anything but an equal. The cook calls her Stacy to her face and Mrs. Flintstone behind her back.

"Oh," she whimpered, "the baby. Where is she?"

"Right over there in her playpen," I told her. "You just about scared her into convulsions with all your screeching."

"I'm just not cut out to be a mother," she whimpered some more. There's nothing like a little self-pity to brighten up your day.

"Well," I told her, "not many people are. My own mother never got the hang of it, but that didn't stop her from popping out six of us at last count and for all I know there may be seven by now."

I said the wrong thing. That set her off again about how she was useless and worthless because she could never have a child of her own. I ask you. In this day and age. There were only about ten zillion things she could do with her time and her money, and there was even Alyssa Morgana who was pretty sweet and cute as babies go, but no, Stacy just wasn't interested.

Alberta, the cook, poked her head in the door about then to ask what Stacy wanted to have for dinner, but really to find out what was going on. I said, "Stacy's sick so maybe she should just have some tea and a poached egg, but I think Carl would

like to have grilled swordfish and spinach soufflé."
He'd told me the night before that he liked those
two things best in the world and they never had them
at home.

"Oh, you do, do you?" said Alberta, getting all
puffed up and huffy. "Well, he's gonna get chicken
and dumplings and boiled carrots. I've already done
the shopping." Alberta is very independent. That's
what comes from Stacy encouraging all this democ-
racy.

"If you already knew, why did you bother to ask?"

"Because she always tells me to cook whatever I
want. And that's what I want. So don't you go getting
any ideas. What's the matter with her?"

It was now or never. I already had the thought.
Now I had to plant the seed. "I don't know," I said
in my meekest possible tiny voice so only Alberta
could hear me. "I came home from the park with
Alyssa Morgana, and there she was in the crib, yelling that she wanted to kill herself."

"Oh, sure," said Alberta. "We've been through
that before with her. She doesn't mean it. She just
wants attention. Don't give it to her. It just makes
her worse."

"But somebody should pay attention," I protested. "What if she really does it?"

"She won't," said Alberta scornfully. "She's too
chicken."

"But what if she does?" I persisted.

"Oh, you are just too young and too dumb." Alberta doesn't like me much. But that's okay with me.
I would hate to have her liking me and wanting to
talk to me over cups of her awful coffee in the kitchen.
She huffed off down the hall to tend to her chicken

and dumplings. It may sound ungrateful, but the food here is worse than Mudville, and that's saying a lot.

So, back I went to the crib. Stacy had quieted down a bit and had her thumb back in her mouth. She stared up at me with those big frightened eyes of hers. What does she have to be frightened of, I asked myself. She's got everything and I've got nothing. Nothing but my hopes and dreams and every day I see them turning into cow chips before my eyes. Like the time I went to an audition, so-called, and this guy, I don't know who he was but he sure wasn't the director, maybe the stage manager or the janitor, said I was perfect for the part but would I mind trying on one of these costumes because they bought the whole show and the costumes came with it. So I said, "Okay, where's the dressing room?" And he said, "Sorry, there isn't one but you can just change right here." And I said, "What are you, a leg man or a fanny man or a titty man? What do you want me to take off first?" And would you believe it, he said, "Take everything off, real slow, and then start in on me." He must have thought I was a real turkey. What I did was, I started in on him. I took his tie, greasy as it was, and yanked it right off his scrawny neck and then I wrapped it back around twice and pulled real hard. I'm kind of strong for a girl. I said, "Do you still want me to take it off real slow?" He didn't say a word, just turned red in the face. I let go before he turned blue.

I didn't get the part.

Six months in New York City and I haven't got a single part yet. All I've got is this au pair girl thing, and Alyssa Morgana, who really likes me. And then there's Carl. I don't know what to do.

Yes, I do. But I guess I don't know how to do it. I've never done anything like this before, even though I've felt like it about a trillion times.

"What do you want, Stacy?" I asked. I didn't expect her to answer me, but she did.

"Sleep," she moaned. "I can't sleep."

"How about some hot Ovaltine?" I said. That's what my mother used to make us drink when we got too hyper. I hate hot Ovaltine.

Stacy did, too, I guess. She made disgusting throw-up noises.

"Well, what *do* you want?" I asked her again.

"Pills," she whispered. "Don't tell Carl."

"What pills?" I asked. As if I didn't know. Carl told me he kept them locked up in his desk and only gave them to her once in a while, one at a time, because one time she took a whole fistful of them and had to have her stomach pumped out.

"Sleeping pills!" she screeched. "God! Are you stupid!"

I'm not stupid, but it's okay with me if she wants to think I am. I won't argue with her. Carl doesn't think I'm stupid. He thinks I'm pretty smart and pretty pretty. He said so. He said, "What's a smart, pretty girl like you doing alone in New York without a boyfriend?"

He laughed when I told him, "There aren't any guys smart enough or pretty enough for me."

"You just haven't found the right one yet," he said, and then he smiled in that wise way he has as if he knew something you didn't know, but if you play your cards right he might just tell you.

I didn't push him on it, but I think I know what he meant.

But back to Stacy and her sleeping pills. "Where are they?" I asked, all innocent and eager to help. I really am a good actress. "I'll get them for you."

"I don't know," she wailed. "They're somewhere in Carl's den. I was looking for them, but I couldn't find them. You go look."

"Okay," I said. "But you mind the baby."

She gave me a look as if I was the crazy one. I'm afraid she really doesn't like Alyssa Morgana much. Beats me why she adopted her. My own mother all over again, only my mother at least had the fun and the pleasure of knowing we were all her own. When I got old enough I asked my mother one time why she didn't take the pill or at least use something. She said she never could remember and anyway wasn't I glad she didn't. I guess I am, but if I'd never been born I don't think I'd have known the difference.

I went over to the playpen to see how Alyssa Morgana was doing. She smiled up at me, her face all smeared with gooey teething biscuit mixed with spit, and held up her arms so I would pick her up.

"Not now, piglet," I told her. "I'll be right back. Be a good girl and take care of your mother. She's a mess."

Alyssa Morgana nodded as if she knew what I was talking about. And I went off to Carl's den to see what I could find.

Stacy'd really done a job, trying to find her pills. All the books from the bookshelves were on the floor, some of them ripped as if she thought the pills could be hiding inside the pages. Carl had a row of tobacco humidors sitting in a row on the fireplace mantel; they were all dumped out and scattered around the floor. One of them, a blue and white china number, was broken, and there was pipe tobacco all over the place. And that's just a hint of the wreckage dear little Stacy had created. Somebody'd have to clean it up, but not me. That doesn't go with the au pair territory.

But she hadn't found the pills. I saw where she'd attacked the desk drawers with a letter opener. Carl wouldn't like it so much that his mahogany was all scratched and chipped. Stacy was so dumb. That was no way to open a lock, especially if you don't want anybody to know you'd opened it.

Over the years, since I was a little kid, I've been collecting mystery keys. You know what I mean—keys that you don't know what they're for. I had about two hundred of them tucked away in my dresser drawer, all sorted by size and shape and so forth. You never know when something like that might come in handy. Like right now.

I zipped into my room and groped under my underwear for the Whitman's Sampler candy box where I kept my collection. Right enough. There was a key ring that had about fifteen or twenty little-bitty keys on it. The kind that open desk drawers.

Stacy was still moaning and sobbing. Not real loud, but loud enough so I could hear her. Alberta wouldn't come snooping around to see what was going on. She'd already done that once, and I knew she didn't want to get mixed up with Stacy's fits. She'd stay in the kitchen, boiling her stupid carrots and glopping up her cannonball dumplings. The coast was clear for what I thought I ought to do.

I went back to Carl's den, stepping over the spilled tobacco as best I could. I reminded myself that after it was all over I'd better clean off my shoes real good so no one could find any tobacco shreds on them. The rest of it was so simple. I unlocked the desk after only five or six tries and found the pill bottle way in the back of the top drawer. It was almost full. I don't know what I'd have done if it had been almost empty. Well, it was about time I got lucky, don't you think?

Alyssa Morgana's room had its own bathroom, which was my bathroom, too, with two doors, one into her bedroom and one into mine. Another stroke of luck. I'd probably need lots of glasses of water. I went in there and filled the first one, and then I went over to Stacy in the crib.

"Here, honey," I said. "Sit up now. I found your pills and I'm going to let you have just one."

She sat up and goggled at me. Red eyes, red nose, and all her makeup smeared. I'd really hate for anybody to see me in that shape. "Two," she begged. "I can't get to sleep without at least two."

"Well, I don't know." It was delicious, teasing her like that. "How many would Carl give you?"

"Oh, Carl," she groaned. "He doesn't want me to have any. Please. Two. I'm so tired."

"Well, okay. But that's all. If that doesn't work, you can't have any more."

She held out her hand for the glass of water, and I opened the pill bottle and shook out two capsules into the palm of my hand. A third one slid out of the bottle sort of by accident. Before I could put it back, Stacy snatched all three and popped them into her mouth.

I didn't say anything, just stood there with the open bottle in my hand.

She gulped them down and drank the whole glass of water. Then she smiled at me. "Thanks," she said.

"You're welcome," I said.

She held the empty glass out to me. "I'm so thirsty," she said. "Would you mind?"

"Oh, sure." I took the glass, put the open pill bottle down on top of the dresser next to the crib right in front of Alyssa Morgana's duck lamp and went back to the bathroom. When I came back with the glass of water, the pill bottle wasn't exactly where I'd put it, and Stacy had a kind of squirrelly look about her face, like she had acorns or something stuffed in her cheeks. She grabbed the glass of water and gulped it down, dribbling all over her chin and practically choking on it.

I didn't think she was going to be so cooperative about it, but *c'est la vie*, as they say.

The pill bottle wasn't quite empty. I picked it up and made as if to put the lid back on. "Guess I better put this back where I got it," I said.

"Wait a minute," she said. "What would you do if you couldn't stand to live with yourself?"

"I can't imagine that ever happening," I said. "But if it ever happened, I guess I'd blow my brains out or go jump in front of a subway train."

She shuddered. "You don't really understand," she said. "You've never done something so bad it'll haunt you all your life."

I had to agree with her. I wasn't the easily haunted type. But she was getting at something, and I wanted to know what it was. "Have you?" I asked.

She nodded, drooping all over herself. "I have to tell somebody. It's driving me crazy. I can't sleep. I can't do anything. It's always on my mind. I think Carl knows, but he doesn't *want* to know, so he won't talk about it and he won't listen. He just wants to pretend that everything is normal and I'll snap out of it after a while. But I won't. I know I won't. Can I tell you?"

"Sure. Why not?" I was all ears.

"It's so hard to say it. You'll think I'm some kind of monster."

"No, I won't."

"Whether you do or not, it doesn't matter. Pretty soon, nothing will matter. Listen."

"I'm listening."

All of a sudden, Alyssa Morgana started crying. She'd been playing quietly in her playpen, and I'd almost forgotten about her. It was past time for her nap, and she was getting cranky. She'd quiet down if she had her bottle, but I couldn't leave right in the midst of things to go to the kitchen to get it. I picked her up and carried her over to the crib.

Stacy glared at her and snarled, "Get her out of here."

"How can I?" I asked, all sweet reason. "You're in her crib and she wants to take a nap."

"I never wanted her in the first place. That's what I'm trying to tell you. It was all his idea." Stacy's words were beginning to slur and her eyes were getting a weird kind of glassy look. "She was supposed to make me forget, but she only makes me remember. I'm afraid."

"Of what?" I asked. Alyssa Morgana put her head down on my shoulder and started sucking on a strand of my hair.

"Oh, God!"

The way she said it sent shivers up and down my spine. It dawned on me that maybe there was more going on here than just a spoiled rich bitch having a tantrum.

"It can't be all that bad," I said. "Tell me what you're afraid of."

She took a deep breath and then blurted it out. "I'm afraid I'll do the same thing to her that I did to them."

I was still in the dark, but I was beginning to see a little spark of light. I didn't much like what I thought that light might show up, but it was too late to stop finding things out. I had to know the whole story.

"What did you do?" I asked.

I knew before she spoke what she was going to say, but I kept hoping it would turn out to be something else. I know I'm no prize package, but I'd never do anything as awful as that. Even what I was doing right at that moment wasn't that bad.

"I killed them," she said. "I held a pillow over their little faces until they stopped breathing. First one, and then a few days later, the other one. Don't ask me why. I can't tell my shrink, so I can't find out."

"Does Carl know?"

"I don't know what he knows. The way he looks at me sometimes, I think he does. But if he knew, why would he have insisted on adopting her?" She grimaced at the baby and then let herself fall back in the crib. She lay there, staring at the ceiling. No more tears, no more moaning. She was quiet. "I'm so tired," she murmured.

"Want some more water?" I didn't know what else to suggest. If she was determined to off herself, I might as well help her. It wouldn't be murder, which is what I originally had in mind. More like justice. How could a mother kill her own kids? As flaky as my own mother was, she loved each one of us in her own way. But I believed what Stacy told me. It accounted for so much, even for Carl coming to my room every night. I might as well take advantage of the situation, I thought.

"More water?" she asked. Her voice was really faint and far away. "Yes. That would be nice. I'm very thirsty."

I put Alyssa Morgana back in her playpen where she just curled up and went to sleep. Poor kid. She'll never know what could have happened to her if I hadn't been around to save her.

I had to hold Stacy up and feed her the rest of the capsules one by one. She was so groggy she could hardly swallow, but she managed to get them all down. Then I let her down gently and covered her up with Alyssa Morgana's bunny rabbit quilt. Except for the smeared make-up, she looked like a sleeping baby. Peaceful and innocent. I cleaned off her face so no one would find her looking like a dead clown. Then I wiped off the empty pill bottle and stuck it under the crib mattress, and I took the water glass back to the bathroom and washed it off and dried it and put it into Stacy's hand. It just flopped over but that was okay. It was empty.

I carried Alyssa Morgana into my room and put her in my bed. She whimpered a little and almost woke up. I didn't like to leave her there alone in case she might roll over and fall off the bed, but I thought I'd better make an appearance for Alberta.

There were horrible cooking smells drifting down the hallway when I headed for the kitchen, hoping

Alberta wouldn't be able to read my mind and figure out what I'd been up to.

She was sitting at the kitchen table, eating a huge chunk of chocolate cake. That was one thing she did do pretty well, eat, but she didn't offer me any. "Stacy's gone to sleep," I told her. "I couldn't get her out of the crib, so I put the baby in my bed."

"If she wets it, you'll have to change it yourself," Alberta grumped.

"I don't mind." I went about warming up a bottle of milk just as I always did for Alyssa Morgana's nap. I wanted everything to be just as normal as possible. "Do you really think she's only trying to get attention? I'd hate it if she really did something to herself."

"Mrs. Flintstone? Hah! If you ask me, she'd be a lot better off if she took care of that baby herself. Of course, that'd put you out of a job, but that might not be such a bad idea either. I've seen him looking at you. Don't let yourself be taken in by that moony look of his. He's got other things in mind."

"Who? Carl?" I'm afraid my innocent façade developed a great big crack right then, and I hoped Alberta didn't notice. Nothing much gets past Alberta. "Looking at me?" I'm embarrassed to say my voice squeaked.

"Yes, you. The same way he's looked at all the girls who came before you, and all the pretty young nurses who've been here to take care of Her Majesty. And they all went off with nothing but a week's severance. That's the way he does it. Once he gets them into bed, it's only a matter of time, poor things. They all thought he was gonna get rid of her and marry them. What they didn't know was that if he ever does get rid of her, he's got the next Mrs. Winston all picked out."

"Is that a fact?" I said, pouring milk into Alyssa Morgana's bottle. "Well, I think that's terrible. Those girls got just what they deserve. Imagine trying to come between husband and wife. I don't think I'll ever get used to New York City ways." I sure didn't want Alberta to stop talking right then, and the surest way to keep her talking was to ignore the juiciest part of what she had to say.

"Well, just listen to her, will you?" Alberta mouthed around a gross mouthful of chocolate cake. "Little Miss Goody Two-Shoes. Thinks I can't see what's going on right under my nose."

What was under her nose right then was a big smear of cake frosting. It was all over her teeth and in her throat, too, and it made her voice all thick and brown and slimy. It was time for me to do the best acting job of my career.

"Oh, Alberta," I whispered, "please tell me what to do. I've got nobody to turn to and if I lose this job, I'll be out on the streets. I'm scared." I tried not to overplay it but I figured the way Alberta loved her soap operas, there wasn't much danger of that.

"And well you should be." Alberta had cornered the market on sanctimonious. That's a word I looked up because I like the sound of it, and there's an awful lot of it going around these days. "I'd hate to think you were carrying on with him, and you so young and all. Them others were older and should have been wiser, but I just know in my heart that you're just young and a little bit stupid."

Did you ever want to smack somebody right in her fat mouth? But there was no stopping her now. I put

Alyssa Morgana's bottle in a pot of water to heat on the stove.

"I hope it hasn't gone any further than looks," she said. "Don't ever let him into your room at night, though. He can't be trusted. You can't trust any of them." The chocolate cake was disappearing as fast as the smirky words oozed past it on the way to my ears. "Some day she'll walk in on you, and then it'll be the same old story all over again. I'm just glad I've got my own place to go home to at night. I couldn't be responsible for what I'd do if he ever tried his silliness on me."

It was all I could do to keep from laughing out loud. Alberta certainly had a high opinion of herself. But then it dawned on me. She was jealous. She'd give anything if Carl *would* pay some attention to her, fat and forty as she was, and that's why she was trying to turn me against him.

"Just supposing something did happen to Stacy," I said, "who's the lucky lady he's got in mind to take her place?"

"Wouldn't you like to know?" she bleated. "You'll just have to take my word for it and don't get your hopes up. I've been keeping an eye on things here for a long time. He'd divorce her if she wasn't such a pitiful mess. Besides, where do you think all the money comes from? He's not going to give that up in a hurry. Isn't that milk getting a little too hot?"

It was, and I didn't want to seem too eager to know more. I said, "Thanks for the advice, Alberta. I really appreciate your taking an interest in my welfare. I had no idea."

"Any time," she said. "Come and have a cup of coffee with me whenever you feel like it. I could tell you plenty more. You're a nice kid, but you need to smarten up."

I got out of there without letting her know how disgusting I thought she was. But she'd certainly given me plenty to think about. If what she'd said was true, I'd done Carl a big favor and I wasn't likely to get anything in return except maybe an invitation to the wedding.

I peeked into Alyssa Morgana's room. Everything was quiet. Stacy hadn't moved from where I'd left her. In a way, I wished I could wake her up and ask her a few things, just to be sure about what I should do next. Carl would be getting home in a few hours. I could wait around and see how he took the news. Or Nadya Nystrom could just disappear off the face of the earth, and I could get the first bus back to Mudville, which wouldn't make me or my mother very happy. Or I could suddenly "discover" that Stacy had scarfed down all those pills and raise the alarm. But that wouldn't change my situation one way or the other.

I hated to admit it, but I really hadn't thought this thing through beyond taking advantage of an opportunity that was right under *my* nose.

Back in my own room, Alyssa Morgana was sleeping in the middle of my bed. I'd really miss her if I went away. I felt more like her mother than Stacy ever pretended to feel. And it was true that I'd entertained the notion of really *being* her mother if Stacy wasn't around anymore. Alberta wasn't wrong about that. So she probably wasn't wrong about all the other garbage she'd told me. Especially the part about Carl having the next Mrs. Winston all picked out.

I sat down on the edge of the bed and tried to think. But the more I thought, the madder I got. And the madder I got, the more I realized that I no more wanted to marry a wimp like Carl than I wanted a bad case of poison ivy. Wasn't he letting me do all the dirty work while he got all the benefit of getting rid of Stacy and being free to do as he pleased?

It was beginning to look like I'd have to do something about *him*, too. But what? I lay down next to Alyssa Morgana to do some heavy thinking.

Well, of course, I fell asleep. Thinking is very exhausting, and I'd been doing a lot of it. When I woke up, the late afternoon sun was blazing right into my eyes and Alyssa Morgana was bouncing up and down on my stomach. "Hi, piglet," I said. "What'll we do now?"

She gurgled and gave me a gummy grin. Nice, but no help at all. I rolled off the bed with her in my arms and went and looked at the two of us in the mirror. We really did look alike, both blonde, both blue-eyed, both of us pretty, if I say so myself. But we both needed a bath. Carl liked to spend twenty minutes or so playing with Alyssa Morgana when he got home from the office, and I liked to be looking my best while he was doing that.

With Alyssa Morgana in my arms, I tiptoed through the bathroom and back into her room. Everything was quiet in there. I didn't want to look at the crib, but I couldn't help it. Stacy hadn't moved. The bunny rabbit quilt didn't move. I didn't go close enough to find out if that was because she wasn't breathing. Quick as a bunny, I gathered up a change of clothes for Alyssa Morgana and went back into the bathroom. Closed the door.

Alyssa Morgana and I had fun in the bathtub. We always did. We played submarine and put bubbles on each other's faces so we looked like Santa Claus, both of us giggling like a couple of loonies. But all the while, in the back of my mind, I was thinking about what I would do when Carl got home and it was time to find Stacy. When we were all dried off, I took Alyssa Morgana back into my room to get dressed. No way did I want to disturb Stacy or even look at her.

I dressed Alyssa Morgana in her blue smocked pinafore and put her down on the floor where she crawled around on the rug while I put on the dress I always wore to auditions for sweet young thing parts, a white number with little blue spriggy flowers all over it and a lacy collar. No makeup except for a little blusher because I was looking pale, and some pink lipstick. I let my hair hang loose, with only a thin blue ribbon tied on top of my head. I looked pretty good, like Alice in Wonderland, but I still hadn't come to any conclusions. I'd just have to improvise, like we did in acting class.

When we were all ready, I carried Alyssa Morgana into the kitchen to see if Alberta had done any snooping while we were asleep. She was brooding over the stove. Probably things weren't overcooked enough to suit her.

"Smells real good," I said, hoping the lie didn't choke me before the dumpling fumes did. "I can't wait till dinner. I'm starving."

"It's my mother's recipe," said Alberta, reverently. "She brought it over from the Old Country."

"Which old country was that?" I asked.

"Bohemia," she said. "I'm a Bohemian. There

aren't many of us left. By the way, there was a phone call for you. I told him you were sleeping." She frowned at me as if sleeping on the job was worth a firing squad at dawn.

"Oh?" I said, indifferently. "Who was it?"

"I don't know. Somebody about a show." Again, the frown, as if shows got you hung, drawn, and quartered.

"Oh, well," I said. "It's probably another thanks-but-no-thanks." But I didn't believe that for a minute. Nobody in New York was polite enough to call you up to say that. "Didn't happen to leave a number, I suppose."

"Yes, well, he did. If I can remember where I put it."

Did you ever want to boil somebody alive in her own chicken stewpot? And then feed the remains to the dogs?

She finally found the number, scribbled on a piece torn off of a page of *Soap Opera Digest*, right there in her apron pocket where she knew it was all along. "I'm not sure I got the name right," she said. "He sounded like he was on drugs or something. Hervy Scurvy's what it sounded like to me." She handed me the scrap of paper as if it was a death sentence.

Harvey Scovill! Oh, my God! Harvey Scovill calling me! He was only the director of the play I'd auditioned for almost two weeks ago. I'd given up hoping. It was a part to die for. True it was by an unknown playwright, and true it was way off-Broadway. But also true, it was about a young girl who lived in a small midwestern town and wanted to write poetry but didn't have anything to write about except the ladies who came into the beauty parlor where she worked as a manicurist. It was called *Fingers*. And *Fingers* was the name of the book of poetry she'd written. And it was goofy and funny and sad, because in the end she kills herself by drinking nail polish remover. And I don't care how awful the play was, it was the *lead* role. And Harvey Scovill was calling *me*!

"Would you please mind Alyssa Morgana for a few minutes?" I said.

"Well, I don't know," said Alberta. "Why don't you leave her with Mrs. Flintstone? I've got to tend to the dinner."

It was on the tip of my tongue to say I couldn't very well leave the baby with a corpse, but I caught myself in the nick of time. I shoved Alyssa Morgana into Alberta's arms and ran to the phone in Carl's den. All the way down the hall, I heard Alyssa Morgana crying and Alberta yelling about how it wasn't fair that she had to do two people's work. I closed the door and picked my way through the debris on the floor to the desk.

It felt good, sitting at that big, important desk, picking up the phone to make the most important call of my life. I dialed the number. The phone rang. And rang, and rang, and rang. When it was finally answered, it wasn't by Harvey Scovill.

"Yello," said a bored woman's voice.

"Is Mr. Scovill there?" I asked.

"Yais. But he cahn't come to the phone. He's with his reflexologist."

I remembered a tall, scrawny woman who'd sat next to Harvey Scovill at the audition and scribbled notes on a clipboard when she wasn't whispering in his ear. She'd whispered throughout my reading and almost destroyed my concentration. I hated her for that. "I'm Nadya Nystrom," I told her. "Mr. Scovill called me this afternoon."

"Oh, yais. We'd like you to come back for a second reading. Ten o'clock tomorrow morning. Can you make it?"

"Yais," I said, and caught myself before I unconsciously mimicked her any further. "I'll be there," I added briskly. "Same place?"

"Yais."

"What's a reflexologist?" I asked. But she'd hung up. I hoped she wasn't mad at me for imitating her peculiar accent. It was something I did automatically. I'd have to watch it tomorrow morning.

When I hung up the phone, Alberta was standing in the doorway, leaning against the open door and looking shocked. She didn't even notice that the room was a mess.

"What's the matter?" I cried, rushing over to her and steering her back out into the hall before she had a chance to come to her senses and start crabbing at me.

"She's really done it this time!" she gasped. "Call the doctor! Call the police!" She sagged against the wall and I had a hard time holding her up. "Oh, my nerves!" she whimpered. "I can't stand this. It'll be the death of me."

"Done what?" I asked. "Where's Alyssa Morgana?"

"In her room," Alberta groaned. "I had to put her down because the carrots were boiling over. You shouldn't have left her with me. You know that's not my job."

I let go of her and she slid down the wall and just

sat there like a beached whale with her huge lumpy legs spread out in front of her.

I ran down the hall to Alyssa Morgana's room. Alberta had left the door wide open. Alyssa Morgana was there in her playpen, googling at me and wanting to be picked up. But first I went over to the crib.

The bunny rabbit quilt had been thrown back. Alberta the Busybody's doing, no doubt. She'd probably tried to wake Stacy up. But it would take more than Alberta screeching at her to rouse her from this nap. Even I could see that. I touched her cheek. It wasn't cold, but it wasn't exactly warm either. As far as I could tell, she wasn't breathing. Well, now.

I picked up Alyssa Morgana. She hugged my neck, and I hugged her warm little body. It was good to have something warm to hang onto. "Piglet," I said, "there's going to be a scene or two around here pretty soon. Wish me luck."

She tried to bite my nose.

Back in the hall, Alberta was still foundered on the floor with her eyes closed and her mouth open. But at least she was breathing. I could hear her from ten feet away.

"Alberta!" I yelled at her. "Do something! Stacy's sick!"

She blinked and rolled her head around on her fat neck. "*You* do something," she muttered. "Can't you see I'm having an attack? What if it's a *heart* attack? Call the doctor. Turn the stove off. If I live through this, I'm quitting."

"What's going on here?" It was Carl. I hadn't heard the elevator door open, but there he was, staring at Alberta and then at me, his handsome face trying to decide whether to be angry or sympathetic. "Has she been at the brandy again?" he asked.

"No. I don't think so," I said uncertainly. But if she had, it would be a darn good thing. "It's Stacy . . ." And then I burst into tears. It was a major asset, being able to do that at a moment's notice. I pointed, with a shaky hand, toward Alyssa Morgana's room.

He dashed past me and ran into the room. Alberta was eyeing me fiercely. "You could have sounded a little more positive," she snarled. "I've never been drunk on the job yet." She lumbered to her feet and staggered away back to the kitchen. I thought she muttered something like "Good riddance."

I tiptoed over to the door to Alyssa Morgana's room and peeked in. Carl was bending over the crib, just staring down at his wife. I'd have given anything to know what was going on in his mind at that moment. Alyssa Morgana chose that moment to say her one word. "Da!"

Wearily, Carl turned his head. His eyes met mine and I made mine well up with tears again. He sighed and then reached down to cover Stacy once again with the child's quilt. "Well," he said. "She's finally done it. Although how she could have done it with both you and Alberta in the house is beyond me."

I blinked away my tears and took a good hard look at his face. There was nothing in it for me. So Alberta'd been right. Well, well. All I could do for the moment was to keep on looking sorry and pitiful. "Should I call the doctor?" I whispered.

"He can't do anything for her this time. But I

suppose we have to have him. It looks like sleeping pills again. But how did she get at them? I had them locked up."

"Just take a look at your den," I suggested.

I trailed along behind him as he mooched along to his den. I didn't want to miss a single moment of his reaction to the mess in there. I needed to know whether or not he was completely sold on suicide. It meant a lot to my future.

He opened the door to his den and just stood there, staring in at the wreckage. Finally, he said, "I guess anybody *that* determined is entitled to get what she wants." And then he turned to me. "Nadya," he said, "I hope this won't drive you away. I need you now."

I didn't say a word, but something like satisfaction began to lighten up the heaviness in my heart. Maybe Alberta was wrong, after all. Maybe I *wouldn't* have to do something about Carl. I tried on a tremulous smile, but the lightness didn't last very long.

"Alyssa Morgana needs you," he went on, "at least until I can straighten things out around here. Stacy wasn't much of a mother—or much of a wife, for that matter. I'd be lying if I said I am sorry she's gone. We haven't been truly husband and wife for a long time. But I guess you know that."

I nodded, waiting for him to continue to dig his own grave.

"I'm going to call the doctor now. And I'll probably have to call in the police. But before I do, I'm going to call a friend of mine. She's a good, kind, sensible woman, and she'll be a big help to all of us. I'd appreciate it if you'd do whatever she asks you to do."

"Okay," I said. And then I couldn't help asking, "Is she *that* good a friend?"

"What?" he said, startled. "Oh, I see what you mean. Well, yes, I guess she is. Only it's a little too soon to think about what might happen six months or a year from now. Nadya, don't think I'm not grateful for the evenings I've spent with you. I was lonely, and you were sweet. I'll never forget that. And you won't be sorry. I'll make it up to you. I hope we'll always be friends."

But not *that* good a friend, I said to myself. "Sure," I told him. "For as long as we both shall live."

He gave me a puzzled look, but then shrugged it off and went into his den and closed the door.

I opened it and said, "I've got an audition in the morning. Is it okay if I get a babysitter? That's what Stacy always did."

"Of course," he said, staring down at his desk drawer and fingering the marks of the letter opener. "You've got your career to think of. Good luck." He picked up the phone and started dialing.

I closed the door and snuggled my face into Alyssa Morgana's sweet baby-powder smell. "It'll have to be soon," I whispered to her. "It'll be something like this. He couldn't live without her. I don't know yet how it'll happen. Maybe he'll jump out a window. Or drink poison in his Tequila Sunrise. Poor guy. He was just so upset and depressed. Blamed himself for what happened. Don't worry. I'll figure it out. If there's one thing an au pair girl has to be, it's resourceful."

Alyssa Morgana gurgled and pulled the blue ribbon off my head. I didn't mind. This particular costume had served its purpose.

And to tell the truth, Stacy'd given me a few ideas about how to play the suicide scene at the audition tomorrow morning. She always said she wanted to help out a future star.

Bodyguards Shoot Second

LOREN D. ESTLEMAN

Loren Estleman lives near Detroit, the turf of his fictional detective, Amos Walker. Successful as both a western writer (he won the Western Writers of America Spur award in 1982) and a crime writer, Estleman feels his cowboy and detective heroes are lone revolutionaries. In a recent interview, Estleman speculated that mystery readers want to read about "characters of extraordinary makeup doing things the police can't because of the Bill of Rights, the Supreme Court, and the inertia of modern American law enforcement." Walker was created for them.

Estleman's most recent novel is *Any Man's Death* (1985), published by The Mysterious Press.

"A. Walker Investigations."

"Amos Walker?"

The voice on the other end of the line was male and youthful, one of those that don't change from the time they crack until the time they quake. I said, "This is he."

"Huh?"

"Grammar," I said. "It gets me business in Grosse Pointe. But not lately. Who's speaking?"

"This is Martin Cole. I'm Billy Dickerson's road manager."

"Okay."

"No, really."

"I believe you, Mr. Martin. How can I make your life easier?"

"Cole. Martin's my first name. Art Cradshaw recommended you. He said you were the best man for what you do in Detroit."

"Sweet of him. But he still owes me for the credit check I ran for his company six months ago."

"That's hardly my business. I need a man."

I parked the receiver in the hollow of my shoulder and lit a Winston.

"Walker?"

"I'm here. You need a man."

"The man I need doesn't pick his teeth with his thumbnail and can wear a dinner jacket without looking like he was strapped in waiting for the current, but doesn't worry about popping a seam when he has to push somebody's face in. He's a good enough shot to light a match at thirty paces on no notice, but he carries himself as if he thought the butt of a gun would spoil the lines of his suit. He can swear and spit when called upon but in polite conversation wouldn't split an infinitive at knifepoint."

I said, "I wish you'd let me know when you find him. I could use someone like that in the investigation business."

"According to Art Cradshaw you're that man."

"I don't own a dinner jacket, Mr. Dickerson."

"Cole. Dickerson's the man I represent. The jacket's no problem. We have a tailor traveling with us and he'll fix you up in a day."

"I didn't know tailors traveled. But then I don't

72

know any tailors. What business are you and Mr. Dickerson in?"

Pause. "You're kidding, aren't you?"

"Probably not. I don't have a sense of humor."

"Billy Dickerson. The singer. Rock and Country. He's opening at the Royal Tower in Dearborn tomorrow night. Don't tell me you've never heard of him."

"My musical appreciation stops around 1962. What sort of work do you have in mind for this cross between Richard Gere and the Incredible Hulk?"

"Protection. Billy's regular bodyguard has disappeared, and he can't leave his suite here at the Tower without someone to stand between him and his adoring fans. Too much adoration can be fatal."

"I don't do that kind of work, Mr. Cole. Bodyguards shoot second. If at all."

"We're paying a thousand. For the week."

I hesitated. Habit. Then: "My day rate's two-fifty. That comes to seventeen-fifty for seven days."

"We'll go that."

"Can't do it, Mr. Cole. I'm sitting on retainer for a local union just now. They could call me any time. Try Ned Eccles on Michigan; security's his specialty. Infinitives don't last too long around him, but he's hard and fast, and he knows how to tie a bow."

"I don't know. Art said you were the guy to call."

"Cradshaw's in the tool design business. He doesn't know a bodyguard from a right cross."

"I thought you guys never turned down a job."

I said, "It's not a thing I'd care to get good at. Tell Ned I sent you."

"Will he give me a discount?"

"No. But he might give me one next time I farm something out to him." I wished him good luck, and we were through talking to each other.

The union rep didn't call that day or the next, just as he hadn't called for a week; not since the day I'd accepted his retainer. Meanwhile I was laying in a hundred and a half every twenty-four hours just for playing solitaire within reach of the telephone. I closed the office at five and drove home. It was November. The city was stone-colored under a gray sky, and there was in the air the raw-iron smell that comes just before a snow.

Out of long habit I flipped on the television set the minute I got in the door and went into the kitchen, stripping off my jacket and tie as I went. When I came out opening a can of beer the picture had come on but not the sound and I was looking at a studio shot of Ned Eccles's fleshy moustached face.

" . . . died three hours later at Detroit Receiving Hospital," came the news anchor's voice, too loud. I jumped and turned down the volume. Now they were showing videotape of a lean young man with stringy blond hair to his shoulders, striding down a stage runway in a gold lamé jumpsuit unzipped to his pelvis. He was shouting song lyrics into a hand mike while the crowd jammed up against the footlights screamed. The anchor continued.

"Dickerson, shown here during his last appearance at the Royal Tower two years ago, was shoved out of the line of fire by a member of his entourage after the first shot and was unharmed. The slain bodyguard has been identified as Edward Eccles, 45, a Detroit private investigator with a background in personal security. Police have no leads as yet to the man who fired the shots." There was a short pause as the picture dissolved to the anchor's grave face. He turned his head and smiled. "How are the Tigers doing, Steve?"

I changed channels. There was a commercial for a women's hygiene product on the next local channel and a guy in a chef's hat showing how to make cheese gooey on the last. I turned off the set and sipped beer and thought. The telephone interrupted my thinking.

"Walker?"

"Yeah."

"This is Carol Greene. You heard?"

Carol Greene was Ned Eccles's business partner. I said, "I just caught a piece of it. What happened?"

"Not on the phone. Can you come to Ned's office?"

"What for?"

"I'll tell you when you get here." After a beat: "You owe Ned. You got him killed."

"Don't hang that on me, Carol. I just made a referral. He didn't have to take the job. Give me twenty minutes." I hung up and retrieved my tie and jacket.

Eccles Investigations and Security worked out of a storefront off Cadillac Square, with an oak railing separating Carol's desk in front from Ned's in back and a lot of framed photographs on the walls of Ned shaking hands with the mayor and the governor and various presidential candidates whose faces remained vaguely familiar long after their names were faded on old baled ballots. The place had a friendly, informal, unfussy look that had set its owners back three grand. The basement vault where the firm's files were kept had cost more than the building. I went through a swinging gate in the railing to Ned's desk where Carol was supporting herself on her small angular fists.

"Give some guys twenty minutes and they'll take forty," she greeted me.

"The rush hour got me by the throat. You look the same as always."

"Don't start." She put the cigarette she was holding between thumb and forefinger to her lips, bit off some smoke, and tipped it down her throat in a series of short, jerky movements like a bird bolting grain. She was a small, wiry woman in a man's flannel shirt and jeans with gray-streaked blonde hair cut very short and unadorned glasses with underslung bows. She had been Ned Eccles's junior partner for ten years. Whatever else she might have been to him wasn't my business today or ever.

"How much do you know about what happened to Ned?" she asked.

"Just that he was killed. Apparently by someone trying to get Billy Dickerson."

She nodded jerkily, ate some more cigarette, ground it out in a glass ashtray full of butts on the desk. "Dickerson stopped to sign an autograph in front of the service elevator on the way up to his suite at the Royal Tower. Ned had told him to avoid the lobby. He'd told him not to stop for anyone either, but I guess Billy-boy didn't hear that part. The guy ducked Ned and stuck a pad in Dickerson's hand, and while Dickerson was writing he pulled a piece. Ned saw it and got between them just in time to get his guts drilled. That was about noon. He spent the afternoon dying. I just got back from the hospital."

Her eyes were a little red behind the cheaters. I said, "Who saw this?"

"Dickerson's manager, Martin Cole. Dickerson. Some gofer, Phil something. I talked to them at the hospital. While they were busy getting the Music Man out of the way of the bullets, the gunny lit out through the rear entrance. Six feet, a hundred and eighty, thirties, balding. Dark zipper jacket. That's as good as it gets. The croakers dug two .38 slugs out of Ned's insides."

"Say anything before he died?"

She shook her head, firing up a fresh cigarette from a butane lighter whose flame leapt halfway to the ceiling. "Outside of cussing a blue streak. That why you turned Cole down? You had dope on the shoot?"

"I was in the clutch when he called."

"Yeah."

I said, "Ned and I didn't get along, you know that. We had different ideas about how the investigating business should be run. But I didn't put him in front of those bullets."

"Yeah. I guess not." She tossed the lighter atop a stack of manila file folders on the desk. Then she looked at me. "I'll go your full rate to look into Ned's death."

"Ned's death was an accident."

"Maybe. Either way you get paid."

"You've got a license."

"I make out the books, trace an occasional skip. That's all I've done for ten years. Ned was the detective. You do this kind of thing all the time."

"Wrong. Mostly I look for missing persons."

"The guy who killed Ned is missing."

"He's cop meat," I said. "Save your money and let them do their job."

"Cops. First Monday of every month I hand an envelope to our department pipeline, a night captain. A thing like that can shake your faith. You still in the clutch?"

I nodded. "Retainer. I sit by the telephone."

"You've got an answering service to do that. Look, I won't beg you." She made a face and killed the butt, smoked only a third down. "I know everyone thought I was sleeping with Ned, including that slut of a wife of his, who should know about that kind of thing. I haven't cared what people thought of me since my senior prom. For the record, though, I wasn't. He was my friend and my partner and I have to do this one thing for him before I can go back to what I was doing. If you won't take the job I'll find someone else. The Yellow Pages are lousy with plastic badges."

"I'll look into it. Courtesy rate, two hundred a day and expenses. Couple of days should tell if I'm wasting your money."

She wrote out a check for five hundred dollars and gave it to me. "That should see you through. If it doesn't, come back here. With an itemized list of expenses. No whiskey."

"You keep the books, all right." I folded the check and stuck it in my wallet. "One question. Don't hit me with the desk when I ask it."

"Ask."

"Did you ever know Ned to be the kind of a bodyguard who would throw himself between a gun and its target, even if the target was the person he was guarding?"

"No," she said quickly. "No, I didn't know him to be that kind of a bodyguard."

"Neither did I."

I cashed the check at my bank, deposited all but a hundred of it, and drove the four miles to Dearborn. The sky was low and the heater took ten minutes to chase the chill out of the upholstery. I parked in the lot behind the Royal Tower. A uniformed cop stopped me at the main entrance to the hotel. "Excuse me, sir, but are you a guest here?"

"No, I'm here to see someone."

"No one goes in without a room key, sorry. We had some excitement here earlier."

I handed him one of my cards. "Would you see that Martin Cole gets that? He's with Billy Dickerson. It's important."

The cop called over another uniform, gave him the card, and told him to take it up. Ten minutes later the second officer returned. "Lieutenant says okay." To me: "306."

More uniforms and a group of men in suits greeted me in the hallway when I stepped off the elevator. One of the latter was an inch shorter than I but half again as broad through the shoulders. It would have been a long time since he had gone through a door any way but sideways. His skin was pale to the point of translucence, almost albino, but his eyes were blue. He combed his short blond hair forward.

"Walker? I'm Gritch, homicide lieutenant with the

Dearborn police." He flashed his badge in a handsome leather folder. "Cole says to let you through, but we got to check you for weapons."

"I'm not carrying," I said, but stood for the frisk by a black officer with hands like Ping-Pong paddles. Gritch meanwhile looked through the credentials in my wallet. He handed it back.

"Okay. We got to play it tight. The description of the guy that tried to kill Dickerson fits you as good as it fits a thousand other guys in this town."

"Anything new?" I put the crease back in my topcoat.

"Now, would I be earning your tax dollars if I answered that, after going to so much trouble to keep the public off the premises?"

"Nothing new," I said. "I thought so. Where's 306?"

"Right in front of you, Sherlock." He stepped away from it.

Before I could knock, the door was opened by a young man in shirtsleeves and stockinged feet. His hair was brown and wavy and combed behind his ears, his face clean-shaven, and his eyes as lifelike as two stones. He had a nine-millimeter automatic pistol in his right hand.

"Let him in, Phil."

The man who spoke was smaller than Lieutenant Gritch but not so small as Carol Greene, with a great mane of styled black hair and a drooping moustache and aviator's glasses with rose-tinted lenses. He wore a dark European-looking jacket with narrow lapels and a pinched waist over yellow-and-red checked pants. His shoes were brown leather with tassels and he had a yellow silk scarf knotted at his throat.

"Walker, is it? I'm Martin Cole. Decent of you to stop in."

At first glance, Cole was as youthful as his voice, but there were hairline fissures around his eyes and pouches at the corners of his mouth that his moustache couldn't hide. I took the moist warm hand he offered and entered the suite. The room was plushly carpeted and furnished as a living room with a sofa and easy chairs, but folding metal chairs had been added. Cole caught me looking at them.

"For the press," he said. "We're holding a conference as soon as the police finish downstairs. Billy Dickerson, Amos Walker."

I looked at the man seated on the end of the sofa with a small barrel glass full of copper-colored liquid in one hand. In person he was older and not as lean as he appeared on television. His skin was grayish against the long open collar of his white jumpsuit and a distinct roll showed over his wide brown tooled leather belt with an ornate gold buckle. His long yellow hair was thinning at the temples. He glanced at me, drank from his glass, and looked at Cole. "He the best you could do?"

"Walker came on his own, Billy," the manager said. Quickly he introduced the man with the gun as Phil Scabarda.

I said, "He must have a permit for that or he wouldn't be waving it around with the cops so close. That doesn't mean he can point it at me."

Cole gestured at the young man, who hesitated, then hung the pistol on a clip on the back of his belt. "Phil is Billy's driver and companion. These days that requires courses in racing and weaponry."

"Ned Eccles's partner hired me to look into the shooting," I said. "I appreciate your seeing me."

"Ah. I thought maybe you wanted his job after all. I'd rather hoped."

"You've got police protection now. What happened in front of the service elevator?"

"Well, we were standing there waiting for the doors to open when this guy came out from behind the elevator and asked Billy for his autograph. As soon as he got rid of the pad he pulled a gun from under his jacket. Eccles stepped in and took both bullets."

"Was Eccles armed?"

Cole nodded. "A revolver of some kind. I don't know from guns. It was still in his shoulder holster when the police came. There wasn't time to get it out."

"What was Phil doing while all this was going on?"

"Hustling Billy out of the way, with me. Meanwhile the guy got away." He gave me the same description he'd given Carol.

"If he was after Dickerson, why'd he leave without scratching him?"

"He panicked. Those shots were very loud in that enclosed space. As it was he barely got out before the place was jammed with gawkers."

"What happened to the pad?"

"Pad?"

"The pad he handed Dickerson for his autograph. Fingerprints."

"I guess Billy dropped it in the scramble. Some souvenir hunter has it by now."

I got out a cigarette and tapped it on the back of my left hand. "Anyone threaten Dickerson's life lately?"

"The police asked that. He gets his share of hate mail like every other big-name entertainer. They don't like his hair or his singing or his politics. That kind of letter is usually scribbled in Crayola on ruled paper with the lines an inch apart. I called Billy's secretary in LA to go through the files and send the most likely ones by air express for the police to look at. But she throws most of them away."

"What's the story on this bodyguard that disappeared?"

"Henry?" Carefully plucked eyebrows slid above the tinted glasses. "Forget him. He was a drunk and he got to wandering just when we needed him most. Flying in from LA day before yesterday we changed planes in Denver, and he was missing when we boarded for Detroit. Probably found himself a bar and he's drying out in some drunk tank by now. If he hadn't ducked out we'd have fired him soon anyway. He was worse than no protection at all."

"Full name and description." I got out my notebook and pencil.

"Henry Bliss. About your height, a little over six feet. Two hundred pounds, sandy hair, fair complexion. Forty. Let's see, he had a white scar about an inch long on the right side of his jaw. Dropped his guard, he said. Don't waste your time with him. He was just an ex-pug with a taste for booze."

"It's my client's time. Any reason why someone would want to kill Dickerson? Besides his hair and his singing and his politics?"

"Celebrities make good clay pigeons. They're easier to get at than politicians, but you can become just as famous shooting them."

"Everyone's famous today. It's almost worth it to

get an obscure person's autograph." I flipped the notebook shut. "Can I reach you here if something turns up?"

"We're booked downstairs for two weeks."

"Except for tonight."

"We're opening tonight as scheduled. Look, you can tell Ned's partner how sorry we are, but . . ."

"The show must go on?"

Cole smiled thinly. "An ancient tradition with a solid mercenary base. No one likes giving refunds."

"Thanks, Mr. Cole. You'll be hearing from me."

"You know," he said, "I can't help thinking that had you been on the job, things would have gone differently today."

"Probably not. Ned knew his business. Your boy's alive. That's what you paid for."

As I closed the door behind me, Lieutenant Gritch came away from his crew next to the elevator. "What'd you get?" he demanded.

"Now, would I be earning my client's money if I answered that, after going to so much trouble to keep the cops out of my pockets?"

His pale face flushed for a moment. Then the color faded and he showed his eyeteeth in a gargoyle's grin, nodding. "Okay. I guess I bought that. We'll trade. You go."

I told him what I'd learned. He went on nodding.

"That's what we got. There's nothing in that autograph pad. Even if it had liftable prints, which nothing like that ever does ever, they'd have someone else's all over them by now. We Telexed this Henry Bliss's name and description to Denver. It won't buy zilch. This one's local and sloppy. If we get the guy at all it'll be because somebody unzipped his big yap. Give me a pro any time. These amateurs are a blank order."

"What makes him an amateur?"

"You mean besides he got the wrong guy? The gun. We frisked the service area and the parking lot and the alley next door. No gun. A pro would've used a piece without a history and then dumped it. He wouldn't take a chance on being picked up for CCW. You got a reference?"

The change of subjects threw me for a second. Then I gave him John Alderdyce's name in Detroit Homicide. He had a uniform write down the name in his notebook.

"Okay, we'll check you out. You know what the penalty is for interfering with a murder investigation."

"Something short of electrocution," I said. "In this state, anyway."

"Then I won't waste breath warning you off this one. You get anything—anything—you know where to come." He handed me one of his cards.

I gave him one of mine. "If you ever have a carpet that needs looking under."

"I'd sooner put my gun in my mouth," he said. But he stuck the card in his pocket.

The sun had gone down, sucking all the warmth out of the air. It still smelled like snow. On my way home I stopped at the main branch of the Detroit Public Library on Woodward, where I knew the security guard. I spotted him a ten to let me in after closing and browsed through the out-of-town directories until I found a list of detective agencies in Denver and copied some likelies into my notebook.

Colorado is two hours behind Michigan, so most of the offices still were open. The first two I called didn't believe in courtesy rates. The third took down the information I had on Henry Bliss, the wandering bodyguard, and said they'd get back to me. I hung up and dialed my service for messages. I had a message. I got the union executive I was working for at home. He had a tail job for me, a shop steward suspected of pocketing membership dues.

"What am I looking for?" I asked.

"Where he goes with the money." The executive's tone was as smooth as ice. No lead pipes across his throat like in the old days. "He's not depositing it, and he's not investing it. Follow him until it changes hands. Get pictures."

The job would start in the morning. I took down the necessary information, pegged the receiver, slid a TV tray into the oven, and mixed myself a drink while it was heating up. I felt like a pretty, empty-headed girl with two dates for Saturday night.

In the morning, after breakfast, I rang up Barry Stackpole at the *Detroit News*. While waiting for him to answer I watched the snow floating down outside the window turn brown before it reached the ground.

"Amos the famous shamus," said Barry, after I'd announced myself. "What can I do you for this lovely morning?"

"You must be in St. Tropez. I need a name on a pro heavyweight." I described Ned Eccles's killer. Barry wrote a syndicated column on organized crime and had a national reputation and an artificial leg to show for it.

"Offhand I could name twenty that would fit," he said. "Local?"

"Maybe. More likely he was recruited from somewhere else."

"Make that a hundred. I can get a list to your office by messenger this afternoon. What's the hit?"

"A P.I. named Eccles. You wouldn't know him. He bought the lead that was meant for Billy Dickerson yesterday."

"That was a hit?"

"I don't know. But the cops are following the amateur theory, and that leaves this way open. I step on fewer official toes."

"When did you get religion?"

"I'm duplicating them on one thing, a previous bodyguard that got himself lost out West. The cops don't put much faith in it. I wouldn't be earning my fee if all I did was sniff their coattails. What's this list going to run me?"

"A fifth of Teacher's."

"Just one?"

"I'm cutting down. Hang tight."

After he broke the connection I called my service and asked them to page me if Denver called. Then I dug my little pen-size beeper out of a drawer full of spent cartridges and illegible notes to myself, clipped it to my belt, and went to work for the union.

The shop steward lived a boring life. I tailed his Buick from his home in Redford Township to the GM Tech Center in Warren where he worked, picked him up again when he and two fellow workers walked downtown for lunch, ate in a booth across the restaurant from their table, and followed them back to work. One of the other guys got the tab. My guy took care of the tip. On my way out I glanced at the bills on the table. Two singles. He wasn't throwing the stuff away, that was sure.

During the long gray period before quitting time I found a public booth within sight of the Buick in the parking lot and called my service. There were no messages from Denver or anywhere else. I had the girl page me to see if the beeper was working. It was.

I followed the steward home, parked next to the curb for two hours waiting to see if he came out again, and when he didn't I drove to the office. Opening the unlocked door of my little waiting room I smelled cop. The door to my private office, which I keep locked when I'm not in it, was standing open. I went through it and found Gritch sitting behind my desk looking at a sheet of typing paper. His skin wasn't any more colorful and he looked like a billboard with the window at his back. My Scotch bottle and one of my pony glasses stood on the desk, the glass half full.

"Pour one for me." I hung up my hat and coat.

He got the other glass out of the file drawer and topped it off. His eyes didn't move from the paper in his left hand. "You got better taste in liquor than you do in locks," he said, leveling off his own glass.

"I'm working. I wasn't when I bought the lock." I put down my drink in one installment and waited for the heat to rise.

"This is quite a list you got. Packy Davis, yeah. Benny Boom-Boom Bohannen, sure. Lester Adams, don't know him." His voice trailed off, but his lips kept moving. Finally he laid the sheet on the desk and sat back in my swivel-shrieker and took a drink, looking at me for the first time. "It isn't quite up to date. Couple of those guys are pulling hard time. Two are dead, and one might as well be, he's got more tubes sticking out of him than a subway terminal."

"You know lists. They get old just while you're typing them up." I bought a refill.

"Some smart kid in a uniform brought it while I was waiting for you. I gave him a quarter and he looked like I bit his hand. Who sent it?"

"A friend. You wouldn't know him. He respects locks."

His marblelike face didn't move. He would have heard worse. "This to do with the Eccles burn?"

I said nothing. Drank.

"Yeah, Alderdyce said you could shut up like an oyster. I called him. We had quite a conversation about you. Want to know what else he said?"

"No, I want to know what brings you to my office when everyone else who has any brains has closed up for the day."

"Your client won't answer her phone. Her office is closed too, but it's been closed all day, and her home isn't listed. And you're harder to get hold of than an eel with sunburn. I didn't feel like talking to the girl at your service. She sounds like my aunt that tells fortunes. I got to find out if there was any connection between Eccles and Henry Bliss, Dickerson's old bodyguard."

A little chill chased the whisky-warmth up my spine, like a drop of cold water running uphill. "How come?"

"No reason. Except the Denver police fished a floater out of the South Platte this morning, with two holes in the back of his skull. We got the Telex two hours ago. The stiff fits Bliss's description down to the scar on his chin."

I struck a match, cracking the long silence, and touched the flame to a Winston. Gritch watched me. He said:

"Dunked stiffs surface after three days. That puts him in the river just about the time Dickerson and Cole and their boy Phil noticed him missing."

"Meaning?" I flipped the dead match into the ashtray on the desk and cocked a hip up on one corner, blowing smoke out my nostrils.

"Meaning maybe yesterday's try on Dickerson, if that's what it was, wasn't a backyard job after all. Meaning maybe the same guy that dusted Bliss dusted Eccles. Meaning that seeing as how the two hits were a thousand miles apart and seeing as how the guy that did it didn't leave tracks either time, he's pro."

"Slugs match up?"

He shook his fair head without taking his eyes off my face. "Nothing on that yet. But they won't. Major leaguers never use the same piece twice. What I want to know . . ."

"You said they didn't take their pieces away with them, either."

"What I want to know," he went on, "is how it happens I come here looking to talk to you and your client about Eccles's hit being a mechanic's job and find a list of mechanics all typed up nice and neat before I'm here five minutes."

"Just touching all the bases," I said. "Like you. You didn't send a flyer to Denver looking for some local nut that doesn't like loud music."

"That's it, huh."

I said it was it. He sipped some more Scotch, made

a face, rubbed a spot at the arch of his rib cage, and set the glass down. I never knew a cop that didn't have something wrong with his back or his stomach. He said, "Well, I got to talk to Carol Greene."

"I'll set up a meet. What makes it look like Bliss and Eccles were connected?"

"Nothing. But if it's Dickerson this guy was after, he's a worse shot than I ever heard of."

"Why make the bodyguards targets?"

"That's what I want to ask the Greene woman." He got up, rubbing the spot. The houndstooth overcoat he had on was missing a few teeth. "Set it up. Today. I get off at eight."

"How'd Dickerson do last night?"

He opened the door to the outer office. "Capacity crowd. But he don't have the stuff he had when the wife was a fan. When no one shot at him they left disappointed."

He went out. I listened to the hallway door hiss shut behind him against the pressure of the pneumatic device. Thinking.

I finished the cigarette and pulled the telephone over and dialed Carol's number. She answered on the third ring.

"Lieutenant Gritch wants to talk to you," I told her, after the preliminaries. "You're better off seeing him at headquarters. That way you can leave when you want to."

"I already talked to him once. What is it this time?" Her voice was slurred. I'd forgotten she was an alcoholic. I told her about Bliss. After a pause she said, "Ned never mentioned him. I'd know if they ever did business."

"Tell Gritch that."

"You got anything yet?"

"A shadow of a daydream of an idea. I'll let you know. Take a cab to Dearborn."

Next I got the Denver P.I. on the telephone. He said he was still working on the description I'd given him of Henry Bliss. I told him that was all wrapped up and I'd send him a check. Then I called Barry Stackpole.

"That list all right?" he asked.

"A little out of date, according to the cops. I may not need it. Who's on the entertainment desk today?"

"Jed Dutt. I still get my Teacher's, right?"

"If you switch me over to Dutt I'll even throw in a bottle of tonic water."

"Don't be blasphemous." He put me on hold.

"Dutt," announced a wheezy old voice thirty seconds later.

"My name's Walker," I said. "I'm investigating the attempt on Billy Dickerson's life yesterday. I have a question for you."

"Shoot."

"Very funny," I said.

"Sorry."

I asked him the question. His answer was the first time I got more than one word out of him. I thanked him and broke the connection. The telephone rang while my hand was still on the receiver. It was the man from the union.

"I'm still working on it," I told him. "No money changed hands today."

He said, "Keep an eye on him. He isn't swallowing it or burying it in the basement. I made some inquiries and found out the house across the street is for rent. Maybe you ought to move in."

"Round-the-clock surveillance costs money."

"Name a figure."

I named one. He said, "Can you move in tomorrow?"

I said that was short notice. He said, "Your retainer buys us that right. Shall I make the rental arrangements?"

"I'll let you know," I said.

I smoked a cigarette, looking at the blonde in the bikini on the calendar on the wall opposite the desk. Then I ground out the stub and made one more call. It took a while. When it was finished I got up and unpegged my hat and coat. Before going out I got the Smith & Wesson out of the top drawer of the desk and checked it for cartridges and snapped the holster onto the back of my belt under my jacket. I hate forcing a case.

No cops stopped me on my way into the Royal Tower this time, and no one was waiting to frisk me when I stepped off the elevator on the third floor. I felt neglected. I rapped on 306.

"What do you want?"

I grinned at Phil. There was no reflection at all in his flat dark eyes. The automatic pistol was a growth in his fist. "This is for the grownups," I said. "Any around?"

"You got a lot of smart mouth."

"That makes one of us."

"Phil, who is it?"

The voice was Martin Cole's. It sounded rushed and breathless.

"That snooper," answered Phil, his eyes still on me.

"Tell him to come back later."

"You heard." The man with the gun smiled without opening his lips, like a cat.

A sudden scuffling noise erupted from inside the room. Someone grunted. A lamp turned over with a thud, slinging lariats of shadow up one wall. Phil turned his head and I chopped downward with the edge of my left hand, striking his wrist at the break. He cursed and the gun dropped from his grip. When he stooped to catch it I brought my right fist scooping up, catching him on the point of the chin and closing his mouth with a loud clop. I stepped back to give him room to fall. He used it.

I got the automatic out from under his unconscious body and stepped over him holding it in my sore right hand. I'd barked the knuckles on his jaw. It was a wasted entrance. Nobody was paying me any attention.

Billy Dickerson, naked but for a pair of blue Jockey shorts with his pale belly hanging over the top, was on his knees on the floor astraddle a scarcely more dapper-looking Martin Cole. The manager's tailored jacket was torn and his neatly styled hair hung cock-eyed over his left ear. It was the first I knew he wore a wig. Dickerson was holding a shiny steel straight razor a foot from Cole's throat and Cole had both hands on the singer's wrist trying to keep it there. Dickerson's eyes bulged and his lips were skinned back from long white teeth in a gargoyle's grin. His breath whistled. Through his teeth, Cole said, "Phil, give me a hand."

Phil wasn't listening. I took two steps forward and swept the butt of the automatic across the base of Dickerson's skull. The singer whimpered and sagged. Falling, the edge of the razor nicked Cole's cheek. It bled.

A floor lamp had been toppled against a chair. I straightened it and adjusted the shade.

"Most people watch television this time of the evening," I said.

The manager paused in the midst of pushing himself free to look at me. Automatically a hand went up and righted his wig. Then he finished rolling the singer's body off his and got up on his knees, listening with head cocked. A drop of blood landed on Dickerson's naked chest with a plop. The manager sat back on his heels. "He's breathing. You hit him damn hard."

"Pistol-whipping isn't an exact science. What happened?"

"D.T.'s. Bad trip. Maybe a combination of the two. He usually doesn't get this violent. When he does, Phil's usually there to get a grip on him and tie him up till it's over." He glanced toward the man lying in the open doorway. "Jeez, what'd you do, kill him?"

"It'd take more than an uppercut to do that. How long's he been like this?"

"Who, Billy? Couple of years. The last few months, though, he's been getting worse. The drugs pump him up for his performances, the booze brings him back down afterwards. But lately it's been affecting his music."

"Not just lately," I said. "It's been doing that for

the past year anyway. That's how long attendance at his concerts has been falling off, according to the entertainment writer I spoke to at the *News*."

He had picked up his tinted eyeglasses from the floor and was polishing them with a clean corner of the silk handkerchief he had been using to staunch the trickle of blood from his cut cheek. He stopped polishing and put them on. "Your friend's mistaken. We're sold out."

"They came to see if history would repeat itself and someone would make a new try on Dickerson. Just as you hoped they would."

"Explain."

"First get your hands away from your body."

He smiled. The expression reminded me of Phil's cat's-grin. "If I were armed, do you think I'd have wrestled Billy for that razor barehanded?"

"You would have. He's too valuable to kill. Get them up."

He raised his hands to shoulder level. I unholstered my .38 and put the nine-millimeter in my top-coat pocket. Go with the weapon you know.

"There was no hit man," I said, "no attempt on your boy's life. The man you intended to get killed got killed. It was going to be Henry Bliss, but in Denver something went wrong and you had to dump him without trumpets. What did he do, find out what you had planned for him and threaten to go to the law?"

He was still smiling. "You're out of it, Walker. If there was no hit man, who killed Ned Eccles?"

"I'm coming to that. You've got a lot of money tied up in Dickerson, but he's a depreciating property. I'm guessing, but I'd say a man with your expensive tastes has a lot of debts, maybe with some people it's not advisable to have a lot of debts with. So you figured to squeeze one more good season out of your client and get out from under. Attempted assassination is box office. A body gives it that authentic touch. After disposing of Bliss you shopped around. I looked pretty good. Security isn't my specialty; my reflexes might not be embarrassingly fast. Also I'm single, with no attachments, no one to demand too thorough an investigation into my death. But I turned you down. Ned Eccles wasn't as good. He was married. But his marriage was sour—you'd have found that out through questioning, as keeping secrets was not one of Ned's specialties—and being an experienced shield he'd have been looking for trouble from outside, not from his employers.

"I called Art Cradshaw a little while ago. That was a mistake, Cole, telling me it was him recommended me. He wasted some of my time being evasive, but when he found out I wasn't dunning him for what he owes me he was willing to talk. He remembered especially how pleased you were to learn I have no family."

Dickerson stirred and groaned. His manager ignored him. Cole wasn't smiling now. I went on.

"What'd you do, promise to cut Phil in on the increased revenue, or just pay him a flat fee to ventilate the bodyguard?"

"Now I know you're out of it. If Phil shot him, where's the gun? His is a nine-millimeter. Eccles was shot with a .38."

"You were right in front of the service elevator. One of you stepped inside and ditched it. Probably Phil, who was more reliable than Dickerson and tall enough to push open one of the panels on top of the car and stash it there. The cops had no reason to look there, because they were after a phantom hit man who made his escape through the back door."

"You're just talking, Walker. None of it's any good."

"The gun is," I said. "I think you have it hidden somewhere in this suite. The cops will find it. They've been sticking too close to you since the shooting for you to have had a chance to get rid of it. Until now, that is. Where are they?"

"I pulled them off."

The voice was new. I jumped and swung around, bringing the gun with me. I was pointing it at Lieutenant Gritch. He was holding his own service revolver at hip level. Phil lay as quietly as ever on the floor between us.

"Put it away," Gritch said patiently. "I don't want to add threatening a police officer to the charge of interfering in an official investigation. Too much paperwork."

I leathered the Smith & Wesson. "Why'd you pull them off?"

"To give Cole and Scabarda here breathing space. I didn't have enough to get a warrant to search the suite. I had a plainclothes detail in the lobby and near the back entrance ready to follow them until they tried to ditch the piece. Imagine my surprise when one of my men called in to say he saw you going up to the third floor."

"You knew?"

He said, "I'm a detective. You private guys forget that sometimes. I had to think who stood the most to gain from two dead bodyguards. What tipped you?"

"Cole's story of what happened downstairs. Ned Eccles wouldn't have stopped a bullet meant for his mother. But it didn't mean anything until you said what you did in my office about Dickerson's fans paying to see him get killed."

"Yeah, that's when it hit me too."

"Couple of Sherlocks," I said.

And then the muzzle of Gritch's revolver flamed and the report shook the room, and if there had been a mirror in front of me I would have seen my hair turn white in that instant. The wind of his bullet plucked at my coat. Someone grunted and I turned again and looked at Cole kneeling on the floor, gripping his bloody right wrist in his left hand. A small automatic gleamed on the carpet between him and Billy Dickerson, the King of Country Rock.

"Circus shooting," Gritch said, disgusted. "If my captain asks, I was aiming for the chest. I got suspended once for getting fancy. Oh, your client's waiting out in the parking lot, shamus. I was questioning her when the call came in. Couldn't talk her out of going. Three sheets to the wind she's still one tough broad. You better see her before she comes up here."

"Yeah," I said. "She might kick Cole's head in."

"Guess I'll be able to get that warrant now. You going to be handy for a statement?"

I wrote the address of the shop steward's house in Redford Township on the back of a card and gave it to him. "Don't try to reach me there. I'll be staying in the place across the street for a while starting tomorrow."

"How long?"

"Indefinitely."

"I got a sister-in-law trying to get out of Redford," he said. "I feel sorry for you."

"Like hell you do."

He grinned for the first time since I'd known him.

Far Eyes

ROBERT SAMPSON

Robert Sampson is a pulp mystery historian and
management analyst at Marshall Space Flight
Center in Huntsville, Alabama. The inspiration
for "Far Eyes" came at a flea market in Huntsville, he says: "One of the old boys was talking,
and he said 'Nobody's going to bother me and
my money.' With that he pulled out a sawed-off
Ivers-Johnson revolver, and I had the seed for
my story." Mr. Sampson's "Rain in Pinton
County," published in *New Black Mask No. 5*,
was awarded an Edgar as the best mystery story
of 1986.

They turned right onto a dirt road. The truck jolted
over heavy red ridges of clay and the thin man's hat
fell off.

"By damn," he said in his reedy voice, "she's sprung
stout, ain't she?" He bent to retrieve the hat, showing a bald patch baked red-brown and fringed by
scraps of brown and white hair.

Mason clutched the steering wheel. By now, ap-
prehension had its claws deep into him. He was involuntarily recoiling whenever the thin man moved.
He said, "Your momma lived a piece out, Silbert."

"Oh, sure. She loved the country, Momma did,
God rest her." His eyes were pale and evasive in a
face stripped of flesh, and he smelled softly sour.

"She had a world of antiques. But Sis got most of 'em."

"Too bad."

"Just a world of them. Valuable, too. She had a dealer to look at them and he said they was worth money."

"She sell them?"

"Now she didn't say." He stared glumly through the windshield, regret for lost money in his face. "She didn't leave hardly nothing but just the stuff under the house. You suppose it's worth shucks?"

"I'll have to see," Mason said. He felt exposed, helpless. He felt as if he sat between a trap's descending jaws. It was hot in the truck and his smooth little face shone with sweat.

Tan dust plumed behind them. They drove slowly along the road, skirting a field run full of Johnson grass and blackberry tangled under a pallid blue sky. They had driven at least five miles from Huntsville. In Mason's pocket, the roll of money glowed and burned.

"I do hate to run you way out here for maybe nothin' a'tall."

"It's part of the business," Mason said. "Driving around. Looking at things."

"You should of seen all that stuff Momma had. It was something."

The truck jounced on. Mason snatched another glance at the thin man lounging in his rancid clothing. Slight but hard. Thin and hard. His stomach jerked. He was a fool to come driving out here. If it came to that, he was way past the age to maybe have to go fighting people out behind the brush.

He pressed his left leg against the truck door, feeling the revolver in his left pocket.

The familiar hardness gave him no reassurance.

Until that morning, he had never seen Silbert or his harsh-faced brother. They showed up at the flea market after ten. It was hot, and Mason was sweating behind his table of Depression glass as he watched Mrs. Kohlenmachen finger the stock. She always talked more than she bought.

". . . and then he opened up this dirty little shed," she continued. "It was just full of his mother's things."

"Uh-huh," Mason said. "Full up, was it?" His round face expressed fascination with her story, anxiety as to its ending.

"And way in the back of the shed, we found it." Her hands with the glittering nails pantomimed excavation. "It was in a bushel basket, all covered with old newspaper. The most darling Tiffany lamp shade." Her face shone at him, a triumphant moon. "It was the Woodbine pattern. So really beautiful. Completely filthy, you can just imagine. But when I rubbed the glass, it just sparkled and glowed."

"Tiffany Woodbine," Mason said. His eyes tested passing faces for an interest in his display. He saw two men in jeans and gray cotton shirts come around the end of a truck and stare toward him. "How much he want for it?"

The two men turned away. The tall one, hard face stained with beard, bit an apple.

Mrs. Kohlenmachen said: "He didn't want to sell it because it was his mother's. But you know, people always say that so you'll beg them. He was a cute little man but very dishonest looking. Anyway, I recognized the lamp pattern at once. I insisted. You know . . ." Her voice lowered as she bent massively toward him. "I finally bargained him down to less than two hundred dollars." She laughed. "Can you imagine a real Tiffany lamp for two hundred dollars?"

"No, ma'am," Mason said. "I can't."

"There, now," she cried brightly. "You see."

She made a purchase after all. He watched her march off, a grand procession of one, holding to her stately self a yellow Depression glass cake plate wrapped in newspaper.

Mason sighed. He wandered over to his wife, who stood at the far end of the tables, polishing Carnival glass.

"That lady bought herself a small-piece Tiffany lamp for less than two hundred dollars," he remarked.

"Oh, dear," she said. "She didn't buy it from Ollie Preacher?"

"Uh-huh. She doesn't know it, but she did that."

"Something ought to be done about that man." She stared fire at him, a small bird outraged. "Did you tell her about him?"

Mason blinked, round-eyed, at her. He was small and stout, a neat, soft man in his early sixties, with the strained set to his mouth and chin that physical trouble sets on a face.

"No, I didn't tell her that. She found that shade herself. All he did was tell her it was Sweet Old Mom's—and maybe it was. Ollie's made enough of those shades for everybody in his family."

"That's terrible. Selling a new thing as an antique."

"He didn't sell it as an antique. She bought it as one. There's the difference." He put a short pipe into his mouth. "He's a fine craftsman. You may not like his way, but it sells lamps."

She said sharply, "He's disgusting. I won't have his lamps on our table. Our glass is real."

"No. He won't ask us again."

Remembered shame stirred in him like an evil mud. He looked sharply away from her and stalked back under the canopy, shoulders stiff. The two men, he noticed, now bent over a box of old shoes. Their eyes flickered toward him and then away, as if memories showed on his face like pictures on a screen.

He poured a foam cup full of cola and carried it back to her. "Here you are, Lady."

"Thank you, El." He thought there might be pity in her voice. As if she, too, remembered Preacher's voice as he turned away from their table.

The two men now ambled slowly toward his counter. He moved to meet them.

"You Mr. Mason?"

"Uh-huh." They smelled of dirty bodies in dirty clothing. They were heavy-boned, red-faced, with the flesh starved off them. Their mouths grinned, showing the evil surfaces of their teeth.

The big one took off his cap with the beer label on the front. "You got some pretty things here."

"Uh-huh."

"We're the Silberts from up to Bexton. This's my brother, Ev. I'm Andy. We got us some glass and stuff. Momma died, and it was all down there under the house."

The thin one, Ev, said, "We was wondering to ask you might be thinkin' on buyin' anything like that."

"I buy antique glass, mainly. Mason jars, plates. Some smaller things, long as it's something I need." Interest stirred in him, and he added, blank-faced, "What do you have?"

"Jus' some old bottles and stuff, I guess," Andy said.

Ev glared at him. "There's some of those things the ladies put flowers in. And all Momma's glass pieces."

The big man put on his cap, tugging it down over thick black hair. "We got maybe ten-twelve boxes out in the shed."

"It's all that glass Momma had on the table," Ev said. "She was proud of those as a hundred dollar in gold."

Mason said, "Bring in a couple of boxes and let me take a look."

Andy rocked his head left and right. "No, sir, they're maybe not worth the carryin'. They're in the shed. We should maybe leave them sit. I hauled them every one from under the house, but not no more."

Ev said aggressively, "Well, now, didn't I haul and carry same as you?"

"Not much you did."

"Shoot. I picked and carried more'n you."

"Thing is," Andy said, "if you was to want to look at them, there they are. If not, there they be."

Ev said, "We thought maybe you might find something you'd be wanting to give us a price for." He added, "No use Sis gettin' it all."

"It's just down the road a mile," Andy said.

"Well, I could look," Mason told them. "Maybe you might gimme about twenty minutes."

"Suits me," Andy said. Sweat blotched his gray shirt.

Ev said, "We're just fixin' to dab around some. Be back."

They drifted away into the crowd.

Lady, at his elbow, asked sharply, "Who were those horrible men?"

"Got some glass to sell."

"Don't you fool with them. They got that look, like bad dogs."

He stood beside her under the canopy that filtered sunlight on their two wooden chairs, on the white cooler of cola cans, on the neat stacks of sacks and newspapers used to wrap their sales. Not much paper used today. Too much money tied up in antique glass and not enough buyers. In the thick heat, the glass glared pale pink, lemon, green; enticements of color.

The Silberts set uneasiness rippling through him. They were the latest waves in a day of ominous tremors and forebodings. Beginning that morning. When, as he stood by his bed, he felt the room tilt and weave.

Not much. Not long. The sensation dissolved, but it was not something that would stay away. It would return, fanged and terrible. For nothing ever got better but only progressively fell apart.

As the day fell apart.

They ran late leaving home. They had to stop for gas. They found no satisfactory place at the flea market. Two black women with racks of pink and purple robes laughed in Mason's accustomed spot. After which he discovered that they had no change. And later no customers.

Events thrust at him. The desperate heart shook his body. His angers and his failures ran together, heated by deep fear, building a pressure that he recognized but could not understand. Resisting that pressure, he found himself resisting Lady as part of it.

He set his mouth. "I'm going to see what they got. Won't take an hour."

"Trouble don't take long to come."

"We need new stock."

"We can't sell what we've got. No call you to go out in this heat, Elwood. It's not good on your heart."

He said, "My heart's fine." She would keep patting at him about his heart, just like a woman patting at dough. Standing erect, pulling in his stomach, he pushed confidence into his voice: "Just fine."

Around them sprawled the North Alabama Giant Outdoor Flea Market. Across the parking lot sweltered disorderly rows of trucks, tables, homemade stands piled with someone's old clothing, paperbacks, plastic toys with violent pasts, chairs you could fix with a little work. Sunlight lay like scalding liquid over tomatoes in their boxes and light green okra, lawnmowers and hand tools, velvet cushions decorated with kittens, hub caps concentrating light to merciless white points. Children's furniture clustered white and pink and blue, decaled with cunning bunnies. Past the displays wandered sun-numbed shoppers, eyed narrowly by sellers huddled beneath large hats and umbrellas. The air smelled richly of frying pork skins, the odor thick enough to spread on bread.

Lady said at last, "Don't you be takin' a lot of money."

"I'll take enough."

"You are the stubbornest man."

She turned slowly from him. He knew she waited for him to change his mind.

"Here they come, right on the dot," he said.

He watched the Silberts slouch toward his stand, and swallowed to clear his throat. "One of 'em's going with me in the truck to show the way."

They did look like dogs: the thin one, fawning and treacherous; the tall one, bony-shouldered and dark, with the look of a hound that would come at you from behind—all teeth and silent savagery.

As he fumbled for the truck keys, he felt a single stir of fear.

They drove a long time through the heat. More than a mile.

Finally Silbert pointed a finger and Mason braked the truck to a stop behind a decayed wooden house. Dust swirled up. He saw bleached boards sealing the windows, waist-high weeds engulfing a stack of tattered window screens. A dozen sparrows whipped past them into the field beyond.

The rear yard was strewn with litter, as if the house had disgorged a stream of decayed cardboard, bits of wood, newspapers, automobile parts. A shabby pickup truck was parked by a small outbuilding. Andy stood inspecting the carcass of another truck, stripped of engine and wheels, sunk to its windows in weeds.

He turned, said, "It all right there in the shed, Mr. Mason," showing his foul teeth.

Like bad dogs, Mason thought. He found himself breathing heavily. He stalked across the bare dirt yard, conscious of the Silberts at either side of him. At the shed door, he turned quickly. "In here?" But he surprised no danger in their faces.

They stood immobile an arm's length away, watching him. The sight was horrifying. At the look of them, silently watching in the sun, he felt emptiness open in his body.

Jerking himself around, he entered the shed.

"They's right over there on the table," Ev told him.

Trash crammed the interior—trash crammed in, tossed in, dropped in. It looked like the backside of Hell. Under a line of dirt-caked windows along the right wall sagged a long bench. It was stacked with cardboard boxes. Among crumpled newspapers glinted the sawtooth edge of a glass bowl, the dull rose and green of pottery.

Mason negligently walked the length of the table, examining nothing. He turned. Ev had stepped into the shed. Andy stood in the doorway, a black outline against the glaring yard.

Mason's stomach clenched. He felt the urgent need to set his back against the near pile of boxes.

With difficulty, he asked, "Is this all?" His voice sounded thin.

Ev nodded. "Every last box. What you think?"

Mason shrugged. "Oh, well. It's not really . . ."

He shrugged again.

From the doorway, Andy said in a kind of controlled bellow, "We might of stuck some more down there under that table."

Mason glanced down. Behind a box of Momma's

glass, he saw part of a curving glass surface, dirt-crusted. He knelt. The hunter's excitement rose in him. Now he could see part of a stained glass lampshade, about a foot and a half across, canting up in its nest of newspaper. He worked the box into the aisle, rubbed the glass with his finger. Complex designs lay under the dirt.

He asked, "Where'd this come from?"

Ev said, "I reckon it was the one hanging in Grandma's hall. It's been layin' around longer'n I know." His reedy voice thickened and he began to cough.

"It was under the house," Andy said. "I jus' fetched it up with all the rest."

"Was there any more?" Mason asked. His finger slipped along the gently rounded solder seams, scrubbed away the dirt clogging the complexly figured aperture cap at the top of the lamp. His heart jarred again.

"Naw. I never seen nothin'."

It was a finely made piece. He could puzzle out the shape of leaves and stems. Small bits of glass jigsawed delicately to form the cups of blossoms.

"Tulip lamp," he thought. A popular Tiffany design. You would expect to find this, or the Acorn shade, or the Dragonfly.

He remained squatting in the aisle. His thumb scrubbed carefully across the dirty surface, revealing the intricate worksmanship.

After some time, he rose, balancing the shade in his hands.

"I'll have to look at this a little more. Let's make some room here."

He turned to the bench and tipped his head at the cardboard boxes. "You want to move some of this?"

Ev gaped blankly at him, screwing up his eyes. "Don't you need none of it?"

Mason said impatiently, "Well, if you carry it out to the truck, I'll give you three dollars a box. Or just toss them over on the lumber."

Money worked in Ev's face. He said with careful reluctance, "Well, now . . ."

Andy said, "That's thirty dollar, Ev."

"That's piddling little."

Mason held up the shade, looking through the hollow curve toward the window light, seeing deep crimson, intense yellow, green. "It's up to you," he said in a remote voice.

"Mightn't you make that fifty, Mr. Mason?"

Mason took his eyes from the shade. "Fifty? For what?"

"They's herlooms."

"Toss them on the floor, then," Mason said, rubbing the shade.

"Thirty's thirty," Andy said. He picked up two boxes and left the shed. Ev hesitated, watching Mason finger the shade, said, "Well, I suppose . . ." He hefted up a box and trudged out, leaving the doorway to the shed empty, full of hot light.

Excitement expanded in Mason's chest. When most of the boxes were cleared away, he set the shade deliberately on the bench. Clearly it was the tulip pattern, a beautiful thing.

All the boxes were gone now. He glanced once about the shed. Then he counted thirty dollars from his roll of money. Sucking in his breath, he stepped through the door to the freedom of the outer yard.

Sunlight struck him. The Silberts stood whispering by their truck.

Mason handed over the money. He said casually, "That's a nice lamp shade. You thinking of selling it?"

He felt, rather than saw, secret glee pass between them.

Ev screwed up his face. "Dunno. You want to sell Grandma's lamp, Andy?"

"Dunno. Let him make a price."

"That's one valuable lamp, that is," Ev said. "Course you're the expert, Mr. Mason."

"He'll be for treating us fair," Andy said.

"But I was thinkin', an old lamp like that, like maybe . . ."

The brothers exchanged looks.

" 'bout maybe eight hundred, around there."

Mason said, "I was thinking more like two hundred."

"Ah, no," Ev cried. "Ah, no, Mr. Mason. That ain't right."

"I don't carry big money like that, anyway," Mason said. He showed them a smile and looked past their shoulders toward his truck, miles away across the yard. "Tell you what. I'll have to think on it some. You bring that shade around next week, so's I can take another look."

"Whyn't you decide now?" Andy asked. He stepped forward, grim face set, bulking between Mason and the truck.

"You don't spend money like that right off," Mason said. His voice was steady, he noticed; never a tremble.

"Now or never," Ev said. "Now or never."

"There's others liking that lamp," Andy said. "Lots of others."

"Well, I can see that," Mason said.

He felt faintly sick. He always felt sick when a confrontation could no longer be stalled off. His thought became shallow and sluggish and he heard his voice talking on:

"It's a nice-looking piece. Made real well. Lots of people'd like to have one like that, just like you say. You might maybe get three hundred for it. You just might."

Hard shame took him as he listened to his voice. His lips clamped off the words.

And, for a moment, he no longer faced two rapacious men, their faces strained, their eyes changing.

For a moment he was again behind his stand, a week ago, and Ollie Preacher faced him, holding out a small-piece lamp shade in the Acorn design. Ollie's soiled craftsman's fingers cupped the edge. His small face, creased and lined, grinned furtively.

"Just tell them," Preacher said in his husky voice, "you got it up North. No call you need say she's new made. Set her by your pretty glass and let 'em price it themselves."

The personality of this shabby little shriveled man enveloped Mason like a furnace's breath. He temporized, evading the moment of refusal. "Now, I couldn't tell people it's Tiffany, Preacher."

"No call for you to tell them anything."

He had not seen her come, but now Lady stood at his side, arms folded, her body stiff. "We don't do our business that way," she said. "We don't handle reproductions. Do we, El?"

He opened his mouth to speak, could not speak.

If she were not standing there as inflexible as a concrete piling, he might have found a carefully worded refusal of Preacher's offer. But that was not Lady's way.

She said: "We sell nice and honest. Honester than some."

"Miz Mason, folks love to buy these old glass shades."

"Not from us," she said. "Not our kind of business."

"That your thought, Mr. Mason?"

That was the humiliation. He did not want Preacher's shades or his business. But when he should stand as unyielding as an iron wall, refusing because it was right to refuse, he could say nothing. Just stare like a kicked dog.

Mason produced a limp grin and spread out his hands. "You know how it is, Preacher."

Preacher's face became harshly grooved as a walnut hull. He said: "Looks like the ladies just got to have their way, Mason."

"Looks so," said Mason, from out of his shame.

Andy jerked off his cap and resettled it hard over thick hair.

Ev said anxiously: "We might could settle for like six-fifty, Mr. Mason."

Remembered shame ran its blazing touch through Mason's mind. He said violently, seeing Preacher's contemptuous eyes, "Not for a new-built shade. One of Preacher's pieces, ain't it? Got you to hide it out here, suck old Mason in. Think I'm a new boy? Think I don't know a Tiffany to touch and look?"

"Hell," Andy said. He spit into the dirt.

"Now, Mr. Mason . . ."

"Shut your fool mouth, Ev," Andy said. "Told you it wouldn't never work."

"Now don't you listen to him, Mr. Mason."

Darkness gathered in Andy's face. "Look at that cold little bastard standing there grinning at us like a sick coon. Think he minds what you say?"

Ev hesitated, puffed out his cheeks. In a different voice, he said, "I 'spect you was right, first off, Andy."

"Sure I was." He whacked one hand hard against his leg.

"Here we're jus' dealing from the other fellow's deck."

"That's a fact," Andy said. "Hell with Old Preacher. Told you it wouldn't work."

Ev stared passionlessly at Mason, slowly shaking his head. "I do hear tell these old flea market boys, they got their pockets round with cash, they do."

"Let's see," Andy said.

They started toward him, grinning like stone masks.

Mason stepped back and again back until the shed boards ground against his spine. The sun glared. Their feet kicked up thin dust. Mason heard a weak little shrill whimpering sound and wondered what it was and realized with horror that it was coming from his mouth.

He took a short-barrelled .38 from his left pants pocket and set the hammer with a solid click.

"Close enough," he said.

They paused, heads forward, bodies bent toward him like waves about to break.

Andy said, "I don't 'spect he'd gun a poor fellow all bare-handed. You jus' better let me have that, Mr. Mason."

116

He stepped forward, hand extended.

Mason watched the blocky fingers reach out, thought, "He's going to take it right out of my hand."

He felt the coming nights of shame, the humiliation that would eat his days, the yelling hole of self-recrimination and disgust that would close in on him, and he shot Andy in the side of the left leg.

Andy fell down on his knee, hands clamped against his thigh. Bright blood tumbled out between his fingers. "Lord a mercy," he said in a startled voice.

Ev yelled furiously: "You didn't oughta."

Sparrows wheeled frantically up across the broken house roof.

Mason shuffled sideways away from the shed through knee-deep grass. He thought vaguely of chiggers. Tipping the gun muzzle toward Ev, he said, "Help him up."

"You got no right hurtin' him."

"Help him up."

Andy said, soft-voiced, "You shut up, Ev, damn it. Not but a scratch."

Mason asked sharply, "You want to lay out here in the sun?" He angled the muzzle toward Ev's crotch.

"Gimme a shoulder," Andy said. He heaved himself erect, leg bent, shining wetness streaking his jeans.

"Into the shed," Mason ordered.

Ev said, "I'll cut the hot heart out of your body." His face jerked. "I'll throw it on the ground."

"You're a barrel of words," Andy told him.

He hobbled into the shed, bent tall over the smaller man.

Mason smacked the door shut on them. He rattled the leaf into the hasp. Then, for one terrible moment, he could find nothing to secure the door. Breath seared his nostrils. Finally he jammed in a piece of wood. It would not hold for long.

From inside the shed, Ev yelled, "He'll get hisself a poisoned leg in here."

And Andy, rough-voiced, "Shut your mouth, you damn fool. You see his eyes. Man with those far eyes, he'll shoot to hear the bang."

Mason listened to them with amazement. He could not relate their words to himself. He was a frightened, sweating old man, clutching the revolver in greasy fingers.

Far eyes, he thought. Man with far eyes.

The words lifted him. He retreated cautiously across the yard to his truck. He placed the gun carefully on the seat. Fitted in the ignition key. Turned the truck toward the road.

No sound from the shed. The disorderly yard simmered silently in the heat.

He drove slowly toward the highway.

They had all misjudged him, every one. Preacher and Ev and Andy and all. He felt as if he looked down from a high place. Far eyes. He had not been tricked. They had confronted him, and he had stood up to them, stood like an iron wall.

A shiver of pleasure rippled through him.

Stood like an iron wall.

He barely remembered the horror as Andy reached for the gun. Far eyes, he thought. That's what they said about me.

Near the main highway, his hands began to shake. He stopped the truck, and the brilliant air faded and became remote, and he heard the strange cadences of his heart. After a time, the shape of the world returned in slow increments, firming and hardening around him.

Sweat bit his eyes.

He headed back toward the North Alabama Giant Outdoors Flea Market, driving with great precision, taking no chances.

Lady appeared at the side of the truck before he set the brake.

"You all right, Elwood?"

"Yes. Fine."

He slipped down from the seat, setting his feet solidly on the hot asphalt.

"Was it all right? I kept wondering."

"It was fine," he said. "No problem at all."

He gestured toward the end of the truck. "It was Heisse glass and Roseville pottery they had. Now just imagine that. Ten boxes of Heisse glass and Roseville pottery, just as nice as you ever did see. It's terrible filthy. But it'll clean up just as pretty as can be."

"Well," she said, "it was worth going out there then. I sort of fretted, you were gone so long."

"We got to talking," he said. And let the tailgate clang down.

The Trouble Shooters

DAN BRENNAN

Dan Brennan began writing between combat briefing sessions during World War II, when he was an American volunteer flying with the Royal Air Force. Since that time, he has been a news reporter and feature writer for the *Minneapolis Tribune* and *Times*, a rewrite man with Harry Reasoner for *60 Minutes*, and press secretary for Senator Hubert Humphrey. He has also written some forty novels about subjects ranging from air war to tennis.

About "The Trouble Shooters," he comments, "In Minneapolis . . . I knew a lot of cops and a lot of crooks in the later 1930s and the postwar 1940s. I knew them personally, even some of the shooters. . . . I was a friend of the bank robbers' friends; knew how and where Baby Face Nelson and Homer Van Meter and Dillinger hung out in St. Paul and Minneapolis. The most interesting bandit I knew personally was a big-time train robber picked up in Kansas City on a golf course with a submachine gun in his golf bag. Did time on the Rock; as polite and mannerly as the Prince of Wales."

The two Sicilians crossed the street toward the brothel. Of red brick, faded by the harsh winters and torrid heat of midwestern summers, the big square apartment building in which the prostitutes lived was owned by the syndicate and faced the railroad yards. The street in front was vacant.

"He won't be here," the first Sicilian said.

"You never know," the second said. It was late afternoon. Shades on all the windows were drawn. The building loomed, looking quiet and empty.

"Yeah. We had a guy like him in Kansas City. Tried to pull the same thing."

"You mean Louie Drucci?"

"Yeah."

The first Sicilian's name was Tony Genna. He was about thirty. They were both men of medium height, lean, wiry like vaudeville dancers, with small heads, narrow, dark faces like two alert, sharp-eyed foxes peering stealthily out behind a screen of bushes. Their hair looked like smooth black leather, shined and oiled, smooth and flat on their heads. Around his left wrist, Tony Genna wore a silver identification bracelet.

"Like I said, after the war there's better rackets than broads. We shoulda kept in slots. No Feds breathing down your neck. Now we gotta worry about getting lousy broads across state lines."

"They stink."

"Yack, yack, yack, anytime the Feds put a little heat on them. No guts. Worse than buying bootleg offa hillbillies."

"And Merlo sits on his can in Florida and never gets the heat."

"Right. You can have this racket. Christ, before the war, with a couple slots in the right spots, a guy could do better."

"You're too young to remember running alky."

"Yeah. I know. My old man was in it. No sweat, no strain."

"A nice bit."

"My family don't even speak to me now. My sister knows."

"My brother, too. Him and his bookie joint. He acts like a Republican every time he sees me."

"There's something about taking money off broads I never did like."

"You said it."

They mounted the steps. It was summer, but a wide wooden winter storm door with a small square window was fastened shut over the front door. There was no sound from within, but they knew what was inside and who they were looking for, ever since Ed Morgan had been killed a week ago. But they did not know if the man they were looking for was here.

There was a main room downstairs, a big room, with china along the wall, and davenports, and tables, and a jukebox in the corner. The floor was bare. In this room the customers met and danced and drank with the whores and made their selections to go upstairs. The shades were drawn, and the light in the room came from the ceiling. It was like coming into a house at night. When the two Sicilians entered with the house madam, the room was full of girls. The two Sicilians sat down at one of the tables.

"Jesus," Tony said. "I shoulda stayed in slots."

"You ain't alone. You and me both," the second said.

"I never seen such crumbs."

"I shoulda kept the crap game. So a few lousy dollars more. It ain't worth it."

"Merlo's crazy. The guy ain't dumb enough to

shack up here." From along the wall, from the other tables, the smell of the girls' cheap perfume rolled over them in waves. "I'm Tony Genna. I'm from Merlo," Genna said to the girls, his eyes roving around the room. The girls stared at him sullenly. "Merlo sent us. Where's Johnny Skidmore?" The girls stared at him. The odors of perfume and disinfectant carbolic soap seemed to fill the hot, airless room. Their eyes, faces, bodies, were motionless.

"All right," Genna said. "You know why we're here. One of you broads is supposed to know where he's gone."

"Maybe they'd like to work in Chicago," the second said. "Maybe they don't know what work is."

"Come on," Genna said. "Start talking. You broads know Johnny?"

"Which one of these hustlers did he go for?" Genna asked the madam.

She was a fat, dark-skinned woman with dyed blonde hair. She wore a red dress.

"Alla time a different girl," the madam said.

"He's gone," the second Sicilian said. "He took off. He'd be a sucker to hang around here. It was like this in Kansas City when Drucci knocked off Nelson and thought he could cut in. We caught up to him in Cape Girardeau. Merlo was screaming all the way from Miami because it took us a week to catch Nelson."

"I never thought Skidmore had the guts," Genna said.

"Yeah. Irish. Like the Greeks. Which is worse? They double cross five ways."

"Let's get outta here."

"Wait. One of these broads knows. I'll betcha.

Four to one. Jesus, with slots we never had trouble like this."

"Yeah. That lousy Skidmore. He took off. Let's get outta here."

The whores stared silently at the two men. Their eyes were expressionless.

"Gutless bitches," Genna said. "What'll we do with them?"

"Let's see Mantello."

"Why should he care? He still gets his end."

"Yeah, he's got the town now," the second man said.

"Maybe he paid Skidmore. Now he gets the Cadillac." They got up and went out. Twilight shone pink and gold in the sky beyond the railroad yard. From a block away came the sound of evening traffic on Minnehaha Avenue.

"He's been driving a Cadillac almost a year anyway, I heard," the second man said.

"Morgan never knew it. It don't matter. The bum's got the town."

"I heard they had a fight about the Cad. I heard Morgan told Mantello that only the top guy can drive one in Cereal City. Mantello didn't like it."

"Yeah," Genna said. "He can drive two Caddies now. Merlo don't care. Just so Mantello delivers the ice right every month. How about that?"

"I don't know," the second said. "I don't like Caddies. Do you?"

"No," Genna said.

"You're smart," the second said.

The apartment building sat on a hill, above the lake, surrounded by elm trees. It was a modern building, designed with a simplicity that was severe. It was five years old. It had been built and paid for by Merlo, out of Chicago, who had been Morgan's boss when Morgan was alive and who was now Mantello's boss. The walls were of gray sandstone.

Merlo had been born in Cicero, one of eleven children, out of the tenements swarm of Little Hell on the North Side; a member of the Market Street gang, a thief, safecracker, and finally a bootlegger; the heir apparent of the Unione Siciliana, the last in the dynasty of bootleggers. Nobody knew exactly how he became boss, save that his competition disappeared suddenly, died suddenly. At that time he controlled syndicate operations throughout the Middle West and shortly thereafter he installed Ed Morgan as head of the rackets in Cereal City, Minnesota. During the war, Merlo began to broaden the brothel operations of the syndicate in his region because police and political heat fell upon the syndicate's gambling empire and intergang warfare between the East and West coasts threatened his wire service. Out of the farms, small towns, slums, girls were recruited.

In the hierarchy of the syndicate local bosses, Ed Morgan ranked high. He ruled his own operation with a group of police and politicians who gathered when the local heat from civic improvement groups and churches required a meeting of the local crime clan in Morgan's rooms in the apartment building Merlo's money had built in Cereal City.

"How's about cutting down on the cat houses?" an alderman said.

"What's to make up for it?" one of Morgan's enforcers asked.

"There are too many cat houses," the alderman said.

"Right," the chief of police said. "Something's got to give. I can't take the heat."

"What about fourteen and sixty-six boards? How about a few spots?" Morgan asked.

"The governor won't buy it," said a state senator who was Morgan's lawyer.

"That phony crumb," Morgan said. "He got more than his end in the last campaign."

They all stared at Morgan, waiting for some solution, some answer.

"Why not talk to him?" the county sheriff said. "The governor's not a bad guy."

"No," the state senator said. "That won't work. He's got to keep the church vote. Passing the antislot law was the only way he could do it. I think you better go down for a while."

"Go down?" Morgan said.

"Yes. Let things cool off for about three months," said the chief of police. "We can open up again in the fall."

"How are we going to make it up?" said another alderman from the city licensing committee. "I quit selling soap two years ago."

Morgan looked at them thoughtfully.

"Merlo ain't gonna like it," Morgan said.

"Let him make it up elsewhere," the police chief snapped. "He's got to understand our position."

So they closed five houses and kept five running and sent the idle girls to houses in Wisconsin, Iowa, and Illinois. Three months later the houses opened again. That winter Morgan went to Florida to see Merlo and came home driving a new Cadillac with a Florida license. It was painted white, a four-door sedan, and the first day home he gave Mantello a ride in it and took it to the dollar car wash which Merlo also owned in Cereal City. Every day after that, Morgan had the Cadillac washed. Chickie Mantello had sleepy eyes, like a cobra; heavy lidded, but the sight of the white Cadillac made his eyes bright, alert, yet somehow veiled.

Mantello was a product of Cereal City: newsboy, bellhop, pimp, alky runner. Within a week after Morgan got his Cadillac, Mantello started borrowing it to run errands. Morgan laughed to himself. Two years later Morgan went to Florida again in the winter and returned with a new Cadillac. Mantello quit asking to use it, but one of the enforcers of the syndicate told Morgan that Mantello had been pricing Cadillacs himself at the local agency.

Morgan sent for Mantello. "Go down to Chase's lot and pick yourself out a second-hand Caddy," Morgan said. He did not smile as he said it. "Send me the tab."

Mantello looked at him with a brief glance.

"Thanks," he said.

Mantello was then about forty-five, unmarried. Both were big men, gross, with florid faces, hairy hands, black hair; one Italian, one Irish.

"You like it?" Morgan said when he saw the car. It was last year's model, only yellow.

"Sure," Mantello said. His eyes were blank and heavy lidded.

"Well," Morgan said, "you got yourself a nice car." He watched Mantello's face.

"What kinda car does Merlo drive?" Mantello said, his eyes still blank, his face wooden.

Morgan looked at him again.

"Two Lincolns and a Caddy," Morgan said. "But he doesn't use them. He hardly leaves the estate. So what? He's got what he wants."

That conversation was three years ago, and now Morgan was dead. He was to meet Skidmore one night; Skidmore, the collector for the houses. He had been stealing from the collections, and though Morgan was only going to warn him, Morgan forgot to take precautions when he changed their regular meeting place from his apartment to his Cadillac. In a vacant parking lot, at midnight, Skidmore shot him in the back of the head.

That was three days ago. Mantello was the new boss, and Morgan had been buried in the best cemetery in Cereal City. Legislators and aldermen and policemen attended the burial service.

"Skidmore's still in town," Tony Genna said, as he and the other Sicilian rode in Tony's car to the apartment where Mantello lived. "The cops've staked out every station. Bus depot. Railroad. Airport. His car's still behind his apartment. Just like Drucci."

The second Sicilian's name was Harry Scalisi. "He'll have to hole up in town here. Everybody knows him."

"With slots we never had this kind of trouble. Only with broads," Genna said.

"He'll have to show in a week."

"We oughta watch all those broads when they change shifts. One of them is probably taking care of him at home," Genna said.

Genna turned into the parking lot beside the apartment building.

"Mantello can drive two Cadillacs now." Scalisi grinned.

"He better keep 'em in the garage," Genna said. Scalisi looked at him. "Maybe Skidmore wouldn't like Mantello looking for him in one of those Caddies."

Scalisi said, "Why should Mantello care? A guy that's got everything now."

"Why not? Maybe Skidmore goes for Caddies."

"Sure," Scalisi said. "But Merlo would never make him boss with Mantello chopped. He's had it."

"Are you sure?"

"Aren't you?"

"I don't know," Genna said, watching him.

Scalisi grinned. "To hell with Caddies. Skidmore is crazy if he thinks . . ." Scalisi stopped.

Genna smiled.

"Yeah. Real crazy," he said.

"Mantello's the boy for this operation."

"Either that or we ain't supposed to be here," Genna said.

The carpets in the hallway of the apartment building were thick. The walls were a cool green; modern chairs and a marble-top coffee table sat in the small foyer entrance. They rode upstairs in the self-operated elevator. On the top floor, in another small foyer with a balcony overlooking the street, sat a young man. He was young, blond, and clean-cut; wearing a camel's hair sport jacket, fawn-colored slacks with too many pleats, black leather loafers, and a purple silk sport shirt buttoned at the throat. When he saw them he started talking.

"This town's goin' to hell," he said. "When's Merlo gonna get us outta the pros business?"

Genna and Scalisi stopped in front of him. He

looked up at them. "You ain't never gonna find Skidmore," he said.

"Sure," Scalisi said.

"You're wasting your time. He's outta state."

"That's what Drucci thought in Kansas City," Genna said.

"Was you . . . ?" the young man said, and ceased. His eyes jerked up at Genna.

"No," Scalisi said. "It was Santa Claus."

The young man looked at them.

"Saint Nick, Buster," Genna said, and they walked past him.

The apartment door was painted a soft gray. The polished knocker glinted. Genna pushed the buzzer and an old man with a wrinkled face let them in. They entered a long room. It contained several white davenports. The walls were white, hung with big modern paintings, and the carpets were white. Mantello was married to a woman fifteen years younger; a former cashier in a theater he owned. She had decorated the apartment to please herself. There was a grand piano in a sun room next to the big sitting room and a huge white television set against the far wall of the sitting room. There was a wide, high, white brick fireplace. Two davenports were set at right angles to the fireplace. Between the davenports squatted a long, low, ebony coffee table. Behind a modern desk, below which his trousered legs showed, sat Mantello.

He was an even six feet, though he did not look it, and he weighed one hundred and ninety pounds. He was perhaps fifty. He wore a white sport jacket and a black sport shirt, open at the throat. His chest was broad; his stomach lean. On his feet were shining black loafers with tassels. He sat rigid behind the desk, with his lean, V-shaped face and narrow-bridged nose and nostrils held back, slightly lifted. There was no expression on his face. His eyes, face, were inscrutable, quite still. He appeared to be staring straight ahead, musing on a point beyond Genna's head.

"We got in yesterday," Genna said.

Mantello said nothing. You could not tell what he was thinking. He did not move.

"Maybe he took off," Genna said.

Still Mantello did not move or speak.

Genna said, "Why didn't you get him picked up right away?"

"Take care of it," Mantello said. "Don't come in here asking why."

Genna watched Mantello's eyes. The eyes did not move.

"Look," Genna said. "Don't get in a sweat. Merlo sends us. He expects a job. He gets a job. Right?"

Scalisi nodded.

"We handled these before," Genna said. "Maybe you never heard of Spangola last year in LA. It took us three months. We got him. Don't go getting in a sweat."

Scalisi nodded. He fixed his eyes on Mantello's face.

Mantello did not move, his face rigid, motionless, lifted slightly.

"We looked for Spangola in three states," Genna said. "We had him figured. Skidmore is a punk compared to Spangola."

Mantello's black eyes stared straight ahead. He appeared not to listen; to be musing on a point beyond both men.

"You're gonna help get Skidmore, ain't you?"
Genna said.

Scalisi said, "You're top man here now."

"You're gonna help."

That day Skidmore lay hidden in a top room in the brothel, listening to the radio. He was thirty; he had a long, straight nose; a big, round head, his forehead was high and his teeth were straight, even, and white. He had started his career before he was ten years old, stealing coal in the freight yards to supply the stove in a dingy apartment of three rooms where he lived with his mother, father, three brothers, and three sisters. He was the youngest. He had worked for syndicate operations in Cereal City since he was sixteen.

The night he shot Ed Morgan, he hurried back to the brothel. In the dawn light the street was vacant. Eva Benson, the madam, let him in the back door: the girls were changing shifts. Nobody saw him save Ruby, a prostitute for whom he had pimped before she had gone to work in the brothel. She was eighteen or nineteen, blond, Swedish, from a prairie wheat town. To her he looked frightened.

"Maybe I didn't kill him," Skidmore said, staring at her.

"Kill him?" she said. "Kill who?"

"Maybe he'll live."

"Who?"

"Morgan."

Her eyeballs seemed to bulge.

"Morgan?" she said. He put his hand over her mouth. The sound of footsteps and voices sounded in the hall below. Skidmore sat on the edge of the bed, panting. He had run the last six blocks to the brothel. His face was sweaty. "You gotta hide me!"

She muttered through his hand.

"You gotta!" he panted.

He knew the madam wouldn't squeal on him because he had been splitting with her part of the collection money he had been holding out on Morgan.

When the cops came the next morning, Eva kept him hidden in the closet in her own room. The police did not search there; the police and the syndicate trusted her. The odor of her hanging clothes struck sharp and rank into Skidmore's nostrils. He could hear the police going up and down the halls looking in the rooms. The girls stood outside in the hall downstairs; silent in the big, long reception room.

From the top front room in the building, with the door locked, Skidmore listened to the radio and watched the street outside. At noon there was a radio broadcast about the killing. No identification of the killer was made. The announcer said Morgan was in the hospital. Jesus, Skidmore thought, surprised, and I shot him in the head.

"He's still living," Ruby told him that night.

"I might as well be dead."

"Don't worry, honey," she said. He felt a longing to be out of this room, even in jail, even with the police—anything to stop the feeling of being trapped in the room, waiting, waiting, not knowing how to escape. He sat beside the curtained window watching the street outside. The next morning he heard on the radio that Morgan was dead.

Two days later, in the afternoon, Ruby brought him the Cereal City *Tribune* and he read about Morgan's funeral, smiling quietly while he read the pallbearers' names. There were two retired aldermen, a retired police captain who owned fifteen old apartment buildings, a lawyer employed by the syndicate, the brother of a retired county attorney, and four names unknown to Skidmore.

The next afternoon, watching quietly from the window, he saw Genna and Scalisi walk down the street and mount the front steps. He waited and watched them leave. When it was dark, he opened the door, listening to all the sounds throughout the building. The hall was vacant. He descended the stairs, walked through the kitchen on the ground floor, and passed a maid sitting at the kitchen table, her hand holding a piece of toast above a cup of coffee while she stared at him, mouth open, her eyes rounding whitely in her face. He ran down the hall past the long reception room. The sliding doors between the room and the hall were closed. Through the doors he heard the jukebox music thudding. He jerked the bolt back on the front door and ran outside into the summer darkness.

He ran up the dark street as far as the corner and turned. Three blocks down the dark silent avenue shone the lights of a busy street. He could see car lights rushing past. He ran again toward the lighted street, toward a taxi parked under the street light. He knew that both the police and Genna and Scalisi would be looking for him in the morning. He knew all the stations would be watched. He tried to remember who he had helped and he thought of a family of Syrians, the Delmites, who were always being picked up by the police on bum raps to cover any heat the cops might be getting from the public.

There were nine Delmite brothers. Some sold pornographic literature, photographs; three ran a floating crap game that was always getting knocked off by the racket squad because it wasn't a syndicate game and, in addition, wouldn't pay off to the precinct police. Several of the brothers sold flowers in night clubs, leftover flowers, purchased from floral shops; on the side and with the flowers they attempted to pimp for free-lance street hustlers.

Skidmore had saved two of the brothers from a safe-cracking rap and two other brothers from a charge of illegally selling fireworks. He had told them who to contact in the police department for a payoff. In exchange, they informed Skidmore on any cops who gave the "go-sign" to nonsyndicate operations. One ran a large newsstand to cover the brothers' criminal operations.

The next morning, lying in the basement beneath the newsstand, Skidmore saw through the single window part of the dragnet. There were two detectives in sport shirts, hatless, carrying their police Colt .38s in bank messenger style: long leather wallets in their hands, big enough to hold a revolver. They were young, lean Swedes—Larson and Peterson. He knew both of them—eager for promotion, not yet in on any payoff, just keeping their mouths shut, turning their eyes the other way, waiting for the day when they had been in the police hierarchy long enough to get their end of the payoff. They were talking to Larry Delmite. Larry shook his head. They didn't have enough on Larry to make him squeal. Skidmore tasted his thirst now, the dry cottony flesh of his mouth; a sharp ache in his throat. God, I could use a cold beer, he thought. He told himself this again but did not move all day or night, lying on the single cot under which sat two cigar boxes filled with loaded dice. It was dark in the room when a hand touched him. He sprang bolt upright. An invisible hand pushed him down.

"You're too hot," Larry Delmite's voice said in the darkness. "You gotta get outa here."

Skidmore's heart thudded. He sat up.

"Jesus," he said, pleading. "Where the hell is there?"

"Here's a couple sawbucks," Larry said. "You'll get us all in the can."

"Yeah, I know. Thanks." His heart was beating faster now. He could see Delmite in the darkness.

"Wanna drink?" Delmite said.

"Got any beer?"

"Beer? Man! What's wrong with whiskey?"

"I'm thirsty."

"Take this jug. I ain't got no beer."

Skidmore took the pint of whiskey, stuck the bottle in his hip pocket. He followed Delmite upstairs. He walked out into the night. He kept walking, past dark houses. "I'll walk straight out of the city," he thought. "I'll hitchhike out of this state." He stopped under an elm tree, took a drink of whiskey, and shook his head. He kept walking. There were no more houses.

It was still dark. On each side of the road fields stretched away into black distances. He entered the fields, crossed a meadow. Out of the darkness a hump of thicker darkness loomed. He walked toward it. When he touched it he lay down, pulling the straw over his body, and went to sleep.

He woke with the sun in his face. An hour later on the highway he turned and stood almost face to face with a state highway patrolman, seated in a car. The patrolman looked quietly out at Skidmore, beckoned to him with one hand. Skidmore did not move. Standing there, looking at the patrolman, he felt suddenly hungry for the first time in many hours. He stared at the patrolman with red-rimmed eyes. The patrolman got out of the car. He was tall, clean-faced; the embodiment of quick justice. Still Skidmore did not move. His trouser pocket still contained the .32 with which he had shot Morgan, but he simply stood there and watched the patrolman walk toward him.

He did not remember hearing the patrolman speak, nor any sound, until the explosion surprised him and a hot, shocking blow struck him suddenly with terrific force in the left shoulder. It was a sledge-hammer blow, and he did not know he had been knocked down until he saw his hands sprawled in front of him in the dirt and felt his utter helplessness as he saw the policeman coming toward him, pistol raised, the patrolman's face growing bigger.

"Don't! Don't shoot!" Skidmore said. "Don't kill me!" He watched the pistol lift and then rise slowly again. The patrolman seemed to be smiling. Skidmore's hand scrabbled at his trouser pocket, his red eyes suddenly wild and steady. Then he moved and fired, still on hands and knees. With the grimace of a smile on his face, the patrolman struck the earth. Skidmore stood up slowly and looked at the gun in his hand and the body on the ground with a dazed expression as if he were waking from a dream. He backed slowly away. Then he turned and scuttled toward the car waiting in the road. By God, he thought, bygodbygodbygodbygodbygod, I'm lucky. But he knew he mustn't drive the car on the highway.

Mantello drove the Cadillac slowly. He liked to drive slowly, feeling the thick, luxuriant ease of the car rolling smoothly along the street. He never drove over twenty miles an hour in the city. He had driven at that speed all day, between each stop, where he spoke to men who worked for him, men who owed him favors, bootblacks, cab drivers, ex-convicts gone legit, waitresses, bar owners, bartenders, all who might know something about Skidmore. To Mantello it was demeaning in a sense, but he questioned them as if they were his partners.

At five o'clock that afternoon, with the Cadillac at the dollar car wash, Mantello relaxed in a booth in a bar owned by the syndicate. He sat reading an advertising pamphlet issued by the local Cadillac dealer. A drink sat on the table before him. He had not touched it. He was sitting there reading the pamphlet for the third time when Genna and Scalisi came in.

"Anything new?" Mantello said.

"He's still in town. He can't get out. We'll get him or the cops will."

"When?"

"Tonight."

"You guys are supposed to be hot stuff."

"Wanna bet?"

"You been here long enough to get five guys."

"Wanna bet?"

"Sure. Five to one not tonight."

"You got a bet."

That was the day the flowers on Morgan's grave began to rot.

The next day they were all brown and nobody ever put flowers on the grave again. It was the day Genna lost his bet, because he didn't get a line on Skidmore that night or the next day. It was a week later when an informer—a hunchbacked, after-hours bootlegger Genna had promised to get in with the cops and the syndicate—phoned Genna at his hotel. The hunchback had news. He had always hated the Delmites because once for five weeks they had been able to bribe the tenth-precinct captain to let them run a card game for some garment workers while he was ducking around corners after midnight trying to sell a bottle of overpriced whiskey without getting picked up by the racket squad.

"He's been shot," said the hunchback.

"Where is he?"

"Delmite's attic. I got a friend watching the house. He's hurt bad."

They picked up the hunchback on a street corner downtown. Delmite's house was in the north end of the city, twenty minutes from the business district. They found the house, talked to a lookout planted in a car down the street, and told him they would park a block away until it got dark.

"If he comes out of the house, honk twice," Genna said. "We'll get him after dark."

They drove down the street and parked. In the twilight they listened to a dance band on the radio from Chicago. They sat with the windows rolled down. Darkness began to rise as though out of the ground between the houses. The street lamp on the corner flickered, then flashed into light. They turned the radio low. Suddenly a horn honked twice, and Genna started the car. The lookout met them at the corner.

"He came out and went back in when he saw me."

"Was he alone?"

"Yeah. He's got one arm all bandaged, shoulder it looks like. He needs a doctor. Ain't a doctor in town'll touch him. Delmites musta fixed him up."

"Park in the alley behind the house," Genna said. "Go with him!" he said to the hunchback. "Honk fast if he comes out the back door."

The hunchback sprang out of the car, cat-like, and entered the other car almost as it was already moving, the back wheels spinning at the corner. A shade lifted in a window on the second floor. There was no one in the window. Genna lifted his .38 from his shoulder holster.

"Let's go," he said.

The two Sicilians walked up the front steps and crossed the wooden front porch, walking heavily, making no effort to approach quietly. Before they rang the doorbell Skidmore opened the front door. They saw his face in the dark doorway with the hall light behind him. He mumbled, half of his sad face in shadow. They looked at him quietly, not moving, their hands thrust in their coat pockets. He stared at them, his eyes red-rimmed. His coat, with sleeve empty, hung over one shoulder. In the dark they saw the white bandage, his arm pressed against his side.

"Let's go," Genna said. "You shoulda shot Mantello while you were at it."

The moon was out full, high and white and naked, and the summer sky was starry as they drove in through the cemetery gates. Skidmore sat in back with Scalisi.

The sweet smell of water at night blew through the trees from the lake beyond the cemetery. Moonlight dappled the grass, the tombstones, the trees big and dark in the white shining light. They followed the winding road. A pheasant scurried across the road in the lights of the car.

"How about a beer?" Scalisi said, shaking Skidmore's good arm. On the floor below the rear seat rested a six-pack of beer. Scalisi punched a hole in top of a can. Skidmore was sitting up, erect, rigid, staring straight ahead. He was taller than Scalisi. His mouth gaped open and he was breathing hard. He looked out the window, from left to right, as if he did not believe what he saw.

"Beer?" Scalisi said. Skidmore did not move. Scalisi pushed the can of beer into Skidmore's hands.

"Thanks," he said dazedly. Then an expression of despair came over his face. He sat there staring at the can of beer, breathing hard.

"Drink up," Scalisi said. "We got a six-pack."

A long moment passed and Skidmore suddenly drank savagely, holding the rim of the can jammed between his lips until the liquid began to run from the corners of his mouth.

He brought the can away from his mouth. He looked suddenly out the window again with a kind of dazed disbelief. Scalisi watched him.

"Give him another beer," Genna said in the front seat, without turning his head, looking at the road curve and climb between the dark trees.

The tar road went around a bend. Trees made long shadows across the road in the moonlight. The night air blew peaceful and quiet over the graveyard. The car stopped.

"Come on," said Genna. "Get out." He spoke softly.

Scalisi reached across Skidmore and opened the door. Skidmore stepped out. He lifted his face to the moonlight. "Give him his beer," Genna said. Scalisi thrust the can into Skidmore's hand. His hand took it. Skidmore looked across the tombstones in the moonlight. "Come on," Genna said.

Skidmore stared straight ahead. "The bastard shot me," he panted. "He shot me first."

"Come on," Genna said. Skidmore seemed to be walking up the slope without making any gain.

"Drink your beer," Genna said.

Skidmore's eyes glared suddenly. "Sure," he said like a sleepwalker. He lifted the can to his lips. They watched him drink. He stopped. The can fell from his hand.

"Come here. Stand right here," Genna said, putting his foot out in the darkness, touching a mound of earth, feeling the top of Morgan's grave in the dark. Skidmore nodded and moved forward.

Murder Most Kind

B. M. GILL

B. M. Gill is the pseudonym of a former teacher
and chiropodist who lives in England. As Mar-
garet Blake, she has written eight romantic thrill-
ers. As B. M. Gill, she writes serious crime fiction
which typically concentrates more on emotional
violence than physical injury. She has published
four B. M. Gill novels, most recently *Seminar for
Murder* (1986), published by Scribners. B. M.
Gill won the Golden Dagger Award in 1985.

"It's like incarcerating a small helpless creature with
a predatory ape," Maybridge protested. "One swipe
of his paw and she's had it."

"If you're trying to tell me my will is unwise you
could express it less dramatically," Miss Lambton
replied calmly. She examined the chess board. "You're
about to be checkmated, Tom. You should forget
you're a detective chief inspector and keep your mind
on the game."

"And mind my own business?"

"But that's precisely what you *are* doing. You're
obsessed by your job. You see crime everywhere."
She suppressed a smile. "Do you know, you're the
only one of my former pupils who has the nerve to
tell me what to do—or not to do." And the only one,
she thought, who has the kindness to visit whenever
he can.

She made the final move, then gathered up the

chessmen. "You shouldn't judge people by the way they look. Walter has never preyed on anyone in his life. Or hurt anyone. And Victoria isn't a small helpless creature."

"The exaggeration was deliberate. I was making a point."

She ignored the interruption. "She's a very capable middle-aged widow. She likes The Beeches—it's what the estate agents call a desirable property. As she's my niece, my only living relative, it's right she should inherit it."

"That I don't dispute." Maybridge pushed his chair back from the table and went over to the kitchen window where he had a view of the garden. Walter Clegg was mowing the lawn. A light rain was falling, and he had a piece of old sacking over his head. Even at a distance he couldn't be described as a desirable property. And the poor unsuspecting niece was inheriting him too.

Maybridge gestured at him. "Does he know?"

"That he won't be put into an old people's home when I die? Yes, he knows. I'd have left him The Beeches outright if I thought he could cope. But he can't manage paperwork, taxes, and all that. He can't read or write. And the roof will need attention at some stage. His pension wouldn't cover the upkeep."

Walter Clegg, a bachelor, had been Miss Lambton's handyman-gardener for years, producing first-class vegetables and enough flowers to keep her happy. When fences blew down, he put them up again. If the chimney smoked, he swept it. Five years previously his cottage had been bulldozed to make room for a bypass, and he had come to live at The Beeches. After all, she had pointed out to him, he was there

144

all day anyway, so why not all night, too? Walter, delighted, had grunted his appreciation and moved his big shabby furniture into the big shabby bedroom on the top floor. No one gossiped. There were no raised eyebrows or sly innuendoes. Walter with his nicotine-stained beard, aversion to washing, and monosyllabic conversation, wasn't a likely bedfellow for a retired Classics mistress who painted pretty flower pictures and liked poetry. Besides they were both too old.

"What if she won't have him?" Maybridge asked.

"There's no question of that," her voice was tart. "The Beeches is worth upwards of eighty thousand pounds, believe it or not." She looked around the kitchen, the heart of the house, a friendly, comfortable room. Walter's favorite chair, the leather roughened by age and the springs sagging a little, was drawn up by the fire. "Walter is seventy-two," she reminded Maybridge, "the poor old boy can't go on forever. When he's dead Victoria can sell—if she wants to. Until that day he's a permanent resident, and they'll just have to put up with each other."

Maybridge tried hard to see the situation through the eyes of someone not contaminated by police work. He couldn't. Miss Lambton's solicitor had presumably warned her of the traps and pitfalls, and she had chosen to ignore them. What she did with her property was her business, and she had confided in him with the quite evident satisfaction of a deed well done. So stop harassing her with common sense.

"You might outlive him," he commented hopefully.

"God forbid!" She was truly appalled by the notion. "He's my crutch. My means of independence.

He does the heavy work I can't manage. He even made meals for me when I had a flare-up of arthritis." She indicated the big old-fashioned range. "On that. Baked beans on toast mostly. Smoky but edible. He can't cope with modern stoves." Her voice softened perceptibly. "And I can't cope without him. Damn it, Tom, I'm eighty. I need Walter. If the Good Lord takes him before He takes me, then He's not a good manager."

The Good Lord managed Miss Lambton's demise very gently the following autumn. She died peacefully of a virus infection—and with a clear and happy conscience, sure that all would be well.

Walter Clegg didn't realize how much he needed the Lamb, as he thought of her, until he saw her being carried out of The Beeches in her coffin. Need was synonymous with grief. Grief was a true understanding that she was dead. Until then, he hadn't believed that she had gone from him. The nurse, treating him as if he were a cretinous and smelly cave-dweller, hadn't let him anywhere near the old woman during her final days. On the day she died he had lurked in the kitchen and fitted a new washer to the tap while the house had filled with strangers. And then he had sat in his leather chair and smoked strong plug tobacco, coughing and hawking into the fire and ignoring everyone who trespassed on his territory.

A few hours after the funeral, when dusk was closing in, he went up to the cemetery and removed all the wreaths from her grave, neatly stacking them against an adjacent headstone. Then he poked little holes on the uncovered mound with a dibber and pushed in corms of *anemone blanda*. The windflowers, she called them. In the spring they'd make a decent-looking bed of color over her.

The evening air was full of an earthy smell of disturbed soil, bruised grass, and the faint scent of the flamboyant blooms of the wreaths. She had been given very posh flowers by very posh people, he thought, but the flowers had short stems and wouldn't last. Cards, black-edged, were tied to the wires under them. The cards said who they were from. Which was daft. The Lamb, lying down there under his anemone corms, dead-eyed, couldn't read them. In time the corms would send down little shoots towards her, like hands trying to touch someone in the dark. They were a link between him and the Lamb. His secret and hers. He crouched beside the grave, loath to leave her. There was an emptiness inside his head, and his stomach gnawed at him like hunger. But it wasn't hunger. He got up at last and replaced the wreaths. Jealously. Contemptuously. Upside down.

The rector didn't see the vandalizing of the grave, as he thought of it, but he caught a glimpse of Walter leaving the cemetery. Obviously he had done it. There wasn't anyone else around and Walter was odd. He hadn't even bothered to change his suit for Miss Lambton's funeral and had clumped into one of the back pews in the church wearing muddy boots. It would have been an act of respect to have made some kind of sartorial effort. The old lady had been exceptionally good to him.

Too good.

He had commented on this to Maybridge after the service. "People like that," he'd said, "take advantage of the weak and the foolish—they leech onto them—suck them dry. I'm totally in sympathy with the niece, God help her."

Maybridge might have murmured "Amen" had the criticism been voiced by anyone else. He wasn't a regular churchgoer and hadn't an idealized conception of men of the cloth, but rectors should make an effort. Walter Clegg might be a Person Like That, a Blood Sucker, even an Ape (his own description), but the light of Christian charity should surely send out a weak beam and illuminate something good. Miss Lambton had liked him.

"Let's hope," the rector had gone on, "that the niece, Victoria Carradine, has a very strong hand."

Mrs. Carradine, who hadn't for some unspecified reason been able to attend the funeral, was due to take up residence in a few weeks.

Her arrival was awaited with interest.

Maybridge, fully occupied with his duties as D.C.I. (rather mundane duties, nothing very spectacular), didn't give Walter and the new owner of The Beeches any thought until a letter arrived from Victoria Carradine on a Saturday morning a week before Christmas. Amongst her aunt's belongings, the letter stated, she had come across a leather-bound volume of the Lake Poets with Meg Maybridge's name inside. She remembered that her aunt had always spoken very warmly of Mr. and Mrs. Maybridge, and it would give her great pleasure to meet them and return the book. Would they care to partake of a glass of sherry on Sunday at midday?

"No," said Meg. She believed that happy memories of Miss Lambton should be preserved. Now that she was no longer at The Beeches, Meg didn't want to go there.

"Yes," said Maybridge whose curiosity had surfaced quite strongly.

"Tell her I prepare tutorials for my university students on Sunday mornings," Meg suggested. "It's a polite lie. And I don't like the verb, 'partake'."

"For an otherwise nice woman," Maybridge teased, "you can be bloody pedantic."

"Rumor has it," Meg retorted, "that Mrs. Carradine is *very* nice. Walter has landed on his feet. And all is hunky-dory."

"Good," said Maybridge, "so let's slurp sherry. Both of us."

She sighed and gave in.

Victoria Carradine received the Maybridges very graciously. The social game had to be played, her manner implied, and it had to be played well. She was a small, spindly woman impeccably dressed in a dark blue suit. Her eyeshadow, carefully applied, was a lighter blue. When she smiled her narrow chin seemed to narrow even more, and she smiled a lot. Her hair—thick, dark, and glossy—was caught up in a small bun at the nape of her neck. She looked youthful from behind; almost girlish. Face-to-face, the years showed.

The house, though centrally heated since she had taken possession of it, seemed chill. In Miss Lambton's time visitors shivered in the hall and then roasted in the small sitting room or the kitchen—usually the latter. The small sitting room now was enlarged by an archway leading to the dining room. The dining room, Maybridge remembered, had been the studio-

cum-storeroom. Miss Lambton's easel had been propped against the wall, and Walter's geraniums had overwintered on the window ledge. The room had smelt of paint, turpentine, and old leaves.

"We eat in there now," Mrs. Carradine told her visitors. "It seemed a pity to let such an attractive room lapse into a state of chaos."

Maybridge noticed the "we." He asked how Walter was.

"Oh, very well. I try to give him every encouragement. After all, he's not a servant here. I always call him *Mister* Clegg. It's a small courtesy, and it should help to build his confidence."

Maybridge, at a loss for words, nodded. Walter seated at the highly polished dining room table and using the best cutlery was difficult to imagine. Not difficult. Impossible.

Mrs. Carradine, interpreting his expression, smiled. "He's still rather an untidy eater—drops crumbs, uses his fork the wrong way—but all that will improve in time. The first hurdle was getting him to come to the table. We have achieved that, and now we progress slowly."

"Wonderful!" Meg said, careful not to catch her husband's eye.

After the sherry and the usual small talk, Mrs. Carradine asked if they would like to see the kitchen. "I was *surprised* at the state of the house when I came here. Putting the kitchen to rights was an urgent priority."

She opened the kitchen door with a flourish. "What, I wonder, would my aunt think of this?"

Meg murmured something appropriate. Maybridge was silent. Bloody appalled, he thought. The wonderful old range had been taken out. The old leather chairs had gone. Chrome and white units gleamed like functional pieces of machinery in a space capsule. Where did Walter sit now, for God's sake, when he came in from the garden? Did he lurk all day in the shed?

He asked her where Walter was.

Walter's whereabouts as she proudly displayed her new kitchen seemed an irrelevancy. "I really couldn't tell you. Spending a convivial hour or so down in the pub, perhaps."

It would make sense, under the circumstances; a cozy retreat. But Walter didn't drink and was awkward in company. Maybridge pointed this out.

She shrugged. "Then walking—or up in his bedroom having a nap. I don't question his comings and goings. My aunt was extremely possessive, from what I can gather. He couldn't call his soul his own."

"They got on," Maybridge retorted bleakly.

"Oh, I've no doubt. But only because the poor man knew no better. He fetched and carried far too much for a man of his age. And she could have given him better accommodations. His bedroom is up on the top floor. Very cold. Furnished with junk. He refuses to move. I wanted to extend the central heating, but he wouldn't get out." She sighed. "And I can't persuade him to be better clothed. He doesn't seem to realize that appearances matter. My aunt could have gently and tactfully taught him a great deal, but she didn't. And now it's up to me. He clings to the old ways because his mind has been conditioned to them. In time he will see things my way. His confidence will grow." She indicated the new range with all its knobs and dials. "When I had this installed, he shied away from it as if it were going to bite him. And he ate his meals standing up—at the sink. Bread and cheese, mostly. I coaxed him to the table in the dining room with my beef casserole. It has a delicious aroma. Naturally I had to demand a degree of cleanliness. Not much to ask, wouldn't you agree?"

Maybridge nodded. If washing your hands warded off starvation, then you washed them. Starvation was too strong a word, of course. Jungle animals weren't necessarily starving when they succumbed to the lure of bait.

Sometimes the bait was noxious.

In this case it would be good and wholesome, washed down by the milk of human kindness.

Or would it?

Maybridge looked contemplatively at the small neat woman. Her eyes, gimlet-green, met his briefly. For the first time since Miss Lambton's death his sympathy was entirely with the old man.

Walter, from a vantage point in the beech wood opposite the house, had seen the Maybridges arriving. Had the Chief Inspector been on his own, he might have gone down to the drive and waited by his car until he came out. But trying to put his case was difficult enough without an onlooker. He wasn't sure what his case was. That he was being done to death, grindingly and slowly, by some means he didn't understand was obvious. In the couple of months since the Witch-Woman had taken over the house he had become alarmingly weak. He couldn't walk briskly anymore, and the walks he was forced to take to get away from the house were becoming shorter. He was always tired these days. Not well. When his head wasn't aching, his stomach was queasy, and sometimes all parts of his anatomy tormented him. There was no peace to be had anywhere. Nowhere to go.

When the Lamb had rough-tongued him, which wasn't often and usually deserved, he had sulked in the shed. Afterwards she had always made him a strong cup of tea, and they had become friends again within minutes. The Witch-Woman, whose tongue was sickly sweet and never rough, had locked the shed. He wouldn't need to go in there in the winter, she had told him, and when spring came she would arrange for a gardener to come every week. "You must rest, Mr. Clegg," she had said, "your days of hard work are over."

He had protested that he wanted to get into the shed to smoke his pipe, since she wouldn't let him smoke it in the house. He'd get lip cancer smoking, she told him. It wasn't that she objected to his smoking in the house because it made a smell (which it did); she objected to him smoking anywhere, for his sake. She was surprised that Miss Lambton hadn't cared more for his health.

If anyone said anything nasty about the Lamb he became very angry and bad words boiled up in his head—and sometimes came out of his mouth. She pretended she didn't hear them. Her constant politeness was like a sharp pair of secateurs lopping away at him—drawing blood.

So what could he tell Maybridge?

Nothing, he decided. Policemen only listened to complaints about ordinary things. Like being poisoned by weed killer. The food she gave him didn't taste of weed killer. It was very fancy—mashed up avocado with prawns to start off with—and then meat with wine in the gravy. The Lamb had made nice plain gravy and hadn't minded when he spooned it up. Her spuds had been good, too, with lots of butter on them. He had known how to grow them, and she had known how to cook them. Meals with the Lamb had been all right. They hadn't worried him. He'd cleaned himself up a bit for her, of course, but she hadn't presented him with a nail brush and a cake of scented soap just before he sat down. By the time he got his hands the way the Witch-Woman wanted them, most of his appetite had gone. And she kept on watching him while he ate so that he had to chew with his mouth shut. It wasn't that she said anything; it was the way she looked. Like a lizard with hard bright eyes crouching on a rock.

Today he didn't feel like eating at all. The policeman and his wife were just about to leave. They were standing on the doorstep talking to her. Dinner would be late. Her voice whispered silkily inside his head: "Not *dinner*, Mr. Clegg, *lunch*. We *dine* at night."

The Lamb had never bothered about things like that.

She had only bothered about things that mattered. Like having proper soles on his boots. Extra blankets on his bed in the winter. Cough mixture when he wheezed.

She never made him feel stupid. About anything. A lot of people couldn't read, she told him. And it didn't matter that he forgot words sometimes—ordinary words when he was talking to her. When they got stuck on his tongue she carried on with whatever she was doing—painting at her easel—making pastry—washing up. Not fussing. He hadn't got all sweaty and worried like he did if he forgot what he was trying to tell the Witch-Woman. She would stand in front of him and smile and make little pulling gestures with her long scarlet nails as if she were pulling the entrails out of a dead rabbit. "My dear Mr. Clegg," she would ask gently, "what *are* you trying to say?"

He hadn't let her know he couldn't read. When she'd started passing him the newspaper every morning and asking him what he thought of the headlines, he'd told her the world was in a bad state.

"But not always in a bad state," she'd suggested, the green eyes gleaming.

"Always," he'd muttered. "Just nonsense. Rubbish."

She had invited him one evening to have a game of Scrabble. He'd told her he didn't play games. Any games. When she was out shopping, he'd found the box of Scrabble and buried it under a mound of leaves in the garden. Afterwards she had made a great fuss about looking for it, smiling to herself all the time.

He had played draughts with the Lamb. The draughts had been friendly objects. When the Lamb had played chess with the Chief Inspector, they had used the same board. It was a sudden friendly memory.

He was sorry how he hadn't gone down to the car, but it was too late. The Maybridges were driving away.

Walter watched them go. He felt helpless, angry, and a little frightened, like a lost child.

As he turned the car into the road, Maybridge glanced up towards the woods and saw Walter walking listlessly toward the house. He looked more stooped than he remembered him. Frailer.

He pointed him out to Meg. "Cause for concern?"

"I don't know." She leaned forward in her seat to watch him. "At his age there can be that kind of deterioration—naturally."

And unnaturally, Maybridge thought, but didn't voice it. It might be wise to visit The Beeches again—sometime in the new year perhaps, when all the seasonal festivities were over.

Mrs. Carradine told Walter she wanted to make Christmas really very happy for him—his first since Miss Lambton had died. How had they always spent it? The question brought a series of pictures into his mind. Cutting holly. Putting it anywhere handy, like along the tops of pictures. Making sure there were lots of logs for the fire. Eating a good plain meal served on the everyday white plates with the blue rims. Afterwards, smoking the tobacco she gave him while she watched the telly or went to sleep. His present to her was something she could paint afterward on her easel—like winter jasmine. It cost nothing. Meant a lot. Pleased her.

The Witch-Woman was waiting for an answer, smoothing her hair, smiling.

"Nothing much," he said.

All that would be changed, she told him. The house would really glow with the spirit of Christmas. She bought tinsel decorations and a small silver tree. The 'fridge was filled with what she called "delicacies," and there were several bottles of wine. The turkey was obviously too big for the two of them. She saw him eyeing it. She was inviting friends, she explained;

a couple from London. Alison and Humphrey. They were tremendous fun. Very witty. They would stay the night. Was there anyone Mr. Clegg would like to invite?

Aware that in some subtle way she was getting at him, he said there wasn't.

"But you must have *friends*, Mr. Clegg. Everyone has."

He shook his head.

She looked sad and then brightened. "They're putting on a party for the senior citizens at the residential home for the elderly—so the matron tells me. I happened to meet her the other day. You must have friends there—of your age—local people you have known a long time. I'm sure you'd be welcome to join them—just for the meal, of course—if you would like to?"

This was less subtle. They looked at each other in perfect understanding. Walter could quit the pain of the battlefield and carry the white flag of surrender into the internment camp.

Or go on fighting.

Shit, he fumed at her silently. Crap-face. Aloud, he told her that Miss Lambton wouldn't like him to eat his Christmas dinner anywhere else. He got the words out slowly and with rough emphasis: "This is my home."

"Of course," Mrs. Carradine patted his hand with her red-taloned fingers. "*Our* home, Mr. Clegg. For many happy years, I hope."

She watched him thoughtfully as he shuffled out of the room. Anno Domini was striking fast—with just a little help. More help was needed. She began planning the strategy for Christmas day. An array of the best wine glasses on the table. A tumbler of fruit juice for him. Paper hats of gold foil. His particularly grand and ridiculous. Neat embroidered napkins. He'd tuck his in his collar and find it too small. Crackers with riddles to be read aloud. Afterwards games involving words—charades, perhaps. Alison and Humphrey, amused, would play along.

It would be interesting to get their professional valuation of The Beeches when they had time for serious conversation. How much longer would it be, she wondered, before she was free to sell?

Walter escaped the pain of the Christmas onslaught by walking in front of a car. Not deliberately. He had been to the pharmacy to buy aspirin for a persistent headache and had stepped off the pavement without looking.

He wasn't badly hurt, but was taken to the hospital.

The casualty doctor, perturbed by his obvious loss of weight and general weakness, diagnosed bruised ribs—and perhaps something more serious. He was kept in for observation and routine tests. The headaches and malaise could be psychosomatic, but it would be unwise to take chances.

Walter was happy in the hospital. The food was ordinary and safe, and he began putting on weight again. The only time he wasn't happy was when the Witch-Woman visited. She brought him grapes. Fat, black, ugly bunches of fruit. He told the nurse they were poisoned. She ate one and survived.

Before discharging him, the doctor took Mrs. Carradine aside. The old man was a little disturbed, he said. The arteries of the brain tended to harden with age, and sometimes there were behavioral problems. He would need to be handled with patience. Eventually, if matters got worse, he might be admitted to a geriatric hospital, but he was by no means bad enough for that yet. At the moment kindly reassurance, good food, and warmth were what he needed.

"Tender loving care," Mrs. Carradine summed it up.

He eyed her a little suspiciously. Somehow the nuance hadn't sounded quite right.

Walter saw the Witch-Woman coming into the ward carrying a suitcase and cringed back among the pillows. She had brought him going-home clothes. But not *his* clothes. Not his old corduroy jacket with the pipe burns in the pocket. Not his old-fashioned widelegged trousers. Not even his thick woollen longjohns and undershirt.

"New underwear," she said briskly. "No holes. Respectable. Not like the ones you had when you were run over." She put them on the bed. "And a new shirt and suit. Socks. Shoes. I matched up the sizes with your old ones. When you get home you'll find more new clothes in your wardrobe. In fact, you'll find a new wardrobe. I've made quite a few changes in your bedroom. I'm sure you'll be pleased."

She left him while he got dressed.

Dumb with misery, he put on the clothes of a stranger. Trendy clothes. Too bright. Too young. When he looked in the mirror in the reception area where she was waiting for him he didn't recognize himself. He touched his face. His flesh didn't smell like his flesh. He was inhabiting someone else's corpse.

The Witch-Woman smiled at him brightly. "Wonderful," she said. "Quite a transformation. Appearances count more than you realize. They really do. You're not the same man, Mr. Clegg."

She chatted on the drive back to The Beeches, casting him amused glances when he didn't respond.

His old bedroom would have given him a sense of identity—had she left it alone. He would have looked at the ugly, heavy, familiar furniture and been reassured. It had all gone. The room he saw now was a coffin—white wood and silk-lined.

She had taken everything he had. Rubbed him out.

Mrs. Carradine indicated the bedcover—white with sprigs of flowers on it. "It's called a duvet. I'm sure you'll find it warmer than that stained lumpy eiderdown you had before." She opened one of the wardrobe doors. "It's spacious, isn't it? And the white wood is bright and modern and pleasant. Look at all your new clothes." There was a maroon blazer with matching slacks. A tweed overcoat. Rows of shirts on hangers. A couple of thick pullovers. Several ties. All garish.

She told him that she had arranged a welcome-home party for him that evening. Mostly local people. Miss Lambton's friends—some of them. The Maybridges were coming. And Proctor, the solicitor, would be there. And the rector. Professional people. He would wear the suit he had on now—the gray pinstripe looked just right—with perhaps a dark red silk handkerchief in the breast pocket to brighten it. The handkerchiefs were in the top drawer of the dressing table. When the guests arrived he could play host and walk around with the tray of drinks—or the canapés—and help her entertain them. "You mustn't be shy." Her eyes were mocking green slits, bright with victory. There's always the old people's home, up on the hill, they were telling him. No one will make a fool of you there, old man.

He watched her in silence.

A little discomfited, but not yet perturbed, she turned and left him.

He heard her going into the bathroom and running the bath. And then, later, returning to her room. The door closing. He had been standing by the window, immobile, for a long time. The sky was darkening, and the setting sun drew a thin line of red over the beech trees like a narrow flame. He imagined the bonfire she had made of his clothes, his furniture, and his bones gradually warmed into life. He flexed his muscles. Moved a few steps. Rage was in his bloodstream, activating him. He took off the suit and kicked it under the delicate little white dressing table with its gilt scrolls. And then he took off all his clothes.

When she came out of her room, dressed for the party in a green silk gown and with pearls at her throat, he was standing in the corner of the landing, near the stairs, waiting for her.

She recoiled, her eyes wide with shock. The doctor had mentioned abnormal behavior, by God, but he could have put it more strongly! Her heart thumping, she tried to edge past him, to get downstairs, to get help.

He reached out his hand and she moved quickly, awkwardly. He didn't push her. He didn't have to. Her high heels missed the top tread of the stairs and she fell heavily, banging her head on the banister.

Dislodging her wig.

Walter, his anger cooled by surprise, walked down to where she lay sprawled in the hall. He examined her head with interest. What little hair she had sprouted in white tufts on her skull. Near her ears were small scars. He had never heard of a face lift.

She tried to speak, but her mouth was twisted to one side and the words couldn't come out. She made a tremendous effort to reach the wig and her fingers just touched it. Her eyes implored him to fetch it for her, to put it back on. She was no longer shocked by his nudity. Her own state was worse. The guests would arrive soon. They mustn't see her looking like this.

Walter voiced what she couldn't say. "Appearances count." It came out parrot-fashion. Easily. Strongly. A cruel parody. But she had been cruel to him.

He moved the wig out of her reach with his toe. The black silky hair was floppy, like a dead cat.

She moaned, and her contorted mouth dribbled spittle down her pointed chin.

He guessed she'd had a stroke. She'd probably die of it. Whoever came first could call the doctor. If she was still alive.

He left the front door open and wedged it with the mat. It was raining, but he was too elated to feel cold. Not sure where he was going, he found himself up in the cemetery by the Lamb's grave. Very soon the anemones would bloom—bright little flowers all over it. He crouched and felt the earth, then patted it. "It's all right," he told her. "It doesn't matter."

He would never go back to the house. He didn't know where he'd go. And that didn't matter either. All he could see inside his head now were the flowers that would surely come soon.

———

When the doctor and the chief inspector found him, shortly after dawn, he was lying on a bench on the church porch. Rigor had set in. His face was tranquil.

Maybridge covered him gently with his coat. A gesture of respect. Why, he wondered, had the old man come out here naked to die of hypothermia? Mrs. Carradine, if she ever recovered her speech, would tell him. Her version. Not worth much.

"Natural causes?" the rector asked, deeply troubled by events he didn't understand.

"It would seem so," Maybridge said dryly, "given the circumstances." He looked across the graveyard to where Miss Lambton was buried. You silly, well-intentioned, *kind* woman, he thought sadly, if you could only see what you've done.

It's a Hard World

ANDREW VACHSS

Andrew Vachss normally writes to make people angry. "It's a Hard World" is different, he says. In this story he is attempting to be faithful to the past, to reflect what fascinates him about the 1940s and 1950s, which he regards as his time.

Vachss does not regard himself as a writer, because that connotes fabrication to him, and he does not fabricate. His novels are based on experience gained in a series of jobs working with the dispossessed. He has run a maximum security prison; he was in Biafra during the civil war in which two million people died between 1967 and 1969; he was a field investigator for the U.S. Public Health Service in Ohio and West Virginia. Presently, Vachss is an attorney representing children victimized by abuse, neglect, molestation, or incest.

His first novel, *Flood* (1985), was highly acclaimed. His second novel, *Strega*, was published in March by Knopf.

I pulled into the parking lot at LaGuardia around noon and sat in the car running my fingers over the newly-tightened skin on my face, trying to think through my next move. I couldn't count on the plastic surgery to do the job. I had to get out of New York at least long enough to see if DellaCroce's people still were looking for me.

I sat there for an hour or so thinking it through, but nothing came to me. Time to move. I left the car where it was—let Hertz pick it up in a week or so when I didn't turn it in.

The Delta terminal was all by itself in a corner of the airport. I had a ticket for Augusta, Georgia, by way of Atlanta. Canada was where I had to go if I wanted to get out of the country, but Atlanta gave me a lot of options. The airport there is the size of a small city; it picks up traffic from all over the country.

I waited until the last minute to board, but it was quiet and peaceful. They didn't have anybody on the plane with me. Plenty of time to think; maybe too much time. A running man sticks out too much. I had to find a way out of this soon or DellaCroce would nail me when I ran out of places to hide.

Atlanta Airport was the usual mess: travelers running through the tunnels, locals selling everything from shoe shines to salvation. I had a couple of hours until the connecting flight to Augusta, so I found a pay phone and called the Blind Man in New York.

"What's the story?" I asked, not identifying myself.

"Good news and bad news, pal," came back the Blind Man's harsh whisper. He'd spent so much time in solitary back when we did time together that his eyes were bad and his voice had rusted from lack of practice. "They got the name that's on your ticket, but no pictures."

"Damn! How did they get on the ticket so fast?"

"What's the difference, pal? Dump the ticket and get the hell out of there."

"And do what?"

"You got me, brother. But be quick or be dead," said the Blind Man, breaking the connection.

The first thing I did was get out of the Delta area. I went to the United counter and booked a flight to Chicago, leaving in three hours. You have to stay away from borders when you're paying cash for an airline ticket, but I didn't see any obvious DEA agents lurking around and, anyway, I wasn't carrying luggage.

With the Chicago ticket tucked safely away in my pocket, I drifted slowly back toward the boarding area for the Augusta flight. It was getting near to departure time. I found myself a seat in the waiting area, lit a cigarette, and kept an eye on the people at the ticketing desk. There was a short walkway to the plane, with a pretty little blonde standing there checking off the boarding passes. Still peaceful, the silence routinely interrupted by the usual airport announcements, but no tension. It felt right to me. Maybe I'd try for Augusta after all; I hate Chicago when it's cold.

And then I spotted the hunters: two flat-faced men sitting in a corner of the waiting area. Sitting so close their shoulders were touching, they both had their eyes pinned on the little blonde, not sweeping the room like I would have expected. But I knew who they were. You don't survive a dozen years behind the walls if you can't tell the hunters from the herd.

They wouldn't be carrying; bringing handguns into an airport was too much of a risk. Besides, their job was to point the finger, not pull the trigger. I saw how they planned to work it; they had the walkway boxed in. But I didn't see what good it would do them if they couldn't put a face on their target.

The desk man announced the boarding of Flight 884 to Augusta. I sat there like it was none of my business, not moving. One by one, the passengers filed into the narrow area. The sweet southern voice of the blonde piped up, "Pleased to have you with us today, Mr. Wilson," and my eyes flashed over to the hunters. Sure enough, they were riveted to the blonde's voice. She called off the name of each male passenger as he filed past her. If the women passengers felt slighted at the lack of recognition, they kept quiet about it. A perfect trap: if I put my body through that walkway, the little blonde would brand the name they already had to my new face, and I'd be dead meat as soon as the plane landed.

I got up to get away from there just as the desk man called out, "Last call for Flight 884." They couldn't have watchers at all the boarding areas. I'd just have to get to Chicago, call the Blind Man, and try and work something out. As I walked past the desk, a guy slammed into me. He bounced back a few feet, put a nasty expression on his face, and then dropped it when he saw mine. A clown in his late thirties, trying to pass for a much younger guy: hair carefully styled forward to cover a receding hairline, silk shirt open to mid-chest, fancy sunglasses dangling from a gold chain around his neck. I moved away slowly and watched as he approached the desk.

"I got a ticket for this flight," he barked out, like he was used to being obeyed.

"Of course, sir. May I see your boarding pass?"

"I don't have a goddamn pass. Can't I get one here?"

"I'm sorry, sir," the desk man told him, "the flight is all boarded at this time. We have four more boarding passes outstanding. We can certainly issue one to you, but it has to be on what we call the 'modified standby' basis. If the people holding boarding passes don't show up five minutes before flight time, we will call your name and give you the pass."

"What kind of crap is this?" the clown demanded. "I paid good money for this ticket."

"I'm sure you did, sir. But that's the procedure. I'm sure you won't have any trouble boarding. This happens all the time on these short flights. Just give us your ticket, and we'll call you by name just before the flight leaves, all right?"

I guess it wasn't all right, but the clown had no choice. He slammed his ticket down on the counter, tossed his leather jacket casually over one shoulder, and took a seat near the desk.

It wasn't a great shot, but it was the best one I'd had in a while. I waited a couple of heartbeats and followed the clown to the desk. I listened patiently to their explanation, left my ticket, and was told that they would call me by name when my turn came.

I didn't have much time. I walked over to where the clown was sitting, smoking a cigarette like he'd invented it. "Look," I told him, "I need to get on that flight to Augusta. It's important to me. Business reasons."

"So what's that to me?" he smirked, shrugging his shoulders.

"I know you got ahead of me on the list, okay? It's worth a hundred to me to change places with you. Let me go when your name is called, and you can go when they call mine, if they do," I told him, taking out a pair of fifties and holding them out to him.

His eyes lit up. I could see the wheels turning in his head. He knew a sucker when he saw one. "What if we both get on?" he wanted to know.

"That's my tough luck," I said. "I need to do everything possible to get on the flight. It's important to me."

He appeared to hesitate, but it was no contest. "My name's Morrison," he said, taking the fifties from my hand. "Steele," I said, and walked toward the desk.

The watchers hadn't looked at us. A couple of minutes passed. I gently worked myself away from the clown, watching the watchers. The desk man piped up: "Mr. Morrison, Mr. Albert Morrison, we have your boarding pass." I shot up from my seat, grabbed the pass, and hit the walkway. The little blonde sang out, "Have a pleasant flight, Mr. Morrison," as I passed. I could feel the heat of the hunters' eyes on my back.

I wasn't fifty feet into the runway when I heard, "Mr. Steele, Mr. Henry Steele, we have your boarding pass." I kept going and found my seat in the front of the plane.

I watched the aisle and, sure enough, the clown passed me by, heading for the smoking section in the rear. I thought he winked at me, but I couldn't be sure.

The flight to Augusta was only half an hour, but the plane couldn't outrun a phone call. The airport was a tiny thing, just one building, with a short walk to the cabs outside. The clown passed by me as I was heading outside, bumped me with his shoulder, held up my two fifties in his hand, and gave me a greasy smile. "It's a hard world," he said, moving out ahead of me.

I watched as two men swung in behind him. One was carrying a golf bag; the other had his hands free.

Murder

ENRIQUE ANDERSON-IMBERT
Translated by Sara Heikoff Woehrlen

Enrique Anderson-Imbert, an Argentinian by
birth, has taught Spanish-American literature in
the United States for nearly forty years, most
recently at Harvard University, where he has lec-
tured since 1965. He is a prolific author of literary
history, criticism, and fiction. The translator char-
acterizes his stories as "quirky" works in which
"magic and myth invade our 'real' world." "Murder" was included in Mr. Anderson-Imbert's 1971
collection *La locura juega al ajedrez* (Madness Is
a Chess Player). The story has not been previously translated into English.

Sara Heikoff Woehrlen has taught Spanish literature and translation at the college level and
has published translations of Spanish stories and
poetry.

This is the first time since I've been in the United
States that I've descended from the paradise that is
Harvard to the inferno of a Southern university. I
needn't add it will be the last. It was a mistake to
sign a contract with Southern College in Alabama.
My plan was to stay here for a few weeks, earn a
little money teaching summer school, and then continue on to Mexico, where at least I would be able
to speak Spanish. But even so I must have been crazy
when I accepted the invitation. The heat is suffocat-

ing. The light hurts my eyes. The town is dirty. Men, women, and children drag their poverty through the streets, and the defeated look in their eyes is proof enough of the stagnation in which they live.

"There must be a lot of suicides here," I said to myself; but immediately changed my mind. "No, instead of committing suicide these people would rather kill." Haven't we an image of the South as a place where violence is directed against others? Lynch mobs, masters who beat their slaves, men who avenge their honor by fighting duels, riverbank quarrels between the crews of flat-bottomed boats, bands of hooded riders who streak the terror-filled nights with white. . . .

I was given a hint of this violence the very day I arrived.

Professor Hamilton, whom I had bumped into on the street, had invited me to a bar as squalid as any you might imagine. We were drinking at the counter when I heard a thump and a scream. I turned and saw a furious man standing at one side of a table and on the other side a woman who had fainted, her hair dripping with blood and beer. The brute had hit her with a bottle! I moved closer—out of curiosity more than compassion. I must confess, since this is about confessing, that the blood which flows from a real person moves me less than that from a fictional character. In reality, bleeding is sudden and takes me by such surprise that my first reaction is to find out what happened. In stories, the bloodshed is printed in black and white, and if I do see it, it is because the author's clever manipulation of words has sensitized me to the fantasy. More curious than compassionate, then, I started to move closer, but Hamilton threw some coins on the bar, took my arm, and dragged me onto the street.

"Don't get involved," he told me. "The police will come, and we can't let them find us here. It's off limits to the faculty. Besides, who's to say she didn't deserve to have her head bashed in? If I were to challenge the guy he might attack me, and then I'd have to kill him."

I looked at Hamilton, a giant bird with rapacious eyes, and knew he really was capable of killing someone.

Professor Collins also is a violent man. He is married to a pretty Panamanian girl, he says from a distinguished Spanish family. If I am not mistaken, in her dark-skinned past—she came here as a child and no longer speaks Spanish—there are drops of mulatto blood. Perhaps it is to avert suspicion that Collins rants against the Negroes. When I told him I wanted to hear songs with an African rhythm in the black district, he dissuaded me with arguments as obvious as the robes of the Ku Klux Klan. I wouldn't be surprised if he were a member of that secret society, because he defended the lynching of a Negro I had just read about in the local paper.

The others—Ford and Tracy—are more reserved, but instinct tells me that academia hasn't dominated the bestiality in them, either. Ford, for example, admitted to me that the incidence of homicide is higher in the South than in other places, but he explained it with logic: "Of course, in the South there are more people who need killing." Tracy, whom I asked why Southerners are so violent, preferred a historical explanation: the War of Secession, defeat, the end of slavery, the struggle against Northern carpetbaggers who, under the guise of Reconstruction, flocked to take advantage of their misfortune; the presence of the Negro; the feeling that the entire region was always under attack and that they were persecuted from without by scorn and newfangled notions. All of this must have created, or so he judged, a Southern personality with a state-of-siege psychology which felt itself the victim of a hostile environment and hateful threats. Neither Ford nor Tracy was interested in hearing my less fanciful logic or history. . . .

Tracy is chairman of the department. According to what I was told, he's a millionaire, and if he continues teaching it's because he enjoys it. Almost every night he would invite us to his house for a drink. The house was magnificent. It was in the middle of a small grove of trees. At least you could breathe there.

I didn't like having to attend these gatherings. Not all of them, at least. The truth is that Southerners bore me to death. In the first place, it was impossible to have a serious conversation. As soon as anyone brought up a professional matter, the women protested: "Please, don't talk shop!" Even my colleagues were reluctant to risk exposing their intellectual mediocrity. They dedicated themselves, instead, to frivolous pleasures. They thought this kept them young. Nonsense! To delight in repeating the innocent things they had done as boys, at those gay parties before the war, does not rejuvenate; it magnifies one's age. Reflecting upon the past doubles the years as a mirror doubles distances. Changes in contemporary custom are so swift that anyone who stops to take a nostalgic look back at his own childhood will find that, upon returning to reality, today's young people are not in the same place he left them. So, mingle with young people? Delighted! Pretend to be young? God forbid! Those couples—I was the only unclaimed man—bowed to the moralizing of their adult generation but wanted to entertain themselves with adolescent giddiness. What did they do? They played games. One night they played "Twenty Questions," on another, "Who am I?"—and so forth. Sunday, July 9—I will never forget that day—they showed me how to play a game they called "Murder."

Here are its rules: On one piece of paper is written: "Assassin." On another: "Detective." These are mixed with pieces of blank paper. In all, there are as many pieces of paper as there are players. Whoever picks the one marked "Detective" has to produce it. The others silently hide the pieces of paper fate has dealt them. No one knows, then, who has the paper marked "Assassin." The lights are turned off and the Detective goes away. The other players scatter throughout the house, under the cover of absolute darkness, until the Assassin puts his hands around somebody's neck and squeezes: this signals that the murder has taken place. The victim screams so that the Detective can hear and from that moment everyone stays put. Everyone but the Assassin, that is, who can now sneak silently away and place himself where he can best carry out the deception. A minute after hearing the scream the Detective comes back, turns on the lights, searches the rooms, observes the position of the victim and of the other players, collects everyone in the living room, and begins the interrogation. Just as the Assassin was the only one who, after the crime, could move, he is now the only one who can lie. The

Detective tries to discover if someone has moved or lied. Finally he asks a suspect: "Are you the killer?" If the answer is "No," the Detective loses. If the Assassin is found out, he loses, because at this point in the game there can be no more lies: he must confess. Understand?

As I said, on July 9 I was initiated into the game called "Murder." There was a full moon that night. The blinds were closed so that no light could enter the house. Nine little pieces of paper. Hamilton picked the one that said "Detective." He lit a pipe and, before taking it out to the garden, turned off the lights.

The darkness seemed to blot me out. It was as if I had just awakened at midnight in the bed of one of the many hotels in which I stay when traveling in a foreign country. I didn't know what I was doing there, stuck in a coffin. I no longer felt that the living room was in a house, and the house in a garden, and the garden in a neighborhood, and the neighborhood in a town, and the town in the state of Alabama. What my feet touched was the geography of a dream. The mantle of air I breathed was my entire world. Although it contained me alone, this world seemed absolute, without boundaries, so it didn't seem small: I had grown to fill it up like a sightless god. It was no longer the physical space which recedes discreetly into the night until it disappears from view, taking with it the things that do not matter to us. No. This space, instead of unfolding, fell back upon me. My body was its control center—a center in motion because, obeying the rules of the game "Murder," I began to walk.

At first my steps were rapid. There was no danger:

I remembered the position of the nearby furniture pretty well. Before, I had seen this furniture as connected to the real world; but now it was detached, a mere figment of my memory, and I could feel the spaces between the furnishings the way an amputee feels his missing limb.

As I explored lesser-known places, my steps grew slower and slower. Space undulated in time. "I've just touched the back of a chair; now there's a little table with a vase I must not tip over; then right away the television. . . ." It was a series of curves, surfaces, heights.

Finally came the moment I forgot how to walk, and had to learn all over again: an apprentice pedestrian, like a toddler swayed between obstacles which attract and repel at the same time. I could no longer guess what I might bump into on my cautious march. Untied from its moorings, the furniture existed only as a series of threats. In the depths of caves, hedgehogs waited in ambush with their spines erect. Things, things that flee with the light of day—night things, in the dark—attacked me from all sides. Then, on each finger, an eye opened. I walked uncertainly, using a tactile rather than a visual geometry. Hands, arms, elbows, feet, legs, knees were not enough: antennae and tentacles grew from my body as a cane grows from the hands of a blind man. I wanted to feel my way, for I had fallen into a shadowy well; I clung to its walls and, instead of climbing, I circulated. I was a pilgrim without sanctuary, surprised by an unwished-for adventure on a path that led nowhere.

"Bah," I said to myself, "there's no need to exaggerate! It's not a mystical rapture! It's nothing more than a game!" A game, yes, but while playing it there is nothing to do, nothing to think about. With action and thought abolished, space becomes an amusement; time a diversion. Space and time are reborn freely in that suspension of life and, suspended outside of life in this way, one becomes a ghost.

Something touched my face and I jumped. "Ah," I said to myself, "it's a leaf sticking out from the vine which winds around the window." But I felt as if I'd been touched by a ghost. This was too much. To think I was a ghost and that another ghost had touched me? No sir. Humiliating enough that I, an adult, was there playing games like a child. No. I was not a ghost. I was a man, and the men and women who had scattered throughout the house were friends. At the outset, when the lights went dark, I lost sight of this community. But the game itself, solitary as it seemed to me in the beginning, was collective.

Though I recovered the sense of being within a group, I continued to feel isolated from the other players, whose steps responded in echo to my own. I no longer felt like a ghost; rather I felt like a night-blind felon in another lifetime. Not the infallible Max Carrados, the blind detective invented by Ernest Bramah, but more like Fantomas, the nyctalopic criminal created by Allain-Souvestre—the only one who, in the shadows, could have defeated Max Carrados.

I began to develop a criminal mind. For example, when I bumped into a lamp shade I grabbed it quickly before it fell, not with the hope of avoiding an accident, but, like a nocturnal criminal, with the evil intent of suppressing a noise which might alarm the sleeping owners. With this new psychology of wickedness, I felt again the sensation of being imprisoned in a murky circle—this time as a premonition of the punishment I would receive once I committed my crime. Because, fatally, I had to commit a crime. What would it be? I had a presentiment. And I prepared myself. Since one can't be immoral except within a group of people, I tried to align myself with other men. Just by my imagining them, the room became real again.

A glimmer of moon had managed to filter in through the blinds, reflecting its disquieting spell in a mirror. At first I saw practically nothing—non-forms slid past me and dissolved.

Then my body began to dominate space. I now was able to perceive my companions in the game. Suddenly, I could distinguish the men from the women. In the dusk I couldn't determine if a particular figure was Tracy or Collins or Ford, but I could distinguish the rustle of a man's suit from the swish of a woman's dress. I could distinguish a heavy step from a light tap. I could distinguish the breathing. I could distinguish the perfumes. The women laughed nervously or screamed, pretending to be frightened. Perhaps the wives of Tracy and Ford, the stupidest ones, really were frightened by the dark, by that slow parade of bodies as shocking as a resurrection of the dead, by the very idea of "Murder." Controlled by a burning impulse from my vital force, space expanded in the presence of the men, contracted in the presence of the women. Intimate, so intimate is the presence of a real woman—a woman of flesh and bone whom one longs to possess.

In the midst of all this a hysterical scream rang in

my ears, separating the light from the darkness like a bolt of lightning. I remembered the rules of the game. I didn't move. There was laughter. In a moment Hamilton appeared. He was framed by the door, stamped in silhouette against the brightness of the moon: his pipe was that of Sherlock Holmes, but once he turned on the lights, the Detective was a huge bird with cruel eyes.

I was surprised to see Mrs. Hamilton at my side. Happy to have been the victim, she was motioning to her husband and smiling in a way no corpse would. Her smile was a frenzy of white and red, her parted lips so highly painted that the red had smeared. At a distance, next to the window, was Collins. I saw Ford in the vestibule, and his wife, with Tracy's wife, in the middle of the next room. Tracy and the pretty Panamanian girl had disappeared. At least I couldn't see them from where I stood.

Hamilton looked at us, eyeballing the distance between each person. He then searched the house, found Tracy and the Panamanian girl somewhere and, having finished his visual inspection, herded us all into the living room.

He began to interrogate us. "After the scream, did you hear anyone move?" "Just before the scream, if someone near you did move, did you recognize who it was?" "Ah, you bumped into a piece of furniture! Let's see, which was it?" He wanted to discover the identity of the Assassin, of course, not by the testimony of the players but by the expressions on our faces. Careful, then, about laughing too much! Or, conversely, about being too serious! He grilled us with those beady eyes of a bird of prey which had so impressed me outside the bar that day. Only on that day Hamilton had shrugged off the violence—now he was an agent of the law.

When he finished his examination he approached me again and asked:

"Are you the Assassin?"

According to the rules I had to confess. Yes. It was I.

Loud laughter, and then Tracy served us cocktails. It was a bad sign: the evening was going to last another couple of hours. I invented a reason for leaving. No, no! The night is young! What. . . .

"I'll take him home," interrupted Hamilton decisively.

"Don't bother. . . ."

"It's no trouble. I'll take him." Turning to Tracy, he said, "I'll be right back."

I said goodbye to my hosts and their guests and went off with Hamilton.

To get to my house we had to cross a park that rose and fell in abrupt hills. We were on top of the highest hill when Hamilton stopped the car and asked: "Tell me: there's something that intrigues me. You were the Assassin. Why then, after committing the murder, didn't you leave the scene, to better hide your guilt?"

"Well," I answered with a smile, "for several reasons. In the first place, it's expected that the murderer will flee, right? Well, it occurred to me that if I didn't flee I would look less guilty. In the second place, I was tired and didn't want to run the risk of bumping into any more furniture. In the third place, there's no reason to take the game too seriously. It is a game, nothing more than a game . . . "

I was going to add, "and I'm surprised that, at

your age, an important professor like you would take a child's game so seriously," when Hamilton surprised me by asking, "Isn't there another reason, other than the ones you gave me?" Suddenly he plucked the handkerchief from my pocket, turned on the dome light, and pointed out the lipstick stains—lipstick from his wife's lips which I had brushed clean with mine.

That handkerchief is what put the police on the right track. They found it in Hamilton's pocket. Starting from there and with each succeeding clue they soon guessed he had not gone over the cliff while returning to the Tracys' after taking me home (as they first suspected), but that I, having knocked him out with a rock, put him in the car and pushed it over the side.

Why? Because, crazed with honor, jealousy, and cocktails, Hamilton got out of the car, dragged me from my seat, and began to pummel me with the evident intention of doing me in. When he bent over to pick up a stick with which to finish me off, I was already standing and had the rock in my hands.

Hamilton forgot that in "Murder" the Detective cannot murder the Assassin. But in accordance with the rules of the game, I, after killing his wife, killed him. Tell me, Your Honor, what else could I do?

A Flash of Red

EDWARD D. HOCH

A past president of the Mystery Writers of America, Ed Hoch has had over seven hundred short stories published and has written or edited over thirty books, including his annual anthology of best mystery stories of the year published by Walker.

Of "A Flash of Red," he says, "This is my fourth published story about freelance bodyguard Libby Knowles. At the time I created the character, a few years back, the woman bodyguard-for-hire idea seemed unique to me. I still believe it offers a change from the women private eyes increasingly appearing in mystery fiction, and it allows for a greater variety of plots and settings."

It was not until Peterson put his hand on her leg that he realized she was wearing a small automatic pistol strapped to her thigh. His hand drew back in alarm as if it had encountered an unexpected tumor. "What's this?" he asked.

Libby Knowles replied calmly. "What does it feel like? It's a pistol, of course. You hired me as a bodyguard and that's what I'm being. If you had some other arrangement in mind, you should have told me."

"No, no—it's just that I thought you carried a revolver in your purse."

"This is a spare, for emergencies. Purses have a way of getting away from you in a struggle."

"Ah—isn't it uncomfortable?"

"Damned uncomfortable. That's one of the reasons my fee's so high."

He smiled at that. "What're the other reasons?"

"Because I'm good at what I do and because I'm going to keep you alive."

Rick Peterson had hired Libby three days earlier to accompany him on a week-long trip to England and back. He was a handsome man in his mid-thirties who hardly looked as if he needed the services of the Libby Knowles Protection Service. But as he'd explained it, "I'll be visiting some very unsavory characters operating outside the reach of the law, quite literally. I don't want to show up there with a couple of ex-wrestlers at my side and provoke trouble, but at the same time I'd like a bodyguard. You seem to be the perfect answer. They'll take you for my girl and nobody'll get nervous."

The "unsavory characters" Peterson had flown to London to meet were in truth a group of young Americans engaged in an illegal but unofficially tolerated business—the operation of a pirate radio station from a ship anchored seventeen miles off the British coast. Libby had read about such things in the papers from time to time, but only with casual interest. Now she was about to meet some of the people actually involved in such an enterprise.

Their first two days in London had been spent arranging the meeting through intermediaries. The offshore pirates were not allowed to land in Britain, and it was against the law for anyone from the mainland to take them supplies. Such pirate radio ships had been supplied in the past from Amsterdam or some other foreign port, but Peterson seemed to know this ship was different. "They've been seen in London," he told Libby. "I want to meet with them and arrange a visit to their ship."

"Whatever for?" she asked. "Are you a groupie?"

"It's a business matter."

So the meeting was finally arranged, at the Park Lane hotel where Libby and Peterson were staying, sleeping in separate beds in the same three-hundred-dollar-a-night suite. The young man and woman met them in the lobby for tea shortly after Peterson's discovery of the gun strapped to Libby's thigh. They were properly dressed for the occasion, and if either was armed Libby saw no hint of it. They looked like upper-class Londoners who'd stopped in after an autumn stroll around Hyde Park. Only their voices betrayed them as Americans.

"Glad to meet you," the young man said, shaking Peterson's hand. "I'm Kurt Frollic and this here's Susan Vash." He was a bit older than the girl, who seemed barely out of college. She spoke with a slight Boston accent and Libby wondered if she'd gone to Radcliffe.

"I'm one of the disc jockeys," Susan told them in her proper accent. "They wanted someone who sounded educated to the British. Upper-class, you know?"

"Pleased to meet you," Libby said. "We've been listening to your station at night but I haven't heard you yet."

"Early morning's my time," the girl said. Her dark hair framed her face nicely, and Libby envied the fresh windswept look of it. Living on a trawler in the North Sea obviously agreed with her.

Rick Peterson came right to the point. "Libby and I would like to come aboard to see how you operate. I'm doing a story for *Audio* magazine back in the States. It would be nice publicity for you."

"We're not in the habit of running tours," Frollic answered dubiously.

"Sometimes the fans come out on weekends," Susan explained. "They ride out on fishing boats to cheer and take photos, but we don't let them on board. We've never let anyone on board except the people who bring us supplies."

"You've been at it six months, challenging the BBC."

"Oh, there are lots of underground stations like ours over here," Kurt Frollic said. "More than a hundred, really—some operating out of basements and others quite well established. They play music the people want to hear, whether it's reggae, soul, rock, or whatever. A lot of it's ethnic music, of course, of the sort the BBC would never touch."

"But you're among the first Americans to be broadcasting from offshore."

"There are two of us now. We're run from New York by a satellite hookup. Listeners can even make requests, but they have to mail them to a post office box in New York. They're transmitted to us by computer."

"Who owns your ship, the *Skyhigh*?"

"It's a trawler," Susan answered. "Almost two

hundred feet long. There are five of us on board, plus the crew."

"But who owns it?"

Frollic shrugged. "American businessmen. Probably a tax shelter, you know? We don't ask questions."

"Can we come aboard?" Peterson asked again.

The two of them exchanged glances, and finally the young man shrugged. "Sure, why not?"

"When? We're only over here till the end of the week."

"Tomorrow afternoon? It's about an hour and a half journey by fishing boat from Great Yarmouth, but we don't want you to be seen coming aboard. It's best if you leave port in late afternoon and arrive after dark. We'll watch for you to flash a red light as you approach. Then we'll flash a red light in return. Take Captain Olaf's boat."

"Very well," Peterson agreed. "Seems a bit melodramatic, though."

"Sorry. That's the way it has to be."

When their visitors had left, Peterson seemed pleased. "We'll wrap this thing up tomorrow night, Libby. Maybe we can even take in a play before we head home."

"They certainly seemed cooperative enough. You could have come alone and saved my fee."

"I haven't regretted a minute of it. You're a lovely young woman. You know, when I put my hand on your leg earlier . . ."

"Must we go into that again?"

He signed the check and they headed for the elevator. "Whatever made you get into this line of work, Libby?"

"That's a long story. It's a living and I enjoy it."

"Traveling around with strange men, sharing their bedrooms but never sleeping with them?"

"I guard women, too," she answered. "But I don't mix business with pleasure."

They left the elevator at their floor and walked to the suite at the end of the corridor. "Maybe I can change your mind over dinner," Peterson said, unlocking the door and stepping aside to let her enter.

Libby's first thought was that the room was oddly dark for later afternoon. Then she realized the drapes had been closed. "Rick, there's . . ."

Someone's arm grabbed her around the neck, jerking her backwards off her feet. She heard Peterson yell at the same instant. Then she was fighting for her life, trying to ease the tightening pressure on her throat. She swung her gun-heavy purse by its strap and felt it connect with something. The grip on her neck loosened just a trifle, but that was all she needed. She wrenched free, kicking backward with her high heel at the same instant. Off balance, she hit the rug hard, but was satisfied to hear a grunt of pain from her assailant. Then she rolled over, pulling the automatic from her thigh holster, and fired a quick shot at the ceiling. There was no time to aim, but the crack of the weapon had the desired effect. She saw one assailant dive for the door, while the other paused only long enough to shout at the fallen Peterson, "Stay off the *Skyhigh!*"

Libby started after them but Peterson grabbed her. "No—let them go!"

"They might have killed us!"

"But they didn't. You did exactly what I hired you for. You saved my life."

She opened the drapes and inspected his face. He'd been hit with something hard, probably a pair of brass knuckles, but otherwise he seemed all right. She went to her bag and took out something to treat his cuts. "I think you'd better tell me what's going on here. Who were those men?"

"The one who hit me and shouted as they ran out is named Amid Jebel."

"An Arab?"

He nodded. "I didn't recognize the other one."

"What's their connection with a pirate radio station?"

Peterson didn't answer right away. Instead he walked over to the window and looked down at the traffic on Park Lane. Finally he said, "If things go well tomorrow, maybe we should fly home early on Friday."

"I thought the sound of my shot would at least bring a house detective running, but if anyone heard it they ignored it."

"The hotel is owned by Arabs. I was a fool to meet those two in the lobby."

"Yes, you were," she agreed. "You were inviting trouble and you got it. I suppose someone on the staff gave them a key to our room. Maybe we should call the whole thing off while you're still in one piece."

"No," he said without hesitation. "The stakes are too high."

For the rest of the evening she had the distinct feeling they were being followed.

Rick Peterson vetoed her suggestion that they move to another hotel. "If Frollic or the girl wanted to contact us, they wouldn't know where we were.

There'd be no point in leaving a forwarding address if we were trying to hide."

"Just what are you involved in?" she asked again over dinner in a small Soho club. The small piece of tape she'd placed on his right cheek to protect his wound gave his face the look of a boxer's in the restaurant's candlelit interior.

"I can't tell you any more than you already know. It just wouldn't be safe for you to know too much."

"Are you a spy or something?"

He chuckled at the suggestion. "If I were, I'd hate to think I needed to hire a bodyguard. No, I'm just an American businessman trying to make an honest buck."

"Or a dishonest one."

"I can assure you there's nothing dishonest in what I'm doing."

By the time they finished dinner it was too late for the theater, and they strolled back down Piccadilly to the hotel. "If there's nothing dishonest in what you're doing, why did those men assault us? And why did you need a bodyguard in the first place?" she asked, resuming their dinner conversation.

"I explained to you that I wanted a bodyguard along when I visited the ship."

"What do you fear from five young disc jockeys?"

"I just want to be safe, that's all. That thing with Amid Jebel this afternoon shows how dangerous London can be."

"Sure. There are always Arab thugs waiting to pounce on you in your hotel room."

They stopped in the lobby for an after-dinner drink before returning to their suite. Libby felt good, but she was looking forward to completing the assignment and returning home. She was listening to Peterson's long involved story of his youth in West Texas when they heard a bellman paging him. "A phone call for me?" he asked with a puzzled frown. "Excuse me, Libby."

She was instantly on the alert, scanning the lobby for anything suspicious. But there was no sign of anyone waiting to ambush him. He took the call, spoke briefly, and then hurried back to her. "It was Kurt Frollic. He's across the street and he says he has to see me alone."

"Where across the street?"

"At a call box."

"I'm going with you. It could be a trap like this afternoon."

"No." He thought about it and then said, "Look, I'll go over and talk to him while you wait in front of the hotel. I'll be in sight all the time, if anything goes wrong."

She reluctantly agreed and they went out together. The call box was halfway down the block. Libby dropped her hand to her shoulder bag, unzipping it so the revolver would be within easy reach. Peterson crossed the street casually and made directly for the call box, as if anxious to use the phone. She couldn't see if it was occupied.

Peterson opened the door and seemed to jerk back in surprise. He stepped out and waved to Libby. She crossed the street quickly and reached him within seconds. "It's Frollic," he said, pointing into the call box. "He's been stabbed."

A quick glance at the knife in his side and the widening circle of blood told Libby that Kurt Frollic had been dead only minutes. If they reported it to the police, they were certain to be detained for lengthy questioning. "Come on," she told her client. "There's no one within a block of us. We walk away fast and leave it for the next person to report."

He obeyed her as if in a daze. They circled the block once, in case someone had been watching, and then entered their hotel by a side door. "Who could have killed him?" Peterson asked when they were back in their suite.

"How about that Jebel character?" Libby suggested.

"But why?"

"Kurt had something to tell you, obviously. He was killed to keep his mouth shut."

They pondered the implications of the killing on their planned visit to the *Skyhigh* the following day. Peterson was afraid the police would want to question Frollic's coworkers, even though the trawler was anchored in international waters. But the morning paper the hotel left at their door quickly revealed there was no problem. Kurt Frollic had carried no identification, and the unidentified body in the call box was reported as the work of muggers who had stabbed the man and stolen his wallet.

"Maybe that's what happened," Libby suggested.

"No. It was more than that."

They decided to take an early train to Great Yarmouth and spend the day out of London. A taxi pulled up outside the hotel after breakfast, and Libby climbed in while Peterson told the driver to take them to the Liverpool Street Station. Libby had worn wool slacks and a sweater for their evening on the trawler, which precluded the thigh holster. Instead, she'd taped the spare automatic to her leg just above the right ankle.

She had never been to London before, and it was not until the cab made a sharp left turn into an open garage that she realized something was amiss. By that time Peterson was jerking at the door handle, trying to get it opened.

The cab came to a stop as the overhead door closed behind it. Then she saw a dark-haired man walking toward them. He almost casually held an Ingram submachine gun with its cylindrical silencer in one hand. Libby knew it could fire its thirty-two-round magazine in a matter of seconds. And she knew the man holding it was Amid Jebel.

Upstairs above the garage was a large ornate office. Libby and Peterson were led to it after having been handcuffed and searched. Jebel's rough, probing fingers had found both of Libby's weapons, and the tape had been yanked painfully from her ankle. "Beware of taxis that are too convenient," she told Peterson, with an attempt at a smile. "I was a fool to get us into this."

"It may be just as well," he said. "We'll meet the person who hired Jebel."

Almost at once a door opened and an extremely tall Arab entered. Libby guessed him to be close to six and a half feet in height, and he carried himself like some desert sheik. "Well, Mr. Peterson," he said, ignoring Libby, "we meet again."

"I should have known it was you behind this, Azig. Libby, I want you to meet Mudar Azig, one of the most powerful businessmen in the Middle East."

"You praise me too highly, Mr. Peterson. I am only a speculator like yourself."

"How about taking these handcuffs off and behaving like a civilized person for a change?"

Azig's eyes flashed for just an instant, but then he turned to Jebel. "Release them. They are my guests."

The handcuffs came off and Libby rubbed her wrists. She noticed that Jebel still held the Ingram with one hand, though it was pointed toward the floor. "Now suppose you explain what's going on," Peterson said, staying on the offensive. "Why did you kill Kurt Frollic?"

Azig smiled slightly. "The body in the call box? So that is who it was. I assure you we had nothing to do with it. Perhaps one of his friends from the trawler did him in, or a passing mugger as the police say."

"He was killed because he had just phoned me at the hotel across the street. He had something to tell me."

"Interesting," Azig said. "We assumed the killing was somehow connected with you, and with your visitors from the *Skyhigh*. What is your interest in this pirate radio station?"

"The same as yours, I imagine."

The tall man leaned forward across his desk. "Then it would be to my advantage to keep you here and out of mischief until I have completed my own arrangements."

"Keep me if you wish, but release Miss Knowles. She knows nothing of this."

Mudar Azig snorted. "The young woman was carrying two pistols, one taped to her leg. Is she the latest example of an American 'hit person'?"

"Hardly. She's a bodyguard I hired to protect me on board the *Skyhigh*."

"So you fear them, too."

"Don't you? If you didn't kill Frollic, you're probably correct in assuming one of them did."

"You're a clever man, Mr. Peterson. I've always regretted that we were on opposite sides in the great economic war."

"Let us go so we can keep our date on board the trawler. It can't do you any harm, and it might do you some good."

"How is that?"

"If my report is negative it'll save us both a great deal of time."

Azig considered that. "Very well," he said finally. "I will release you provided you agree to report any negative findings to me." He reached a long slender hand across the desk and Peterson shook it.

The meeting was over as quickly as it had begun, and Jebel escorted them out. He instructed the taxi driver to continue to their destination. As he helped Libby into the cab, his hand strayed to her thigh. "We will meet again, sweet lady," he told her.

"Not if I can help it. Do I get my guns back?"

He grinned and showed a row of blackened teeth, then tossed the weapons on the floor at her feet.

Libby was finally able to relax when the cab was under way. "Did Jebel frighten you?" Peterson asked.

"Yes," Libby admitted. "I was afraid I might have to kill him, and I didn't want to do that."

The train ride through the English countryside was uneventful, and Libby passed the time watching the city vistas gradually turn to suburban homes and finally to country woods. When they reached Great Yarmouth, they left the train and headed at once for the docks. Their sightseeing time had been lost by the forced detour to Azig's office, and now they had to find Captain Olaf's fishing boat and arrange transportation out to the *Skyhigh*.

Libby had tried to engage Peterson in conversation about Mudar Azig, but he was reluctant to tell her more than she already knew. "He's a ruthless man. That's all you have to know."

"Then why are you bargaining with him?"

"To save our hides. We got out of there in one piece, and you've got your guns back. I hope you won't lose them a second time."

"Don't worry," Libby told him.

They found Captain Olaf in a pub near the waterfront. It was past the time for the mandatory afternoon closing, and a barmaid was in the process of shooing him out. Olaf was a bearded man of indeterminate middle age who spoke English with a slight Scandinavian accent and walked with a limp. "We want to go out to the *Skyhigh*," Peterson told him.

He squinted at them. "Fans, are you?"

"Not exactly. Kurt Frollic and Susan Vash said you could take us out there."

"Against the law to make deliveries to them pirates. Could get myself in trouble."

Peterson offered him some ten-pound notes. "They assured me you were the one to see."

Captain Olaf's lips curled into a sort of smile. "Well, now, I do favors for friends at times. I can at least take you out to look at the *Skyhigh*, and we'll see what happens from there."

He led them to a medium-sized fishing boat docked

at the end of a busy wharf. A few crewmen were already on board, repairing nets and otherwise keeping busy. "They said it was best to arrive after dark, with the red signal," Peterson told the captain.

He nodded. "It will be dark by the time we arrive. Get aboard."

Already, behind them, the sun was low in the western sky. Peterson and Libby went below to the captain's cabin, keeping out of sight until the fishing boat had cleared the harbor. She used the time to check over the revolver and automatic Jebel had returned.

"Everything in working order?" Peterson asked.

"They seem to be. I was afraid he'd tampered with the ammunition."

"Jebel isn't as devious as all that."

"Who are the other people on the *Skyhigh*?"

"The one I'm most interested in is a technician named Scott Burrows. I expect the other two are announcers like Frollic and Vash."

"What's so special about Burrows?"

"We'll see."

Later they went out on deck as the fishing boat headed into the unruly North Sea waters. Captain Olaf was at the wheel, guiding his craft on a heading he seemed to know by heart. "Do you make this trip often?" Libby asked him.

"Often enough." Now that they were clear of the port, he seemed more willing to talk. "I'm the only one they allow to transport and supply them. I sneak them in and land them down the coast when they want to come ashore."

Libby had a sudden thought. "When did Frollic and Susan Vash come back last night?"

"He's not back yet. I took her over a little after midnight."

"What about the others? Were they on shore too?"

"Oh, that technician Burrows is always slipping in to the pub. He says it's worth the three-hour round-trip boat ride for a few hours' relaxation. I guess he does all his work during the day. The big Irishman, Maguire, went with him last night. But not the other girl, Rachel. She was on the air spinning records."

"What about their crew?"

"Don't see much of them. They stay on board."

As darkness descended and they moved further away from shore, the sea grew rougher. Presently Captain Olaf announced, "There she is, dead ahead."

Libby squinted through the cabin window. "I don't see a thing," she admitted, but almost at once detected a blinking light ahead of them.

"All right," Peterson said. "Give them a flash of your red signal light."

A responding red light came from the ship. It was the *Skyhigh*, waiting to receive them. As they drew nearer, Libby could see the outlines of the trawler, riding smoothly in the choppy waters. Captain Olaf maneuvered them alongside, and she could see a metal stairway being lowered for them. The beat of rock music could be heard, apparently from a loud-speaker on deck that was monitoring the station's transmission.

"How will you know when we're ready to go back?" Peterson asked the Captain.

"I'll hover nearby. Tell them to give me a flash of red and I'll come get you."

There was still a fairly stiff breeze blowing on deck

as Libby made the little jump up to the stairs, and she was glad she'd worn her slacks. A young sandy-haired American was standing on the stairs to help her. "I'm Scott Burrows," he said. "Welcome aboard."

"Thank you," she responded, taking his hand. "It's a long way out here."

Rick Peterson was right behind her. "Pleased to meet you, Burrows. I'm glad you allowed us to visit you."

They went up the iron stairway to the trawler's deck. "Actually it was Kurt Frollic who set it up with you," Burrows said, "and he hasn't returned to the ship. We don't know where he is. Susan Vash was with him in London yesterday and she says he just went off by himself."

The rock music paused and a female voice came over the loudspeaker. "This is *Skyhigh*, the offshore station with the beat of your life! If you like what you hear, tell your friends about us. This is Rachel Rogan, and coming right up is more music!"

Her enthusiasm was infectious and Libby commented on it. "*Skyhigh* must be quite a change from the usual radio fare over here."

"We're teaching the British about modern music," Burrows agreed.

"Are you one of the disc jockeys?"

He laughed and shook his head. "Only a technician. Here's our Irishman, Maguire. And you know Susan. They both spin records."

Maguire was a big man with coal-black hair and a ready smile. He shook Libby's hand and welcomed her aboard. But Susan Vash was tense and unsmiling. "Did you hear anything more from Kurt? I'm worried about him. When he left me in London, he said something about calling you with some sort of information."

Peterson and Libby exchanged glances. After a moment's hesitation he told her, "I think Kurt might have been killed last night."

"Oh no!'

He told them about the body in the call box, omitting the fact that he had found it. "I got a glimpse as they took it away, and it might have been Frollic."

"No one would kill poor Kurt," Maguire said, shaking his head.

"I'm sure you're mistaken," Burrows agreed. "He'll turn up in a day or two."

"Were you in London yesterday?" Peterson asked.

Burrows shook his head. "Captain Olaf's crew took us to the mainland after dark. I hit a few pubs and met Maguire back at the boat after midnight. Susan was there by that time too, and Olaf took us all back here."

"We can at least report to the police and ask to see the body they found," Susan insisted. "If it's Kurt we have to identify it."

"And admit we're from a pirate radio ship, in the country illegally? They'd slap us in jail!" Maguire was having none of it. "They'd probably even try to claim I was involved with the IRA."

Scott Burrows seemed eager to change the subject. "Here, let us show you around the ship as long as you've come this far."

For the most part it seemed like any other fishing trawler, with a pile of nets on the aft deck and cargo booms waiting overhead. But even in the dark Libby could make out the high mast for radio transmissions.

"The trawler is one hundred eighty-six feet long," Maguire told them, "but we use very little of the space for our station. The rest is mainly living quarters."

The loudspeaker music shifted to a heavy metal sound as they made their way below decks to the studio. It was surprisingly cramped—little bigger than a hot tub—but the young woman spinning the records didn't seem to mind. Rachel Rogan was more attractive than Susan, with a more open, breezy personality. Even Susan's news that Frollic might be dead did nothing to dampen her spirits. "Oh, he'll turn up," she decided. "He always has."

"How long are you on duty?" Peterson asked.

"Well, if Kurt's not back by midnight one of these other jokers will have to take over. That's when I hit the sack."

"He has no way of getting here until we go back," Peterson pointed out, speaking as if Frollic were still alive. "Captain Olaf is out there waiting for us, and no one else comes out here, do they?"

"They're all afraid of the law," Scott Burrows confirmed. "The British government doesn't want us here, but they can't take direct action, so they harass us in little ways."

Burrows led the way to the galley, where there was space for them to sit around a table. But Susan and the Irishman soon wandered off. There seemed to be an unspoken agreement that Scott Burrows was their representative. Or perhaps even their boss, Libby thought. "Susan said you wanted very much to come on board," he began. "What for?"

"To see your operation."

He glanced from Peterson to Libby and back again.

Seeing him now in the harsh light of the galley, she decided he was older than he'd first appeared. Probably in his mid-thirties. "You've seen it. Now what?"

"I don't believe I've seen all of it," Peterson remarked quietly.

"Whatever do you mean?"

"I'll be frank with you, Mr. Burrows. I don't represent a magazine. I represent an American corporation that's most interested in . . ."

Suddenly the music in the background was cut short. Rachel Rogan's voice came over the loudspeaker. *"Help me,"* she said, quite distinctly, and then the rock beat of the music returned. The three of them stared at each other for a moment.

It was Burrows who broke the silence. "I'd better see if something's wrong."

They followed him quickly down the narrow passage toward the tiny studio. Susan and Maguire had appeared from their rooms, and they, too, started toward the studio.

"Oh my God!" Susan gasped, staring through the window.

Rachel Rogan was slumped over one of her record turntables. She'd been stabbed in the side, much as Frollic had been. She was dead.

"Search the ship!" Burrows commanded. "Make sure there's no one else on board."

"There's someone on board, all right," Libby pointed out. "There's a wet footprint here on the steps to the deck."

Then they saw him, dressed in a black rubber scuba suit, his face obscured by an air mask. He'd been trying to get out the other end of the corridor, but

202

they'd arrived too soon. Peterson was in front of her, paralyzed with fear. Libby saw the diver's hand go to the waterproof holster on his belt. She pushed Peterson aside and yanked the revolver free of her purse. Her shot was an instant faster than his. He toppled backward and went down in the narrow corridor.

"Good shooting," Burrows said, hurrying forward.

He pulled off the dead man's air mask and Susan asked, "Does anyone know him?"

"We do," Peterson said. "He's Jebel's friend from the hotel room. The one who grabbed you, Libby—remember?"

"How could I forget? But if he's here, so is Jebel."

The muffled spatter of an Ingram submachine gun reached them from the deck. "My God, what's that?" Susan Vash gasped.

"They're trying to take over the ship," Peterson said. "They killed Rachel first so she couldn't send out a radio call for help."

"Who are they?" Burrows demanded.

"A man named Amid Jebel. He works for Mudar Azig."

"Azig!"

"I thought the name would be familiar."

Wondering how many there were against her, Libby sprinted up the steps to the deck. The body of one of the crewmen partly blocked the gangway. Ahead she saw another black-suited diver outlined in the moonlight. She fired two quick shots and he dove for cover.

Peterson was right behind her. "Give me your other gun," he said. "Let me do something here."

She pulled it from her ankle and tossed it to him. "If we ever get out of this alive, you've got some explaining to do!"

There was shooting near them and Peterson returned the fire. "I'll keep this one pinned down," he told Libby.

"Good! I'm going to the bridge."

She went up the stairs, keeping low. It was the radar room she wanted, and she found it just behind the radio shack. No one was there, but a quick look showed her the location of the single green bleep that had to be Captain Olaf's vessel. They needed help, and Olaf was their only chance. She ran outside again, hearing more shots from below, and finally located the red light used to signal Olaf. She pointed it at the direction shown on the radar screen and began blinking it on and off, hoping he received the message. The screen had indicated he was about a mile away.

Libby had just finished flashing the light when she heard a metallic sound behind her. She turned and saw another black-suited scuba diver, his mask thrown back. She swung the spotlight around and aimed it at his face, blinding him for an instant.

It was Jebel himself, and as she raised the revolver to fire she realized that his weapon had jammed. "Stand right there and drop it, Jebel," she warned. "I have a gun."

The shooting on the deck had ceased, and she could see the lights of Captain Olaf's fishing boat moving in to the rescue. There were just the two of them now: herself and Jebel.

He put one hand up to shield his eyes from the

light. "Well, Miss Knowles! We meet again, as I knew we would."

"Drop the gun, Jebel," she repeated.

He let it clatter to the metal deck. "I don't need a gun for you, my dear," he said, moving forward in the glare of the red spotlight. "For you I need only my hands."

"Stay right there!"

He merely smiled. "You would not shoot an unarmed man."

"Try me!"

He kept coming and she shot him in the right kneecap. He went down hard.

The other three members of Jebel's team were all dead, and they strapped him onto a makeshift stretcher for the boat trip back to the mainland. "I will radio ahead and have an ambulance waiting at the dock," Captain Olaf assured them.

Since they did not want the British authorities landing on the *Skyhigh*, Scott Burrows agreed to accompany the bodies and their prisoner to the mainland and add his statement to those of Peterson and Libby. Maguire and Susan remained on the ship, caring for a slightly injured crewman. Another crewman had died, along with Rachel, and their bodies were also on board Olaf's little boat.

"We're lucky to get out of that alive," Peterson said as they headed back through the darkness toward shore.

"No thanks to you," Libby said. "I think you could have explained to me what we were in for."

"Meaning what?"

She gripped the rail of the fishing boat, feeling the cool night spray on her face. "Meaning Azig's men and all the rest of it. Meaning your own true position in this. I should have known sooner, of course. Mention North Sea and Arabs in the same breath and only one word comes to mind: oil."

"Yes," Peterson said sadly. "Oil. I never knew it would lead to so many deaths."

"There were too many parts of the *Skyhigh* we didn't get to see," Libby added. "That whole pirate broadcasting station is simply a cover for an oil exploration ship, isn't it? Pretend you're doing something slightly illegal to cover up the bigger, more important secret."

Peterson nodded. "North Sea oil has never been found this close to shore, but there are oil wells off the coast of Louisiana, California, and southeast Asia. Oil could be here too. The Americans financing the *Skyhigh* mission certainly believe it is. But it was important for them to complete their preliminary surveys before anyone else got the same idea, either in America or the Middle East. While the *Skyhigh* anchored there broadcasting its rock music, test borings of the sea floor were being made."

"How do you fit into this?" she asked. Far ahead she could see the first faint lights of Great Yarmouth.

"I'm employed by a rival American drilling firm. They're the ones who are paying your fee. The idea was for me to get aboard, confirm what they were doing, and offer them money for their test results. It never came to that, of course, because Jebel and his gang decided to take the test results by force."

"But how did you confirm that your theory was correct?"

"I knew it as soon as I met Scott Burrows. He's a technician, all right, but his expertise is in offshore oil drilling, not radio broadcasting. I heard him speak once at a convention in Houston."

"So Frollic was stabbed because he was going to tell you about the test boring?"

"Of course."

"By Burrows?"

"More likely by one of Jebel's men, or by Jebel himself."

"There's another possibility," she said quietly. They were making good time, and the shoreline was drawing closer. She could make out some of the buildings in the town.

"What would that be?"

"You could have stabbed him, Rick. The call box blocked my view, but I saw you jerk back when you opened the door. It could have been surprise—or the act of stabbing him."

He turned to stare at her. "Do you believe that?"

"No. You'd have had no motive for keeping him quiet before he'd told you anything. But I had to consider the possibility."

"I hired you to protect me, not accuse me of murder!"

The floodlit dock had come into view now, and Libby could see the waiting ambulance. A tall man in a white uniform stood by the door.

Tall.

Captain Olaf limped onto the deck, ready to throw a line to the waiting dockhands.

Tall.

"Rick . . ."

Peterson turned to her again. "What is it now?"

"Rick, this is a trap! That's Azig himself over there by the ambulance. He can't disguise his height."

"But how did he know?"

"Captain Olaf is in league with him! Olaf's the one behind all this."

Olaf came at them then, his knife catching the reflection of the shore lights. Peterson tried to grab him and fell on the slippery deck. "You know too much, young lady," the Captain snarled.

Libby had her gun out. "I know it all now. Scott Burrows said Captain Olaf's *crew* took them ashore last night. You weren't there because you'd followed Frollic and Susan into London to meet us, and you stabbed Frollic in that call box before he could tell Peterson about the oil drilling."

"You'll never prove that!"

"And tonight, when I went to signal your boat, I saw on the radar screen that no other craft was visible. Jebel and his scuba divers didn't swim out seventeen miles from shore. They came with us in this boat, hidden below decks."

He lunged at her then with the knife. She took a step back and shot him in the right kneecap. He kept on coming. "That's a wooden leg, lady. Better luck in your next life!"

Then Peterson reached up and grabbed his ankle, throwing him off balance. The knife nicked Libby's arm and clattered against the railing. She brought the barrel of her revolver down hard on Olaf's temple.

When he saw that Olaf was out of action, Azig tried to flee in the stolen ambulance. He and his henchmen were arrested by the police a short time later. Libby and Peterson were on a plane back to New York the following afternoon.

"Olaf will be tried for murder," Peterson told her over the Atlantic. "And Jebel too, for killing those two on the *Skyhigh*. If they decide to implicate Azig, it could be the end for him. Otherwise they might only get him for stealing that ambulance after Olaf radioed him to set up the trap. Of course, once they had Jebel safely in the ambulance they'd have killed us and made their getaway."

Libby turned from the window to look at him. "You know, I was hired to protect you and you ended up saving my life."

"You saved us both by unmasking Olaf before we docked."

She smiled with satisfaction and leaned back in the seat. "The guns are both in my luggage," she said. "It's safe to put your hand on my leg if you want to."

Bale Jumpers

RICHARD B. HARPER

Richard B. Harper is an engineer who builds what he calls "medium-tech sport boats" in Vermont. "I grew up dreaming about fast cars and slow boats," he says. "Now I invent things that whirr and swish and characters to explore more dreams. In this perfect honeymoon, I get paid for both."

About "Bale Jumpers," Harper comments, "Vermont farmers buy hay by the ton from their Canadian brothers. The bales, which weigh about fifty pounds, are stacked in wobbly ten-foot piles. They arrive listing dangerously on flatbed trailers or rickety work trucks. Unloading is the itchy, heavy labor no customs inspector willingly tackles. Inspectors have long poles for checking cargo. I wonder how often they come out bloody."

"Bale Jumpers" is Harper's first short story.

"Vermont State Police."

"Ya gotta come out right now! They're dropping 'em everywhere," the man screamed into his telephone.

"Calm down, sir. Tell me what happened."

"Ya gotta come quick! They're dropping them bales all over the place!"

"Please calm down, sir. Now, who is dropping what bales?" the female dispatcher asked quietly.

"Why it must be them Colombians I read about. They've got a helichopper flying around above the tracks here. They're just dropping them bales all over the tracks."

"Can you tell me exactly where?"

"Just a couple a miles East of Marlboro Center, in the woods off Ethanville Road. You can't miss it. It's where that helichopper's making all the racket."

Six minutes later a green and yellow patrol car bounced to a halt in John Machia's north pasture, about two hundred feet from the road. A Vermont statie climbed out and gestured to the National Guard helicopter hovering above him. As it touched down he ducked under the twirling blades.

"We outgrew our training camp, so we rented this area for maneuvers," the pilot told him. "I'm just scouting a little before we set up here."

They talked a while about the old man so sure he had witnessed the crime of the century, about their plans for duck hunting, and other important topics. Smiling, the trooper turned toward his car.

"Well, since I can't arrest you, I guess I'll do a little hunting next door."

Adjacent to the field, in the old Joyville Park with its eight ramshackle mobile homes, three teenage boys passed a hand-rolled cigarette back and forth and watched the men with interest. They sat on a ragged wooden stoop attached to the oldest trailer in the park, shielded from view by a piece of steel siding dangling from the trailer's side. When the patrol car eased down the rutted drive into the park, they slipped unnoticed into the woods ten steps away. Ringing sounds from a pair of two-cycle engines rose above the thumping background noise of the helicopter.

The trooper knocked and announced himself. No

answer. Hands on his hips, he swivelled, surveying the grounds. A ground-out butt and a partly dissolved blue tablet near the bottom step went into an evidence bag.

Pulling out of the gravel driveway, the trooper paused for a hay-bearing tractor with Quebec plates heading east on the Ethanville Road.

Dennis Wilson sat in his tree house considering the unexpected appearance of law and military so close to his farm. A well-camouflaged observation post, his platform was built in a small maple stand on a knoll separating the Wilson homestead from the long-unused Lamoille Valley railroad tracks. He lifted high-power binoculars for another look.

A tall, cadaverous man—surprisingly pale for a farmer—Wilson spent much of his spare time in the trees. He had protruding blue eyes and a gaunt face scarred by childhood chicken pox. His large head seemed to teeter above his slouched frame. Kids called him Scarecrow behind his back. Oversized hands and splayed feet reinforced the image. His gruff responses in the country store put off the normal neighborly friendliness there; he encouraged his solitude.

"Wait, Peter, you picked up some brambles on your pants." Wilson's daughter Shelley came into view, bending over to pick at the burrs. Peter reached down, rubbed her arm, and smiled as she rose to kiss him. Nearly sixteen, willowy, with thick auburn hair cascading over her shoulders and a way of standing hipshot, smirking, Shelley attracted every boy in the local high school. As her father watched, they stood kissing and caressing each other before Peter, still smiling, pulled back, took her hand, and led her out of the woods.

Across the road, the boys ran their ATVs through Machia's pasture to assure that no observers remained from the helicopter. Then they returned to the Joyville trailer. From his tree house, Dennis watched the tallest boy slip a bill through the mail slot on the steel door. In return he received a fresh package of grass and papers. Hunkering down on the stoop, the boy began rolling. He sat and looked at the result while his two friends waited. Finally satisfied, he passed it to the nearest boy for the first drag.

Two grocery stores, an ironmonger, PJ's bar, and three churches line the single main street in Marlboro Center. None looks much like the postcard country store popularized by *Vermont Life*. Jim Morrill's grandfather started out as the county's first grain dealer. The business had grown when he turned it over to Jim's father, who had to add rooms and sheds to the original building to accommodate the disparate stock accumulated over the years. Now Jim's hardware store carried goat feed, boat anchors, television antennas, and, if hard-pressed, he could probably find a part for a '34 Ford. Most mornings townsfolk wandered in for gossip and coffee.

Morrill's potbelly stove had given way to a wood-fired hot air furnace in 1936. A small fire burned to clear away the early June chill, the hot air rising through a four-foot-square grate. A rickety yellow table held a thirty-cup coffee urn, a Dixie dispenser on its side, and a dozen unmatched cups left by various regulars.

Wearing a heavy plaid shirt, Dennis Wilson came in for 200 pounds of feed. He nodded to the men standing around chatting.

"Did you hear that Mike Racine's boy got busted down to St. Albans?" Dale Bishop, a bluff man in a cowboy hat, spoke from the center of the hot air grate.

Wilson poured a cup of coffee, dropped a dime in the can, and shook his head. He gave his order to Jim Morrill. The owner slowly walked out back.

"Yep. State Police picked him up last night with the rest of his gang. They sold that cocaine all the way to Burlington."

"Cop told me they was all over the state," said Hap Edwards from his corner of the grate. Dennis glanced over, gave a half grin, and looked back down at the floor.

"Can you imagine it?" Edwards continued. "That stuff here? How do they pay for it? I can't even keep up with my bar bill at PJ's!"

"Some thieves right here in town," shouted Morrill through the open warehouse door. "Somebody broke in again last week, and I lost another TV. And a bunch of radios before that. Say, Dale, didn't they get into your barn the other day?"

"Took off with my kids' three wheeler, they did. And before that, it was pieces of my milking stand. I don't know what on earth they thought they could do with that."

"And all these flatlanders coming in," Jacques Powers said in his favorite refrain, "they bring plenty money with them."

"Maybe this bust takes care of the townies, but

what about that trailer park across from you, Dennis? Are they still going strong?"

Wilson shrugged and headed for the door. Conversation ceased until he was gone. Bishop followed, stopping at the threshold and watching as Wilson climbed into his orange pickup truck.

"Just last week I overheard Shelley tell Pete he could get all the pills and grass he wanted there at Joyville. I whaled him good 'til he said he hadn't. But I think she's doing some business there. Plenty of kids always crowded around there, or on the tracks behind Wilson's place."

"Wonder if Dennis knows," Edwards said quietly.

"Can never tell what he's thinking," Bishop replied.

Traditional Vermonters, at least those in the parts of Franklin County tempered by Lake Champlain, have their kitchen gardens in before Memorial Day. Farmers may slog over their fields six weeks before that, risking fifty-thousand-dollar tractors in the mire, but gardeners don't plant before they can walk on the soil. Dennis Wilson had brought his smaller rig around to the back of the house on the last Monday in May. Two short swipes with an eight-bottom plow exposed new soil and turned the winter weeds into fertilizer. Shelley then spent her after-school time raking, hoeing, and picking rocks. Her mother once told her that they first planted there in 1967. Shelley wondered what caused the Vermont soil to continue to grow rocks through all those years. She picked up another one and pitched it onto her mounting pile. Fletcher, her old farm collie, lay still but gave a little woof each time a stone landed.

Shelley had been four years old the Christmas morning Fletcher bounced onto her bed. She had told him all her secrets ever since. Now she turned the earth and asked him to compare the two great loves of her life, Peter Bishop and his best friend, Ralph Carvey. She didn't think, she told Fletcher, that they knew they were serious rivals, even though Ralph worked after school and summers for Peter's dad. She wondered how she could be attracted to two such entirely different boys. Peter, so boisterous and friendly, loved practical jokes. He dreamed up the best dates, taking her to shows or canoeing, to the amusement park or the waterslide. Ralph, so quiet and standoffish, rarely even told a joke. He never took her out in public; his idea of a good time was to crash together in some forgotten corner and get high.

A red and white hay truck arrived Friday afternoon, just as Shelley stepped down from the school bus. It waited, diesel thrumming, as the bus driver backed into her driveway. She had been the last stop on the bus route for as long as she could remember, losing an hour every day after school. When the bus pulled back out the way it had come, the hay driver blocked traffic as he also backed in.

Dennis Wilson stepped out of the barn and directed the trailer under the conveyor. Standing atop his six-high load, the driver dropped bales one after another onto the moving chain. High above him in the loft, Wilson grabbed each bale and tossed it into his own growing stack. They had unloaded nearly half the trailer when the chain shuddered. The driver paused and looked up questioningly. Wilson shrugged.

"Keep 'em coming."

A dozen bales later, the chain lurched again, this time shrugging off its load, and stopped. Wilson climbed down, discovered a frozen bearing, and called Jim Morrill. With a replacement part only minutes away, he asked the driver to stay, jumped in his pickup and headed for the store.

Driveway dust still hung in the air when an ATV bounced up the back lane from Dale Bishop's farm. Attracted by its noise, Shelley peered around the line of lilacs separating the garden from the barn. She watched Ralph Carvey dismount and, slowly turning only his head, inspect the yard for observers. He sprinted into the barn and greeted the driver, who waddled rapidly out to his truck. A gap showed white flesh between his well-stretched T-shirt and drooping jeans as he reached into a side compartment and pulled out a small garbage bag. Carvey glanced in it and stuffed it into the book bag slung over his left shoulder. He offered the man a tiny paper sack in return.

As the boy remounted the ATV, Fletcher finally gave a soft woof. Startled, Ralph jerked around, staring at the lilacs. He started the trike. It roared and carried him through the bushes, nearly landing on Shelley. She fell backwards over her rake as he appeared.

"Hello there, sweetheart." Looking up at him, she thought he sounded just like Bogart. Unintentionally.

"Hi, Ralph. Whatcha up to?"

"Oh just arranging some more fun. You remember our little party last week? You sure liked what I brought!"

Shelley licked her lips. "Ummm." She nodded and

her deep red hair danced down across her forehead.

Reaching around behind him, Ralph drew up his book bag and rummaged around inside. Shelley noticed three plastic-wrapped green bricks before he found the pill bottle he sought. He held it invitingly close to her, jiggling it slightly to let the sunlight dance off its contents.

"If you wander across the road tonight, we could finally have a super party. Maybe the best ever."

"That'd be real nice, Ralph, but you know I'm not allowed there."

"Now, sweetie, you've just gotta begin believing you're a grownup." He glanced over her figure, only slightly obscured by her flannel shirt and baggy jeans. "You certainly look all grown up to me."

"We've been over this before. I'm not going to one of those trailers with you. There are plenty of other places around here we can be together."

"OK. Suit yourself." He flipped her two of the capsules. "I'll be too busy to come back here this evening, but these'll take you wherever you want to go. And I'll show you a good time tomorrow."

Shelley slipped the pills into her shirt pocket and smiled.

The ATV had vanished into the woods by the time Dennis Wilson returned with a bearing for his conveyor. In minutes, the hay was moving into the barn again.

Swaying slightly, his legs spread for balance, Ralph Carvey blocked Shelley's path to her bus. "I sure would like to give you a ride, Miss Shelley," he said with an exaggerated, courtly bow.

She glared at him, curling her upper lip slightly.

She wondered what she saw in the tall, football-player-sized boy with a shock of brown hair and glazed eyes. Shelley brushed by him, upsetting his balance and causing him to stumble back into the side of the bus. He grabbed her arm.

"Now that was unkind to your best connection, Shelley. Did you forget that I'm the one who carries a pocketful of fun? You sure were interested Saturday night."

"I don't like the way you behaved. I don't think I ever want to see you again, Ralph." She flounced onto the bus unaware that his expression had become grim as he looked over the remaining students watching him. He marched away muttering.

Attending her first prom, with Peter of course, she had glimpsed two new worlds. The school gym had been transformed by the magic of lights and tinsel. Now it was a chic nightclub with conversation nooks, dance floor, and even a papier-mâché grotto surrounding the band. The pale blue Victorian dress her mom had selected covered her from neck to toes, but its silky conformity to her figure attracted boys. Never were there less than a half dozen fawning over her; occasionally hissing at each other, always ready to perform some little service in hopes of a dance, or more. Their attention enraged Peter, driving him to stand around with the group of stags. Carvey's sudden appearance at her side sent the others scuttling for their own dates. He swept her out to the parking lot before Peter, watching from yet another corner, could react.

Ralph had sauntered around the lot, right arm protectively around her waist, left hand gently holding both of hers. At the far end, he stopped and pulled a flask from his pocket. She accepted eagerly. They strolled toward the lush lawns and trees surrounding the Agriculture Department's greenhouse, alternating swallows until the flask was empty. Ralph sat down on a rough bench with his back against a broad elm. Giggling and tipsy, Shelley wandered away to pirouette around the green. Her skirt swirled out around her. After several moments, Ralph held out a hand to her. Returning, she accepted the red capsule he offered.

Nearly two hours later, Peter had found her, crying and alone, leaning over the hood of his car.

The coiled yellow phone cord snaked around the corner of the attic stairway where Shelley perched, talking to Alice Rollins. Sitting crossways on one step, she told her friend about her last few nights.

"Have I ever lied to you?"

Alice had no answer.

"All right, have I lied to you more than, say, twice since first grade?"

"I don't think it's even that much," Alice said after another pause.

"And my mom said I wasn't fair to Peter, leaving him standing there all alone. Well! I think he should have paid more attention to me. When Ralph came along I thought he'd show me something real."

"You were outside with him for the longest time."

"Uh huh."

"Did you . . . did you do it with him?"

"Well . . ."

"Did you?"

"I was ready to, that's for sure. He is so good-looking. And he started out awfully nice. He really had me flying. But he started pawing me, not gentle like Peter. Then he shoved me down on the ground and ripped my new dress . . ."

"Oh, Shelley."

". . . and I just couldn't. I told him I had to go back inside."

"What did he do then?"

"His face got bright red and he started cursing me. He was so mad he was spitting!" Shelley giggled and Alice joined in. "It wasn't so funny then! And Peter wouldn't even speak to me. I had to call Mom for a ride home."

"Was she mad?"

"I told her what Ralph tried and she didn't believe me. She says I made it up. What a grouch! So she grounded me again."

"For how long?"

"She won't tell me. Last night, I thought I'd sneak out and see Peter—you know, to tell him about being grounded and all. But Ralph was there, waiting. He wanted me to go over to Joyville with him."

"You didn't!"

"Are you kidding? I tried to get away from him, but he hung around, so I went back to the house. And Mom caught me coming back in, so now I'm not allowed to use the phone or anything. And I can't get hold of Peter, so he's still mad at me, too."

"What are you going to do now?" Alice asked.

"What can I do? On top of everything else, some-body threw a rock in my bedroom window last night."

"Ralph?"

"It must have been. He was awful mad."

"Could be. You know, I heard his ATV in the

woods out back. It was around midnight last night. He was headed toward the trailer."

Both girls fell silent.

"Now I'm going to be stuck here for the rest of my life! They'll never let me get my license, and it's all Ralph's fault." Shelley stopped talking. Alice could picture her chewing on a loose strand of hair. "Oh no. Peter will take up with that dorky Pauline Edwards."

"The junior with the big . . . ?"

"Yeah, that one. What am I going to do now, Alice?"

"I could call Peter for you."

Dennis appeared in the attic doorway, pointed at his daughter and drew his index finger across his throat.

"Uh oh. Thanks Alice. I've gotta go. Bye."

"Ralph tried to get you over to Joyville?" His voice was grim.

Shelley cowered back onto her step, head bowed. She squeaked an answer.

"You ever go there?"

She shook her head.

"And you think Ralph threw the rock 'cause you wouldn't come across."

"Yes."

Dennis stomped out to his tree house, striking one huge hand over and over into the palm of the other.

Flames dancing across the flat roof of the last trailer jumped up to try to engage the dead locust tree that separated the trailer from its faded blue neighbor. A trail of trash and garbage between the two units flashed, carrying the fire under the blue trailer just as the Marlboro VFD arrived. Three men ran from the pumper, dragging twin hoses toward the blaze. Gasoline stored in a jerry can under the skirt exploded with a great whump. The firemen trained both streams on that eruption, quelling it quickly.

While the firemen contained the destruction to the pair of trailers, two state policemen evacuated the rest of the park. Entering the last unit, they discovered Ralph Carvey cowering in the small bathroom. Plastic bags of the multicolored pills he had tried to flush down an overflowing toilet surrounded him. Headlines the next day bespoke the last great bust in Vermont.

Still a juvenile, Ralph was remanded to the custody of his parents the following morning.

Several days later, Simon Fullerton sat watching the Customs House from his own rusty brown Camaro. The pale-green government-issue sedan he usually drove was a dead giveaway whenever the customs agent wanted to work incognito. A man of medium height and build with curly black hair, Fullerton had grown a full beard to blend in with other farm workers and woodsmen. Each time a hay wagon appeared, he slouched down in the seat. His horseshoe-shaped belt buckle caught on the steering wheel.

Loaded with hay, Pierre LaRocque's red and white tractor trailer sat alongside the border station. LaRocque strutted out to his truck. He was a short, squatty, bowlegged man with greasy hair hanging down to his dirty undershirt. The brand-new Peterbilt rumbled to life and moved across the uneven macadam. Columns of baled hay swayed perilously over each bump. The agent slipped behind La-Rocque's rig.

They turned off the first interstate exit and followed unpaved roads through Marlboro Springs. Just as Fullerton crested the fourth small hill from the exit, Marcel Gagne began to drive his Holstein herd across the agent's path. Finished with their early morning milking, the one hundred twenty head were returning to Gagne's rock-strewn west pasture. The hay truck continued out of sight. Fullerton banged on his steering wheel and cursed under his breath. Finally he backed up, turned around and headed for the Customs House.

Rounding the curve at Joyville, LaRocque slowed down, changed gears, and looked over the blackened hulks. He waved to Dennis Wilson, standing on the shoulder, and continued on to Dale Bishop's farm on the banks of the Missisquoi River. As the hay truck turned into the driveway, Ralph Carvey drove up the back lane pulling a load of fence posts with his ATV. He scooted in front of LaRocque, beating him to the barn.

A helicopter swept into a tiny clearing next to the rusted and weed-covered railroad tracks. Two men climbed out into the deepening dusk and scanned the trees around them. An empty, rundown barn stood at the edge of the clearing. A three-wheeler leapt into the open area and skidded up to the tracks. It pulled a four-by-four stake-sided trailer with two half-bales wrapped in kraft paper lashed to its bed. Quietly drawing guns, the two men faded into the shadows of their aircraft.

"You can come on out. It's only the bogeyman. I won't eat you until after dark." The man on the ATV kept his helmet on, its plastic bubble distorting his features and voice.

"Did you bring our load?" the older man materializing behind the rider asked.

"Only this little bit today, boys. There has been so much activity across the street that I had to cut back for a while."

"We just opened a new retail chain in Philadelphia. The kids there have a big appetite for your stuff. The man won't like this slowdown. When can we tell him to expect the next shipment?"

"Take it easy." The rider made a calming motion. "My Colombians say they have better than 27,000 pounds sitting in a barn up to Stanbridge."

"Why don't we just cut you out, fly there, and get it?"

"Are you really dumb enough to fly over the border, making all that racket, with near fourteen tons of grass? That's a whole tractor trailer load, man! Kind of hard to disguise."

"So what do you recommend?"

"Take what you can get for now. In two weeks, the National Guard begins maneuvers. There'll be big transport helicopters in and out of here day and night."

"And you think if we had the right markings, we could get lost in the shuffle?"

The rider handed over a folder of pictures of the Guard machine that had inspected the site. "I'll be bringing that load over in two weeks," he said.

"How?"

"My secret, boys. You just be ready with the chopper. We'll send it out full every other day."

They exchanged the contents of the trailer for a satchel of cash, and the rider buzzed down the tracks into the darkness.

"I don't like it," said the younger man. "We got no protection here in the sticks."

"Don't worry, Tony," said his partner. "I'll put a couple of guard dogs here right away."

Pierre LaRocque lay spreadeagled on the damp ground in front of his own barn near Stanbridge. Morning dew flocked the front of his coveralls. Two men with the mixed Indian and Latin features typical in South America watched him. The taller man lounged in the barn doorway, picking at a broken tooth with a throwing knife.

"I tell you, things they are too hot right now," LaRocque said in entreaty. "Somebody took out Ralph's stand in the trailer, and I think I'm being followed."

"We care not about your nickel-dime trailer operation. This is big, big load. It is bound for all the States."

"No. Too many men watch. Even the army is nearby."

The shorter Colombian looked up at his partner and shrugged.

"Why do we care about your army? It is not like Colombia. They do not watch for us here."

"I tell you, this is a bad time . . ."

"No, I tell you! You will take this load in just as you have before. And José will help you put it in your truck, just to make sure you get it right. Now stand up. You make yourself disgusting."

Bales lined the opposing walls of LaRocque's barn, leaving only a narrow aisle for his trailer. Selecting the darker ones from those on the left side, the two men quickly built a pile covering the center of his flatbed. When it was stacked four high, they began picking light-colored Canadian hay to disguise their special load in the center.

Just two hundred yards from the customs buildings, the state information center parking area offered a perfect vantage point for all incoming traffic. Tinkering under the hood of his son's elderly Blazer, Simon Fullerton awaited the hay truck's arrival.

The big Peterbilt belched a cloud of black smoke as LaRocque pulled out of the truck lot behind the Customs House. Simon slammed the hood, wiped his hands leisurely on an old piece of flannel shirt, and drove out just as LaRocque passed him. In tandem, they again took the first interstate exit and headed for Marlboro Center.

Fullerton caught only occasional glimpses of the trailer as it crested hills or before it headed out of sight around corners. The cloud of dust from the gravel roads hung long after its passage, his homing beacon. Entering the village, LaRocque turned east on Ethanville Road. Seeing Dennis Wilson driving a tractor and manure spreader down his driveway, Pierre gave three short blasts on his air horn and waved without slowing. The fragrant wagon pulled out in front of Fullerton. Driving mostly in the middle of the curving road, trailer wagging, he blocked the agent's progress for nearly half a mile. When he turned down a narrow wooded lane toward his easternmost pasture, the hay truck had vanished. Simon drove another ten miles before admitting that LaRocque could have turned into any of a dozen farms or side roads.

"Hi, Shelley. Will you talk to me?" Peter Bishop sounded distraught.

"Only for a minute. Mom is out in the garden. Didn't Alice tell you I'm not allowed to use the phone?"

"I wasn't sure whether she meant it or whether you were trying to, you know, brush me off. You sure have seen a lot of Ralph, lately."

"That's not true! And besides, I've made sure he's history."

"What's that supposed to mean?" Peter asked.

"Uh oh. Here comes Mom. They'll both be gone tomorrow morning. Will you meet me at the tree house?"

Debra Wilson, a tiny woman with the same thick auburn hair as her daughter, strode into the kitchen.

Shelley hung up as Peter said yes.

"Who was that on the phone?"

"Wrong number."

Three Customs agents met in the Ethanville headquarters building well before dawn the next morning. Fullerton assigned one of them to play leapfrog with him as they trailed their quarry to Marlboro Center.

"Joe, you should sit at the exit from the port," he told the second man. "When that hay truck comes in, you front-tail him while I pick up the rear. I sure wish we could spring enough manpower to do this right."

Joe Rogers looked at his watch. "I do too, Simon," he said. "You know the boss gave me only this morning for what he called your wild duck chase. I don't think he really believes there is all that much dope coming in this way, right under his own nose."

"The girl who called me was specific. She gave us both LaRocque and his connection. Carvey abused her, she said. And it all makes sense. She told me the bales come in in the middle of an ordinary hay truck and get dropped somewhere near Joyville."

Rogers cleared his throat. "I'll admit I've never seen the inspectors tear apart a load of hay," he said.

"Yeah, but the trailer park got burned out, Simon," the third man said. "What makes you think this stuff's got anywhere to go now?"

"Remember last month's DEA bulletin, Frank? It reported on the increased traffic that they have pinpointed coming through Vermont. That girl is right; I can feel it in my bones. And nobody would set up a nice operation like this only for Joyville."

"Yeah, but LaRocque's no more than a mule."

"Uh huh. A well-connected one."

"So you think they're running other trucks in as well?"

"Sure. And we should be able to get a line on the whole organization if we can just find out where he drops those special loads."

"So what is today's plan, Simon? Do we catch 'em or sit on 'em?" Rogers asked.

"Watchful waiting. I don't want any heroics today. I just want to find out who's doing what and to whom."

Red streaks splashed across the horizon as the sun

paused just below the tall black locust stand behind the border station. Joe Rogers leaned against the open trunk of his car, an ice box, a small cardboard carton, and three suitcases spread over the pavement around him. His face exhibited the resigned frustration of a thorough car search. Tapping one foot against a suitcase, he whistled a tuneless melody while he waited. The brown Camaro was parked next to the third agent's sports car in the rest area. He and Fullerton stood in the shingle-sided information building, memorizing all the maps.

Pierre LaRocque drove slowly behind the Customs House to the truck lot and stopped. He sat in his cab for several minutes, pretending to do some paperwork, while he stared at every person, car, and bush in sight. Satisfied, he grabbed his manifest and waddled into the building.

"Nervous Nellie has arrived," Rogers whispered into the mike pinned to his shirt. Two clicks from Fullerton acknowledged him.

The convoy passed over the anticipated route. Joe Rogers paced the hay truck perfectly, keeping it just in his rear view mirror. The brown Camaro and the sports car traded places at each intersection. Fullerton was immediately behind LaRocque as they passed through Marlboro Center.

In an encore performance, the manure spreader swung into the highway with a fresh load. It blocked Fullerton from the swaying hay truck. A brown glob bounced high and sailed onto his windshield; Fullerton ducked involuntarily.

"Do you still have him, Joe?"

"Yeah, he's still there. Hey, he's put on a real

burst of speed. Just about running over me. Now what?"

"Keep your course and speed, buddy. No sense scaring him away now."

"Right." He paused while he negotiated a curve. "Hey Simon?"

"Speak to me, son."

"LaRocque just fell off the edge of the world. He must have turned off just before the last curve. A long right-hand sweeper."

"Okay. Where are you now?"

"I'm coming up on a farm now. Ahh, it belongs to . . . ah, there's a sign. Bishop Farm."

"Good. Stop there, Joe. We still have him boxed between this slop wagon and you."

Dennis Wilson again turned down his narrow lane. Fullerton drew up on the opposite shoulder and called in his other two cars. He gave orders to park them out of sight.

"Joe, you head back to the last farm. There is a lane that seems to lead in the direction they headed. Frank, stay here and make sure they don't sneak out on us."

The agent ran down the lane after the tractor. Branches snapped from overhanging trees lay in the path. A side trail diverged to the right. Missing bark and paint scrapes on a red oak marked the many times the tractor had turned there. Cocking his head to one side to listen, he picked out the deep rumbling of two diesel engines. Although muffled by the trees, Fullerton thought they were idling directly ahead of him.

Peter had just helped Shelley mount the tree house

ladder when the red and white Peterbilt appeared in the clearing. He scrambled up after her. They ducked down behind the low wall.

Simon Fullerton stepped off the trail. Carefully bending branches aside, he slipped through the underbrush toward the noise. He arrived at the clearing moments after the two engines shut down. He blended into a group of cedars facing a ramshackle barn. Great gaps in its siding showed a man waiting within. The agent raised his small camera.

Tossing the last two rows of hay off the trailer, LaRocque exposed the green marijuana bales. Fullerton snapped three pictures. He continued taking snapshots as LaRocque threw the bales into the old barn.

Finding her father's field glasses, Shelley scanned the small tract. She gasped and dropped them when she saw Dennis emerge from the building. The glasses bounced once on the wooden floor. They disappeared out the opening and crashed on a rock below. The noise echoed across the clearing.

LaRocque dove under the trailer. Yanking on the baling twine, he pulled hay around himself as a small fort. Dennis Wilson charged into the barn. A flock of grackles screeched and took flight. The falling binoculars nearly hit Joe Rogers. He jumped to his left, looking for another haven. He turned his back on the clearing just as Wilson, carrying an Uzi, popped out the far side of the barn and dissolved into the woods.

Both agents wondered who else was spying on the field. Fullerton pocketed the camera and drew his service revolver. He slowly began to work his way around the edge of the trees. Still playing who's who, he would not risk starting a firefight. Using brush and shadows for cover, he silently moved in to back up Joe Rogers.

Crouching, searching for other sounds, Dennis tried to pinpoint the crash site. The woods were silent. He inched around a majestic elm, making for the safety of his tree house. Pushing softly through a copse of scrub sumac, he looked uphill at his fort. No one was visible above its low walls. Then he spotted Rogers scaling a tree behind his refuge.

Firing a short burst, Wilson leapt for the tree house ladder. Rogers fell. Hearing the sharp *brraaap* of the Uzi, Shelley shrieked and grabbed Peter's arm. Dennis vaulted over the low railing. He landed in a crouch, Uzi aimed at the kids.

"Daddy! No! What are you doing?" Shelley shrank even closer to Peter.

"I really wish you kids hadn't been here. You've put me in a very tough spot." Wilson squinted and looked out over the clearing. He made his decision. "OK. I'm climbing down. When I'm on the ground, I want you to follow me. Shelley first."

He backed to the opening and surveyed the tract again. Shelley gathered her feet under her. Her father's head jerked back toward her, the Uzi following.

"Don't move," he said. "Not yet." He felt for the top rung and rapidly slid down the ladder. Crouching slightly, he scanned the clearing once more.

"OK, Shelley. Your turn."

Shivering, placing one hand on each shoulder, Shelley crossed her arms over her breasts and stood up. She walked hesitantly across the wooden floor. Peter started to rise. A single gesture from the Uzi stopped him. The girl reached for the sidewall and turned to climb down the ladder. Plaited from swamp grass, the treehouse sides were tied to two-by-fours nailed to the platform. Shelley stumbled on the first step. She grabbed for an upright to save her balance. It pulled free and she lurched backward. Peter jumped to his feet. Startled, Wilson jerked his weapon toward Peter as his daughter dropped on him. The gun went off. The rounds tore a hole through the treehouse floor. Woodchips sprayed over the boy. Man and girl tumbled down the small hill.

Stepping out from the brush, Simon Fullerton stooped and pressed his revolver into the side of Wilson's neck.

"I think everything's over now, my friend." He reached around Wilson and took the Uzi.

Tubes coursed across Joe Rogers. Three in his chest, one in his nose, and two more in his arm held him prisoner. Simon Fullerton sat in a plastic chair next to the hospital bed, reading a magazine. He looked up periodically at the man in the bed. Awakening, Rogers grunted softly. His left eye rolled open and trembled. Room light knifed in, slamming it shut in reflex. The eyelid cracked open again. Light filtered through the lashes until he could stand to open it fully. It jerked from target to target around the room, finally lighting on his partner. He opened his right eye and stared. He closed both eyes, inventorying the pains throbbing over his body. Several minutes passed. Both eyelids popped simultaneously. He winked.

"Well, Joe. Welcome back."

The patient closed his eyes, sighed, and opened them again.

"The doc told me you're likely to be out of here in a couple of weeks."

Rogers waggled one hand, palm down. The movement was scarcely discernible.

"I stopped by to bring you up to date. Except for this, everything went real well." Fullerton looked down at his feet. "There were two other men in the woods," he said. "They took off when the Uzi opened up. Ran straight up the lane. When they saw Frank and the cars, they surrendered on the spot. Turns out they were the guards for the Philadelphia interests. One of them is singing a great song to the FBI. And Pierre LaRocque rolled over on his Colombian friends. The RCMP is rounding them up right now."

"What about the two kids?" Rogers croaked.

"Both are okay. Scared witless, but okay."

Joe Rogers closed his eyes for another long count. "Tough on the girl."

"Yeah. First she tells us about LaRocque, then it turns out it's her old man we're really after, and she all but captures him for us, too. While you've been lazing around in here, she has spent the last couple of days with my wife. She'll bounce back."

"For a change, it looks like the good guys won." Rogers went back to sleep.

Deceptions

MARCIA MULLER

Marcia Muller received both a B.A. and M.A. from the University of Michigan and has been writing mystery fiction since 1977. "Deceptions" is the fourth story Muller has written featuring Sharon McCone, the detective who appears in eight of her novels.

About "Deceptions" she comments: "The setting for this story was suggested to me by a visiting friend with whom I was playing tourist; she said it was eerie and perfect for a murder. I had to agree. Fort Point itself—plus a newspaper article on a dubious suicide—suggested the type of crime."

San Francisco's Golden Gate Bridge is deceptively fragile-looking, especially when fog swirls across its high span. But from where I was standing, almost underneath it at the south end, even the mist couldn't disguise the massiveness of its concrete piers and the taut strength of its cables. I tipped my head back and looked up the tower to where it disappeared into the drifting grayness, thinking about the other ways the bridge is deceptive.

For one thing, its color isn't gold, but rust red, reminiscent of dried blood. And though the bridge is a marvel of engineering, it is also plagued by maintenance problems that keep the Bridge District in constant danger of financial collapse. For a reputedly romantic structure, it has seen more than its fair share of tragedy: Some eight hundred-odd lost souls have jumped to their deaths from its deck.

Today I was there to try to find out if that figure should be raised by one. So far I'd met with little success.

I was standing next to my car in the parking lot of Fort Point, a historic fortification at the mouth of San Francisco Bay. Where the pavement stopped, the land fell away to jagged black rocks; waves smashed against them, sending up geysers of salty spray. Beyond the rocks the water was choppy, and Angel Island and Alcatraz were mere humpbacked shapes in the mist. I shivered, wishing I'd worn something heavier than my poplin jacket, and started toward the fort.

This was the last stop on a journey that had taken me from the toll booths and Bridge District offices to Vista Point at the Marin County end of the span, and back to the National Parks Services headquarters down the road from the fort. None of the Parks Service or bridge personnel—including a group of maintenance workers near the north tower—had seen the slender dark-haired woman in the picture I'd shown them, walking south on the pedestrian sidewalk at about four yesterday afternoon. None of them had seen her jump.

It was for that reason—plus the facts that her parents had revealed about twenty-two-year-old Vanessa DiCesare—that made me tend to doubt she actually had committed suicide, in spite of the note she'd left taped to the dashboard of the Honda she'd abandoned at Vista Point. Surely at four o'clock on a Monday afternoon *someone* would have noticed her. Still, I had to follow up every possibility, and the people at the Parks Service station had suggested I check with the rangers at Fort Point.

I entered the dark-brick structure through a long, low tunnel—called a sally port, the sign said—which was flanked at either end by massive wooden doors with iron studding. Years before I'd visited the fort, and now I recalled that it was more or less typical of harbor fortifications built in the Civil War era: a ground floor topped by two tiers of working and living quarters, encircling a central courtyard.

I emerged into the court and looked up at the west side; the tiers were a series of brick archways, their openings as black as empty eyesockets, each roped off by a narrow strip of yellow plastic strung across it at waist level. There was construction gear in the courtyard; the entire west side was under renovation and probably off limits to the public.

As I stood there trying to remember the layout of the place and wondering which way to go, I became aware of a hollow metallic clanking that echoed in the circular enclosure. The noise drew my eyes upward to the wooden watchtower atop the west tiers, and then to the red arch of the bridge's girders directly above it. The clanking seemed to have something to do with cars passing over the roadbed, and it was underlaid by a constant grumbling rush of tires on pavement. The sounds, coupled with the soaring height of the fog-laced girders, made me feel very small and insignificant. I shivered again and turned to my left, looking for one of the rangers.

The man who came out of a nearby doorway startled me, more because of his costume than the suddenness of his appearance. Instead of the Parks Service uniform I remembered the rangers wearing on my previous visit, he was clad in what looked like an old Union Army uniform: a dark blue frock coat, lighter blue trousers, and a wide-brimmed hat with a red plume. The long saber in a scabbard that was strapped to his waist made him look thoroughly authentic.

He smiled at my obvious surprise and came over to me, bushy eyebrows lifted inquiringly. "Can I help you, ma'am?"

I reached into my bag and took out my private investigator's license and showed it to him. "I'm Sharon McCone, from All Souls Legal Cooperative. Do you have a minute to answer some questions?"

He frowned, the way people often do when confronted by a private detective, probably trying to remember whether he'd done anything lately that would warrant investigation. Then he said, "Sure," and motioned for me to step into the shelter of the sally port.

"I'm investigating a disappearance, a possible suicide from the bridge," I said. "It would have happened about four yesterday afternoon. Were you on duty then?"

He shook his head. "Monday's my day off."

"Is there anyone else here who might have been working then?"

"You could check with Lee—Lee Gottschalk, the other ranger on this shift."

"Where can I find him?"

He moved back into the courtyard and looked around. "I saw him start taking a couple of tourists around just a few minutes ago. People are crazy; they'll come out in any kind of weather."

"Can you tell me which way he went?"

The ranger gestured to our right. "Along this side. When he's done down here, he'll take them up that iron stairway to the first tier, but I can't say how far he's gotten yet."

I thanked him and started off in the direction he'd indicated.

There were open doors in the cement wall between the sally port and the iron staircase. I glanced through the first and saw no one. The second led into a narrow dark hallway; when I was halfway down it, I saw that this was the fort's jail. One cell was set up as a display, complete with a mannequin prisoner; the other, beyond an archway that was not much taller than my own five-foot-six, was unrestored. Its waterstained walls were covered with graffiti, and a metal railing protected a two-foot-square iron grid on the floor in one corner. A sign said that it was a cistern with a forty-thousand-gallon capacity.

Well, I thought, that's interesting, but playing tourist isn't helping me catch up with Lee Gottschalk. Quickly I left the jail and hurried up the iron staircase the first ranger had indicated. At its top, I turned to my left and bumped into a chain link fence that blocked access to the area under renovation. Warning myself to watch where I was going, I went the other way, toward the east tier. The archways there were fenced off with similar chain link so no one could fall, and doors opened off the gallery into what I supposed had been the soldiers' living quarters. I pushed through the first one and stepped into a small museum.

The room was high-ceilinged, with tall, narrow windows in the outside wall. No ranger or tourists were in sight. I looked toward an interior door that led to the next room and saw a series of mirror images: one door within another leading off into the distance, each diminishing in size until the last seemed very tiny. I had the unpleasant sensation that if I walked along there, I would become progressively smaller and eventually disappear.

From somewhere down there came the sound of voices. I followed it, passing through more museum displays until I came to a room containing an old-fashioned bedstead and footlocker. A ranger, dressed the same as the man downstairs except that he was bearded and wore granny glasses, stood beyond the bedstead lecturing to a man and a woman who were bundled to their chins in bulky sweaters.

"You'll notice that the fireplaces are very small," he was saying, motioning to the one on the wall next to the bed, "and you can imagine how cold it could get for the soldiers garrisoned here. They didn't have a heated employees' lounge like we do." Smiling at his own little joke, he glanced at me. "Do you want to join the tour?"

I shook my head and stepped over by the footlocker. "Are you Lee Gottschalk?"

"Yes." He spoke the word a shade warily.

"I have a few questions I'd like to ask you. How long will the rest of the tour take?"

"At least half an hour. These folks want to see the unrestored rooms on the third floor."

I didn't want to wait around that long, so I said, "Could you take a couple of minutes and talk with me now?"

He moved his head so the light from the windows caught his granny glasses and I couldn't see the expression in his eyes, but his mouth tightened in a way that might have been annoyance. After a moment he said, "Well, the rest of the tour on this floor is pretty much self-guided." To the tourists, he added, "Why don't you go on ahead and I'll catch up after I talk with this lady."

They nodded agreeably and moved on into the next room. Lee Gottschalk folded his arms across his chest and leaned against the small fireplace. "Now what can I do for you?"

I introduced myself and showed him my license. His mouth twitched briefly in surprise, but he didn't comment. I said, "At about four yesterday afternoon, a young woman left her car at Vista Point with a suicide note in it. I'm trying to locate a witness who saw her jump." I took out the photograph I'd been showing to people and handed it to him. By now I had Vanessa DiCesare's features memorized: high forehead, straight nose, full lips, glossy wings of dark-brown hair curling inward at the jawbone. It was a strong face, not beautiful but striking—and a face I'd recognize anywhere.

Gottschalk studied the photo, then handed it back to me. "I read about her in the morning paper. Why are you trying to find a witness?"

"Her parents have hired me to look into it."

"The paper said her father is some big politician here in the city."

I didn't see any harm in discussing what had already appeared in print. "Yes, Ernest DiCesare—he's on the Board of Supes and likely to be our next mayor."

"And she was a law student, engaged to some hotshot lawyer who ran her father's last political campaign."

"Right again."

He shook his head, lips pushing out in bewilderment. "Sounds like she had a lot going for her. Why would she kill herself? Did that note taped inside her car explain it?"

I'd seen the note, but its contents were confidential. "No. Did you happen to see anything unusual yesterday afternoon?"

"No. But if I'd seen anyone jump, I'd have reported it to the Coast Guard station so they could try to recover the body before the current carried it out to sea."

"What about someone standing by the bridge railing, acting strangely, perhaps?"

"If I'd noticed anyone like that, I'd have reported it to the bridge offices so they could send out a suicide prevention team." He stared almost combatively at me, as if I'd accused him of some kind of wrongdoing, then seemed to relent a little. "Come outside," he said, "and I'll show you something."

We went through the door to the gallery, and he guided me to the chain link barrier in the archway and pointed up. "Look at the angle of the bridge, and the distance we are from it. You couldn't spot anyone standing at the rail from here, at least not well enough to tell if they were acting upset. And a jumper would have to hurl herself way out before she'd be noticeable."

"And there's nowhere else in the fort from where a jumper would be clearly visible?"

"Maybe from one of the watchtowers or the extreme west side. But they're off limits to the public, and we only give them one routine check at closing."

Satisfied now, I said, "Well, that about does it. I appreciate your taking the time."

He nodded and we started along the gallery. When we reached the other end, where an enclosed staircase spiraled up and down, I thanked him again and we parted company.

The way the facts looked to me now, Vanessa DiCesare had faked this suicide and just walked away—away from her wealthy old-line Italian family, from her up-and-coming liberal lawyer, from a life that either had become too much or just hadn't been enough. Vanessa was over twenty-one; she had a legal right to disappear if she wanted to. But her parents and her fiancé loved her, and they also had a right to know she was alive and well. If I could locate her and reassure them without ruining whatever new life she planned to create for herself, I would feel I'd performed the job I'd been hired to do. But right now I was weary, chilled to the bone, and out of leads. I decided to go back to All Souls and consider my next moves in warmth and comfort.

All Souls Legal Cooperative is housed in a ramshackle Victorian on one of the steeply sloping side-streets of Bernal Heights, a working-class district in the southern part of the city. The co-op caters mainly to clients who live in the area: people with low to middle incomes who don't have much extra money for expensive lawyers. The sliding fee scale allows them to obtain quality legal assistance at reasonable prices—a concept that is probably outdated in the self-centered 1980s, but is kept alive by the people who staff All Souls. It's a place where the lawyers care about their clients, and a good place to work.

I left my MG at the curb and hurried up the front steps through the blowing fog. The warmth inside was almost a shock after the chilliness at Fort Point; I unbuttoned my jacket and went down the long deserted hallway to the big country kitchen at the rear. There I found my boss, Hank Zahn, stirring up a mug of the Navy grog he often concocts on cold November nights like this one.

He looked at me, pointed to the rum bottle, and said, "Shall I make you one?" When I nodded, he reached for another mug.

I went to the round oak table under the windows, moved a pile of newspapers from one of the chairs, and sat down. Hank added lemon juice, hot water, and sugar syrup to the rum; dusted it artistically with nutmeg; and set it in front of me with a flourish. I sampled it as he sat down across from me, then nodded my approval.

He said, "How's it going with the DiCesare investigation?"

Hank had a personal interest in the case; Vanessa's fiancé, Gary Stornetta, was a long-time friend of his, which was why I, rather than one of the large investigative firms her father normally favored, had been asked to look into it. I said, "Everything I've come up with points to it being a disappearance, not a suicide."

"Just as Gary and her parents suspected."

"Yes. I've covered the entire area around the bridge. There are absolutely no witnesses, except for the tour bus driver who saw her park her car at four and got suspicious when it was still there at seven and reported it. But even he didn't see her walk off toward the bridge." I drank some more grog, felt its warmth, and began to relax.

Behind his thick horn-rimmed glasses, Hank's eyes

became concerned. "Did the DiCesares or Gary give you any idea why she would have done such a thing?"

"When I talked with Ernest and Sylvia this morning, they said Vanessa had changed her mind about marrying Gary. He's not admitting to that, but he doesn't speak of Vanessa the way a happy husband-to-be would. And it seems an unlikely match to me—he's close to twenty years older than she."

"More like fifteen," Hank said. "Gary's father was Ernest's best friend, and after Ron Stornetta died, Ernest more or less took him on as a protégé. Ernest was delighted that their families were finally going to be joined."

"Oh, he was delighted all right. He admitted to me that he'd practically arranged the marriage. 'Girl didn't know what was good for her,' he said. 'Needed a strong older man to guide her.' " I snorted.

Hank smiled faintly. He's a feminist, but over the years his sense of outrage has mellowed; mine still has a hair trigger.

"Anyway," I said, "when Vanessa first announced she was backing out of the engagement, Ernest told her he would cut off her funds for law school if she didn't go through with the wedding."

"Jesus, I had no idea he was capable of such . . . Neanderthal tactics."

"Well, he is. After that Vanessa went ahead and set the wedding date. But Sylvia said she suspected she wouldn't go through with it. Vanessa talked of quitting law school and moving out of their home. And she'd been seeing other men; she and her father had a bad quarrel about it just last week. Anyway, all of that, plus the fact that one of her suitcases and some clothing are missing, made them highly suspicious of the suicide."

Hank reached for my mug and went to get us more grog. I began thumbing through the copy of the morning paper that I'd moved off the chair, looking for the story on Vanessa. I found it on page three.

> The daughter of Supervisor Ernest DiCesare apparently committed suicide by jumping from the Golden Gate Bridge late yesterday afternoon.
>
> Vanessa DiCesare, 22, abandoned her 1985 Honda Civic at Vista Point at approximately four p.m., police said. There were no witnesses to her jump, and the body has not been recovered. The contents of a suicide note found in her car have not been disclosed.
>
> Ms. DiCesare, a first-year student at Hastings College of Law, is the only child of the supervisor and his wife, Sylvia. She planned to be married next month to San Francisco attorney Gary R. Stornetta, a political associate of her father. . . .

Strange how routine it all sounded when reduced to journalistic language. And yet how mysterious—the "undisclosed contents" of the suicide note, for instance.

"You know," I said as Hank came back to the table and set down the fresh mugs of grog, "that note is another factor that makes me believe she staged this whole thing. It was so formal and controlled. If they had samples of suicide notes in etiquette books, I'd say she looked one up and copied it."

He ran his fingers through his wiry brown hair. "What I don't understand is why she didn't just break

247

off the engagement and move out of the house. So what if her father cut off her money? There are lots worse things than working your way through law school."

"Oh, but this way she gets back at everyone, and has the advantage of actually being alive to gloat over it. Imagine her parents' and Gary's grief and guilt—it's the ultimate way of getting even."

"She must be a very angry young woman."

"Yes. After I talked with Ernest and Sylvia and Gary, I spoke briefly with Vanessa's best friend, a law student named Kathy Graves. Kathy told me that Vanessa was furious with her father for making her go through with the marriage. And she'd come to hate Gary because she'd decided he was only marrying her for her family's money and political power."

"Oh, come on. Gary's ambitious, sure. But you can't tell me he doesn't genuinely care for Vanessa."

"I'm only giving you her side of the story."

"So now what do you plan to do?"

"Talk with Gary and the DiCesares again. See if I can't come up with some bit of information that will help me find her."

"And then?"

"Then it's up to them to work it out."

The DiCesare home was mock-Tudor, brick and half-timber, set on a corner knoll in the exclusive area of St. Francis Wood. When I'd first come there that morning, I'd been slightly awed; now the house had lost its power to impress me. After delving into the lives of the family who lived there, I knew that it was merely a pile of brick and mortar and wood that contained more than the usual amount of misery.

The DiCesares and Gary Stornetta were waiting for me in the living room, a strangely formal place with several groupings of furniture and expensive-looking knickknacks laid out in precise patterns on the tables. Vanessa's parents and fiancé—like the house—seemed diminished since my previous visit: Sylvia huddled in an armchair by the fireplace, her gray-blonde hair straggling from its elegant coiffure; Ernest stood behind her, haggard-faced, one hand protectively on her shoulder. Gary paced, smoking and clawing at his hair with his other hand. Occasionally he dropped ashes on the thick wall-to-wall carpeting, but no one called it to his attention.

They listened to what I had to report without interruption. When I finished, there was a long silence. Then Sylvia put a hand over her eyes and said, "How she must hate us to do a thing like this!"

Ernest tightened his grip on his wife's shoulder. His face was a conflict of anger, bewilderment, and sorrow.

There was no question of which emotion had hold of Gary; he smashed out his cigarette in an ashtray, lit another, and resumed pacing. But while his movements before had merely been nervous, now his tall, lean body was rigid with thinly controlled fury. "Damn her!" he said. "Damn her anyway!"

"Gary." There was a warning note in Ernest's voice.

Gary glanced at him, then at Sylvia. "Sorry."

I said, "The question now is, do you want me to continue looking for her?"

In shocked tones, Sylvia said, "Of course we do!" Then she tipped her head back and looked at her husband.

Ernest was silent, his fingers pressing hard against the black wool of her dress.

"Ernest?" Now Sylvia's voice held a note of panic.

"Of course we do," he said. But the words somehow lacked conviction.

I took out my notebook and pencil, glancing at Gary. He had stopped pacing and was watching the DiCesares. His craggy face was still mottled with anger, and I sensed he shared Ernest's uncertainty.

Opening the notebook, I said, "I need more details about Vanessa, what her life was like the past month or so. Perhaps something will occur to one of you that didn't this morning."

"Ms. McCone," Ernest said, "I don't think Sylvia's up to this right now. Why don't you and Gary talk, and then if there's anything else, I'll be glad to help you."

"Fine." Gary was the one I was primarily interested in questioning, anyway. I waited until Ernest and Sylvia had left the room, then turned to him.

When the door shut behind them, he hurled his cigarette into the empty fireplace. "Goddamn little bitch!" he said.

I said, "Why don't you sit down."

He looked at me for a few seconds, obviously wanting to keep on pacing, but then he flopped into the chair Sylvia had vacated. When I'd first met with Gary this morning, he'd been controlled and immaculately groomed, and he had seemed more solicitous of the DiCesares than concerned with his own feelings. Now his clothing was disheveled, his graying hair tousled, and he looked to be on the brink of a rage that would flatten anyone in its path.

Unfortunately, what I had to ask him would probably fan that rage. I braced myself and said, "Now tell me about Vanessa. And not all the stuff about her being a lovely young woman and a brilliant student. I heard all that this morning—but now we both know it isn't the whole truth, don't we?"

Surprisingly he reached for a cigarette and lit it slowly, using the time to calm himself. When he spoke, his voice was as level as my own. "All right, it's not the whole truth. Vanessa *is* lovely and brilliant. She'll make a top-notch lawyer. There's a hardness in her; she gets it from Ernest. It took guts to fake this suicide . . ."

"What do you think she hopes to gain from it?"

"Freedom. From me. From Ernest's domination. She's probably taken off somewhere for a good time. When she's ready she'll come back and make her demands."

"And what will they be?"

"Enough money to move into a place of her own and finish law school. And she'll get it, too. She's all her parents have."

"You don't think she's set out to make a new life for herself?"

"Hell, no. That would mean giving up all this." The sweep of his arm encompassed the house and all of the DiCesares's privileged world.

But there was one factor that made me doubt his assessment. I said, "What about the other men in her life?"

He tried to look surprised, but an angry muscle twitched in his jaw.

"Come on, Gary," I said, "you know there were other men. Even Ernest and Sylvia were aware of that."

"Ah, Christ!" He popped out of the chair and began pacing again. "All right, there were other men. It started a few months ago. I didn't understand it; things had been good with us; they still *were* good physically. But I thought, okay, she's young; this is only natural. So I decided to give her some rope, let her get it out of her system. She didn't throw it in my face, didn't embarrass me in front of my friends. Why shouldn't she have a last fling?"

"And then?"

"She began making noises about breaking off the engagement. And Ernest started that shit about not footing the bill for law school. Like a fool I went along with it, and she seemed to cave in from the pressure. But a few weeks later, it all started up again—only this time it was purposeful, cruel."

"In what way?"

"She'd know I was meeting political associates for lunch or dinner, and she'd show up at the restaurant with a date. Later she'd claim he was just a friend, but you couldn't prove it from the way they acted. We'd go to a party and she'd flirt with every man there. She got sly and secretive about where she'd been, what she'd been doing."

I had pictured Vanessa as a very angry young woman; now I realized she was not a particularly nice one, either.

Gary was saying, " . . . the last straw was on Halloween. We went to a costume party given by one of her friends from Hastings. I didn't want to go—costumes, a young crowd, not my kind of thing— and so she was angry with me to begin with. Anyway, she walked out with another man, some jerk in a soldier outfit. They were dancing . . ."

I sat up straighter. "Describe the costume."

"An old-fashioned soldier outfit. Wide-brimmed hat with a plume, frock coat, sword."

"What did the man look like?"

"Youngish. He had a full beard and wore granny glasses."

Lee Gottschalk.

The address I got from the phone directory for Lee Gottschalk was on California Street not far from Twenty-fifth Avenue and only a couple of miles from where I'd first met the ranger at Fort Point. When I arrived there and parked at the opposite curb, I didn't need to check the mailboxes to see which apartment was his; the corner windows on the second floor were ablaze with light, and inside I could see Gottschalk, sitting in an armchair in what appeared to be his living room. He seemed to be alone but expecting company, because frequently he looked up from the book he was reading and checked his watch.

In case the company was Vanessa DiCesare, I didn't want to go barging in there. Gottschalk might find a way to warn her off, or simply not answer the door when she arrived. Besides, I didn't yet have a definite connection between the two of them; the "jerk in a soldier outfit" *could* have been someone else, someone in a rented costume that just happened to resemble the working uniform at the fort. But my suspicions were strong enough to keep me watching Gottschalk for well over an hour. The ranger *had* lied to me that afternoon.

The lies had been casual and convincing, except for two mistakes—such small mistakes that I hadn't caught them even when I'd read the newspaper account of Vanessa's purported suicide later. But now I recognized them for what they were: The paper had called Gary Stornetta a "political associate" of Vanessa's father, rather than his former campaign manager, as Lee had termed him. And while the paper mentioned the suicide note, it had not said it was *taped* inside the car. While Gottschalk conceivably could know about Gary managing Ernest's campaign for the Board of Supes from other newspaper accounts, there was no way he could have known how the note was secured—except from Vanessa herself.

Because of those mistakes, I continued watching Gottschalk, straining my eyes as the mist grew heavier, hoping Vanessa would show up or that he'd eventually lead me to her. The ranger appeared to be nervous: He got up a couple of times and turned on a TV, flipped through the channels, and turned it off again. For about ten minutes, he paced back and forth. Finally, around twelve-thirty, he checked his watch again, then got up and drew the draperies shut. The lights went out behind them.

I tensed, staring through the blowing mist at the door of the apartment building. Somehow Gottschalk hadn't looked like a man who was going to bed. And my impression was correct: In a few minutes he came through the door onto the sidewalk carrying a suitcase—pale leather like the one of Vanessa's Sylvia had described to me—and got into a dark-colored Mustang parked on his side of the street. The car started up and he made a U-turn, then went right on Twenty-fifth Avenue. I followed. After a few minutes, it became apparent that he was heading for Fort Point.

When Gottschalk turned into the road to the fort, I kept going until I could pull over on the shoulder. The brake lights of the Mustang flared, and then Gottschalk got out and unlocked the low iron bar that blocked the road from sunset to sunrise; after he'd driven through he closed it again, and the car's lights disappeared down the road.

Had Vanessa been hiding at drafty, cold Fort Point? It seemed a strange choice of place, since she could have used a motel or Gottschalk's apartment. But perhaps she'd been afraid someone would recognize her in a public place, or connect her with Gottschalk and come looking, as I had. And while the fort would be a miserable place to hide during the hours it was open to the public—she'd have had to keep to one of the off-limits areas, such as the west side—at night she could probably avail herself of the heated employees' lounge.

Now I could reconstruct most of the scenario of what had gone on: Vanessa meets Lee; they talk about his work; she decides he is the person to help her fake her suicide. Maybe there's a romantic entanglement, maybe not; but for whatever reason, he agrees to go along with the plan. She leaves her car at Vista Point, walks across the bridge, and later he drives over there and picks up the suitcase. . . .

But then why hadn't he delivered it to her at the fort? And to go after the suitcase after she'd abandoned the car was too much of a risk; he might have been seen, or the people at the fort might have noticed him leaving for too long a break. Also, if she'd walked across the bridge, surely at least one of the people I'd talked with would have seen her—the maintenance crew near the north tower, for instance.

There was no point in speculating on it now, I decided. The thing to do was to follow Gottschalk down there and confront Vanessa before she disappeared again. For a moment I debated taking my gun out of the glovebox, but then decided against it. I don't like to carry it unless I'm going into a dangerous situation, and neither Gottschalk nor Vanessa posed any particular threat to me. I was merely here to deliver a message from Vanessa's parents asking her to come home. If she didn't care to respond to it, that was not my business—or my problem.

I got out of my car and locked it, then hurried across the road and down the narrow lane to the gate, ducking under it and continuing along toward the ranger station. On either side of me were tall, thick groves of eucalyptus; I could smell their acrid fragrance and hear the fog-laden wind rustle their brittle leaves. Their shadows turned the lane into a black winding alley, and the only sound besides distant traffic noises was my tennis shoes slapping on the broken pavement. The ranger station was dark, but ahead I could see Gottschalk's car parked next to the fort. The area was illuminated only by small security lights set at intervals on the walls of the structure. Above it the bridge arched, washed in fog-muted yellowish light; as I drew closer I became aware of the grumble and clank of traffic up there.

I ran across the parking area and checked Gottschalk's car. It was empty, but the suitcase rested on the passenger seat. I turned and started toward the sally port, noticing that its heavily studded door stood open a few inches. The low tunnel was completely dark. I felt my way along it toward the courtyard, one hand on its icy stone wall.

The doors to the courtyard also stood open. I peered through them into the gloom beyond. What light there was came from the bridge and more security beacons high up on the wooden watchtowers; I could barely make out the shapes of the construction equipment that stood near the west side. The clanking from the bridge was oppressive and eerie in the still night.

As I was about to step into the courtyard, there was a movement to my right. I drew back into the sally port as Lee Gottschalk came out of one of the ground-floor doorways. My first impulse was to confront him, but then I decided against it. He might shout, warn Vanessa, and she might escape before I could deliver her parents' message.

After a few seconds I looked out again, meaning to follow Gottschalk, but he was nowhere in sight. A faint shaft of light fell through the door from which he had emerged and rippled over the cobblestone floor. I went that way, through the door and along a narrow corridor to where an archway was illuminated. Then, realizing the archway led to the unrestored cell of the jail I'd seen earlier, I paused. Surely Vanessa wasn't hiding in there. . . .

I crept forward and looked through the arch. The light came from a heavy-duty flashlight that sat on the floor. It threw macabre shadows on the water-stained walls, showing their streaked paint and graffiti. My gaze followed its beams upward and then down, to where the grating of the cistern lay out of place on the floor beside the hole. Then I moved over to the railing, leaned across it, and trained the flashlight down into the well.

I saw, with a rush of shock and horror, the dark

hair and once-handsome features of Vanessa Di-Cesare.

She had been hacked to death. Stabbed and slashed, as if in a frenzy. Her clothing was ripped; there were gashes on her face and hands; she was covered with dark smears of blood. Her eyes were open, staring with that horrible flatness of death.

I came back on my heels, clutching the railing for support. A wave of dizziness swept over me, followed by an icy coldness. I thought: He killed her. And then I pictured Gottschalk in his Union Army uniform, the saber hanging from his belt, and I knew what the weapon had been.

"God!" I said aloud.

Why had he murdered her? I had no way of knowing yet. But the answer to why he'd thrown her into the cistern, instead of just putting her into the bay, was clear: She was supposed to have committed suicide; and while bodies that fall from the Golden Gate Bridge sustain a great many injuries, slash and stab wounds aren't among them. Gottschalk could not count on the body being swept out to sea on the current; if she washed up somewhere along the coast, it would be obvious she had been murdered—and eventually an investigation might have led back to him. To him and his soldier's saber.

It also seemed clear that he'd come to the fort tonight to move the body. But why not last night, why leave her in the cistern all day? Probably he'd needed to plan, to secure keys to the gate and fort, to check the schedule of the night patrols for the best time to remove her. Whatever his reason, I realized now that I'd walked into a very dangerous situation.

Walked right in without bringing my gun. I turned quickly to get out of there . . .

And came face-to-face with Lee Gottschalk.

His eyes were wide, his mouth drawn back in a snarl of surprise. In one hand he held a bundle of heavy canvas. "You!" he said. "What the hell are you doing here?"

I jerked back from him, bumped into the railing, and dropped the flashlight. It clattered on the floor and began rolling toward the mouth of the cistern. Gottschalk lunged toward me, and as I dodged, the light fell into the hole and the cell went dark. I managed to push past him and ran down the hallway to the courtyard.

Stumbling on the cobblestones, I ran blindly for the sally port. Its doors were shut now—he'd probably taken that precaution when he'd returned from getting the tarp to wrap her body in. I grabbed the iron hasp and tugged, but couldn't get it open. Gottschalk's footsteps were coming through the courtyard after me now. I let go of the hasp and ran again.

When I came to the enclosed staircase at the other end of the court, I started up. The steps were wide at the outside wall, narrow at the inside. My toes banged into the risers of the steps; a couple of times I teetered and almost fell backwards. At the first tier I paused, then kept going. Gottschalk had said something about unrestored rooms on the second tier; they'd be a better place to hide than in the museum.

Down below I could hear him climbing after me. The sound of his feet—clattering and stumbling—echoed in the close space. I could hear him grunt and mumble: low, ugly sounds that I knew were curses.

I had absolutely no doubt that if he caught me, he would kill me. Maybe do to me what he had done to Vanessa. . . .

I rounded the spiral once again and came out on the top floor gallery, my heart beating wildly, my breath coming in pants. To my left were archways, black outlines filled with dark-gray sky. To my right was blackness. I went that way, hands out, feeling my way.

My hands touched the rough wood of a door. I pushed, and it opened. As I passed through it, my shoulder bag caught on something; I yanked it loose and kept going. Beyond the door I heard Gottschalk curse loudly, the sound filled with surprise and pain; he must have fallen on the stairway. And that gave me a little more time.

The tug at my shoulder bag had reminded me of the small flashlight I keep there. Flattening myself against the wall next to the door, I rummaged through the bag and brought out the flash. Its beam showed high walls and arching ceilings, plaster and lath pulled away to expose dark brick. I saw cubicles and cubbyholes opening into dead ends, but to my right was an arch. I made a small involuntary sound of relief, then thought *Quiet!* Gottschalk's footsteps started up the stairway again as I moved through the archway.

The crumbling plaster walls beyond the archway were set at odd angles—an interlocking funhouse maze connected by small doors. I slipped through one and found an irregularly shaped room heaped with debris. There didn't seem to be an exit, so I ducked back into the first room and moved toward the outside wall, where gray outlines indicated small high-placed windows. I couldn't hear Gottschalk any more—couldn't hear anything but the roar and clank from the bridge directly overhead.

The front wall was brick and stone, and the windows had wide waist-high sills. I leaned across one, looked through the salt-caked glass, and saw the open sea. I was at the front of the fort, the part that faced beyond the Golden Gate; to my immediate right would be the unrestored portion. If I could slip over into that area, I might be able to hide until the other rangers came to work in the morning.

But Gottschalk could be anywhere. I couldn't hear his footsteps above the infernal noise from the bridge. He could be right here in the room with me, pinpointing me by the beam of my flashlight. . . .

Fighting down panic, I switched the light off and continued along the wall, my hands recoiling from its clammy stone surface. It was icy cold in the vast, echoing space, but my own flesh felt colder still. The air had a salt tang, underlaid by odors of rot and mildew. For a couple of minutes the darkness was unalleviated, but then I saw a lighter rectangular shape ahead of me.

When I reached it I found it was some sort of embrasure, about four feet tall, but only a little over a foot wide. Beyond it I could see the edge of the gallery where it curved and stopped at the chain link fence that barred entrance to the other side of the fort. The fence wasn't very high—only five feet or so. If I could get through this narrow opening, I could climb it and find refuge . . .

The sudden noise behind me was like a firecracker popping. I whirled, and saw a tall figure silhouetted against one of the seaward windows. He lurched forward, tripping over whatever he'd stepped on. Forcing back a cry, I hoisted myself up and began squeezing through the embrasure.

Its sides were rough brick. They scraped my flesh clear through my clothing. Behind me I heard the slap of Gottschalk's shoes on the wooden floor.

My hips wouldn't fit through the opening. I gasped, grunted, pulling with my arms on the outside wall. Then I turned on my side, sucking in my stomach. My bag caught again, and I let go of the wall long enough to rip its strap off my elbow. As my hips squeezed through the embrasure, I felt Gottschalk grab at my feet. I kicked out frantically, breaking his hold, and fell off the sill to the floor of the gallery.

Fighting for breath, I pushed off the floor, threw myself at the fence, and began climbing. The metal bit into my fingers, rattled and clashed with my weight. At the top, the leg of my jeans got hung up on the spiky wires. I tore it loose and jumped down the other side.

The door to the gallery burst open and Gottschalk came through it. I got up from a crouch and ran into the darkness ahead of me. The fence began to rattle as he started up it. I raced, half-stumbling, along the gallery, the open archways to my right. To my left was probably a warren of rooms similar to those on the east side. I could lose him in there . . .

Only I couldn't. The door I tried was locked. I ran to the next one and hurled my body against its wooden panels. It didn't give. I heard myself sob in fear and frustration.

Gottschalk was over the fence now, coming toward me, limping. His breath came in erratic gasps, loud enough to hear over the noise from the bridge. I twisted around, looking for shelter, and saw a pile of lumber lying across one of the open archways.

I dashed toward it and slipped behind, wedged between it and the pillar of the arch. The courtyard lay two dizzying stories below me. I grasped the end of the top two-by-four. It moved easily, as if on a fulcrum.

Gottschalk had seen me. He came on steadily, his right leg dragging behind him. When he reached the pile of lumber and started over it toward me, I yanked on the two-by-four. The other end moved and struck him on the knee.

He screamed and stumbled back. Then he came forward again, hands outstretched toward me. I pulled back further against the pillar. His clutching hands missed me, and when they did he lost his balance and toppled onto the pile of lumber. And then the boards began to slide toward the open archway.

He grabbed at the boards, yelling and flailing his arms. I tried to reach for him, but the lumber was moving like an avalanche now, pitching over the side and crashing down into the courtyard two stories below. It carried Gottschalk's thrashing body with it, and his screams echoed in its wake. For an awful few seconds the boards continued to crash down on him, and then everything was terribly still. Even the thrumming of the bridge traffic seemed muted.

I straightened slowly and looked down into the courtyard. Gottschalk lay unmoving among the scattered pieces of lumber. For a moment I breathed deeply to control my vertigo; then I ran back to the chain link fence, climbed it, and rushed down the spiral staircase to the courtyard.

When I got to the ranger's body, I could hear him moaning. I said, "Lie still. I'll call an ambulance."

He moaned louder as I ran across the courtyard and found a phone in the gift shop, but by the time I returned, he was silent. His breathing was so shallow that I thought he'd passed out, but then I heard mumbled words coming from his lips. I bent closer to listen.

"Vanessa," he said. "Wouldn't take me with her. . . ."

I said, "Take you where?"

"Going away together. Left my car . . . over there so she could drive across the bridge. But when she . . . brought it here she said she was going alone. . . ."

So you argued, I thought. And you lost your head and slashed her to death.

"Vanessa," he said again. "Never planned to take me . . . tricked me. . . ."

I started to put a hand on his arm, but found I couldn't touch him. "Don't talk any more. The ambulance'll be here soon."

"Vanessa," he said. "Oh God, what did you do to me?"

I looked up at the bridge, rust red through the darkness and the mist. In the distance, I could hear the wail of a siren.

Deceptions, I thought.

Deceptions. . . .

To Sleep, Perchance
to Dream

J. BIRNEY DIBBLE

J. Birney Dibble is a general surgeon in Eau Claire,
Wisconsin, who also has been a freelance writer
for the past twenty years. In nonfiction he has
written about sports and his travels in Africa, the
West Pacific, and Saudi Arabia. He has written
three books of fiction, including a volume of short
stories and two "medical science fiction" novels.
Brain Child, his most recent novel, was published
in the spring of 1987 by Dorchester.

Dr. Dibble says that "To Sleep, Perchance to
Dream" was inspired by a news article in the
Chicago Tribune several years ago. Mike Cellini,
who makes his debut here, is the central character
of Dr. Dibble's novel-in-progress.

The first important clue I found was the last to be
explained. Stuffed in the dead girl's mouth was a page
off her memo pad. On it was written, "Tickets for
A. S.," in English but in a flowing foreign script. I
found it when I rolled her head toward me to check
her jaw for rigor mortis.

I had followed the fire chief up dark stairs which
still dripped with water from the hoses, ducking low
to avoid the smarting smoke still billowing down from
the ceiling. Her naked body lay face up beside a
smoldering pile of charred clothes. I kicked the

blackened remnants aside and pushed my finger against a carotid. Nothing. No surprise, for someone had run a wooden-handled butcher knife through her chest, sprinkled kerosene on the clothes stripped from her body, and lit it. Smoke had filled the corridors, but the smoke-eaters were there long before the room went up in flames. So much for arson with kerosene. And so much for destroying the evidence of a murder.

"Amateur job," I mumbled under my breath. "We'll catch him." Later I wondered how I could have been so cocky. I stuffed the soggy note into an envelope, put the envelope in my pocket, wiped my hands on the carpet, and got wearily to my feet. I looked at my watch. Almost eleven. No wonder I was tired. I moved back a pace, aware that half a dozen men stood in various attitudes of expectancy. But I had learned the hard way not to let anyone rush me.

Even dead she was a pretty little thing. Brown-skinned, black-haired, her big eyes staring up at the ceiling—or at her murderer. Rita Mendiola. Twenty-eight. She lay beside a small knee-hole desk. I checked the memo pad from which the note had been torn. Nothing.

"Okay, boys," I said, and waved a hand toward the corpse. While the body was being chalked down and the parade of photographers, coroner's people, dusters, and other forensic experts earned their pay, I looked around. A woman's one-bedroom apartment. Pictures of family and class graduation on the wall, frilly curtains at the windows, desk with small typewriter and letter holder and the memo pad, matching overstuffed sofa and chair, a beanbag chair, an unplugged TV with its innards pulled out in back.

A kerosene Tilly lamp with a new wick on a small end-table.

Her bedroom was impeccable. In the closet was a row of white uniforms neatly hung on wooden hangers. There was no sign of a struggle. The apartment had not been ransacked. If jewelry or money had been taken, it had not been by wreck and search.

I returned to the living room as the body was being carried away in a canvas bag. My concentration was broken by a grating cigarette voice at my elbow. "Look pretty obvious, Mr. Cellini?"

I turned to the uniformed cop. "Rape-murder? Could be. No signs of a struggle, though."

"May have been in shock."

"Possible."

I didn't like it though.

"Someone she knew," the officer said, "or at least trusted."

I glanced at the dismantled TV. "Like a repair man?"

"She let him in," the officer said, "he worked a while, then . . ."

I eyed the officer. "Possible."

I still didn't like it. The note crammed in her mouth was all wrong. Why would a repairman stuff a note in her mouth?

Why would anyone?

To gag her? She would have spit it out. To get rid of it? He could have shoved it in his pocket and burned it later if it was really incriminating. As a frame? Not very damn subtle. Reverse psychology?

It didn't take me long to find out from talkative neighbors that Rita Mendiola was a Filipina respiratory therapist who worked at the Sisters of Charity

Hospital two blocks away. Unmarried, but known to have an occasional male visitor. Quiet. Friendly. No known enemies. Minded her own business. All that sort of unhelpful information. Why did she have a kerosene lamp? Habit, I was told. In the Philippines, the electric lights went out for hours or days at a time.

The big surprise came the next morning when I got the coroner's report. Rita Mendiola was a virgin.

I sat in my office on the third floor of the Third Precinct Station and stared at the report. Not only had she not been raped, she had never even bedded down with a man. Men visitors who just sat and talked?

I called her parents in the Philippines. They were horrified, baffled, and could not help in any way. Her father, a wealthy physician on Cebu, said he would make arrangements to have her body shipped home when I released it.

The note in Rita's mouth proved to be a dead end. None of Rita's acquaintances knew anyone with the intials A. S. And no one could think of a place or an event abbreviated A. S. I called her hospital and asked the personnel manager to check the employee records. There were half a dozen people with those initials. We checked them all out and drew blanks. There were fingerprints all over the TV set, but our computer said they didn't belong to anyone who had ever been fingerprinted. The knife was Rita's and apparently had been wiped clean. The kerosene came from a can in the kitchen.

Now, I've seen a lot of strange cases, working in homicide. But this was one of the strangest. Usually I can get a handle real soon and at least make a good start at nailing down some suspects. Oh, I know, I blew a big one up north years ago. Since then I've studied hard, worked hard—first in uniform, then in plainclothes—and I've come up in the ranks. Yeah, I still miss those weekends in the woods and on the streams, and I miss Walter Gregg and the howl of his beagle hounds when they hit a fresh snowshoe-rabbit track. Walt says now I'm the hound and I guess I am. And sometimes murderers are as hard to catch as rabbits. This one looked like he'd gone to ground for good.

It began to look like a crime to be put in the file labeled "Open." But a month later, late in the afternoon, a Dr. Ernesto Frontada came to my office. Very precise, he spoke with a heavy Filipino accent. Even elevated on three-inch soles, he was short. He was not a handsome man. Bottle-bottom lenses shrunk his eyes. I wanted to tell him to buy some contacts. Thick black hair, which I quickly spotted as a superbly fitting toupee, hung low on his neck. Though he moved with the agility and grace of a young man, I knew he'd never see fifty again.

I motioned to a chair, but he shook his head and said, "This will not take long, Lieutenant. You will not believe me anyway."

"Good way to get me to listen," I said and waved at the chair again.

"I think then I will sit down now." He moved slowly to the chair, sat down and crossed his legs. His black shoes glistened.

Slowly, in understandable but broken English, he told his story. "I am here," he said, dark eyes somber, "against wishes of my wife. She should be telling you. She won't. Therefore it is being my duty."

"I understand."

"Three days since, Angelina and I are sitting in living room, reading. Without no saying a word, she suddenly go up to bedroom. I think nothing, for bathroom is adjoin the bedroom. But after half hour I realize she is gone long time. Even that is not unusual. She sometimes nap in late evening so she can stay up with me. However, after little while I go up to our room and find her lying dressed on bed. Her eyes are open, staring at ceiling. I ask her is anything wrong."

He stopped, took off his glasses, wiped them thoroughly and put them back on. He uncrossed his legs, put both hands on his knees and leaned forward.

"Do you believe in occult, Lieutenant Cellini?"

"Exorcism, black masses, spirit voices, that sort of stuff? No."

"But you will listen before you expel me?" There was a pleading smile on his face.

"I'll listen."

"I get right to point then, Lieutenant. I ask Angelina what is matter. She answer in voice I am never hearing before. A young woman's voice, educated but not cultured. You understand?"

I nodded. I hadn't heard that term in years.

"She talk," the doctor continued, "in Tagalog, our language in Islands. Partly as doctor, partly as husband, I check for coherency and ask her name. She say, 'Ako 'y Rita Mendiola.' I am Rita Mendiola."

Startled, I tried to keep my tone matter-of-fact. "Do you know anybody by that name, doctor?"

"No. I know name from newspaper, of course. All Filipinos do, I think. I talk to my wife for several minutes before she come out of trance, as she call it. She say she was murder and want me to find man."

I sat forward in my chair. "She told you his name?"

Frontada nodded. "Albert Singer."

A. S.

"When she wake up," Dr. Frontada said, "she remember nothing. But I tell her all she is saying in trance."

"That was three days ago, doctor. Why did you wait to come in?"

"She is not letting me. Too embarrass. Never— even in Philippines where such is often believe—is she dealing with occult, with mediums or astrologers or like that. She say we are look foolish."

"But you're here now."

"Last night she is having same trance. Repeat everything. And again when she wake up she remember nothing. Just very thirsty. And cold."

"Did your wife know Rita Mendiola?"

"Yes. Just vague. Angelina is respiratory therapist, Lieutenant Cellini. She work at Sisters of Charity Hospital where Rita work. But different shift, so she never know her well. My wife is quit full time work." He smiled a little apologetically. "My practice is grow big, even with my not perfect English. Now my wife work once a week or so, just to fill in."

I toyed with the keys of my typewriter. I had one further question. We had never released the information that Rita was virginal. I looked up at the prim little man perched on the edge of his chair. "Did your wife say how Rita was killed?"

"She say she is stab."

"And raped?"

"She say she is not rape."

The next morning I checked again at the Sisters of Charity Hospital to see if an Albert Singer had ever worked there. The personnel manager put me on hold for a long moment, then came back on. "Yes, here it is. Albert Singer, black, age thirty-one, married, part-time work nights as a registered respiratory therapist. Hasn't worked here for almost a year, however."

"Address?"

"Thirty-one thirty-three West Washington. That's also a year ago."

I put down the receiver and tipped back in my chair. It was too much to believe. But not to ignore.

I knew the neighborhood. Middle-class black. Originally built by upper-middle-class whites. It had slowly deteriorated into a slum, but now was being renovated into a nice place to bring up your kids. Respectable people. Not where you'd expect a murderer to be hanging out. But otherwise respectable people did commit murder.

I decided to go myself and right away. I took with me one of my best men, Randolph Jackson, a tall, lean, relaxed black sergeant who could double for Bill Cosby. I told him the story on the way over.

He eyed me with a bemused smile. "And you don't believe a word of it?"

"Have to, don't we? She put a real name to A. S."

"She can read the papers as well as you can."

"Publicity?" I asked with a grim smile.

"It's happened before."

"Her husband came against her wishes."

"So *he* says."

Albert Singer still lived at 3133 West Washington.

A young black woman opened the door, nodded diffidently to Jackson, stonewalled me. She wore designer blue jeans and a loose overblouse. Her hair was corn-rowed with a wisp of pigtail on either side. A gold pendant hung from a thin gold chain around her neck. A huge diamond flashed on the long finger of her right hand.

"Mrs. Singer?" Jackson asked.

"She's away. I'm Hattie Carter, the housekeeper."

"We'd like to talk to Mr. Singer."

We flashed our badges and she backed away, her body undulating like a professional model's. Jackson followed her movements with unconcealed interest, his eyes rippling up and down several times. She met his gaze frankly but with no hint of welcome.

Singer, a husky man with a restrained Afro and bushy sideburns, sat at the dining room table facing the doorway. He glanced up, continued his game of solitaire with a slightly bemused smile as if policemen entered his home on a regular basis.

The apartment was furnished with good—if not lavish—furniture. Lined drapes were pulled back from the windows. A huge color TV stood in a prominent place in the room. On a built-in bookcase bereft of books lay an expensive stereo set. Through an archway I could see a well-equipped, modern kitchen.

I switched off the TV. Jackson moved up to the table and leaned forward on it. "Looks like the devil's taking you this time, man."

"Yeah, mostly does." He glanced up at Jackson, ignored me, looked in vain for a place to play a card, then methodically gathered the cards together and put them aside.

"You got a problem?" he asked Jackson.

"Maybe you do. Like to know what you can tell us of a Rita Mendiola."

Singer nodded. "Poor kid. Sure, I knew her. Met her couple years back, at the hospital. Used to stop up and fix things for her. You know, change a washer, tape a 'lectric cord, fix her TV. I'd started a little job on the TV just a few days before she was killed. Was gonna go over there later and finish. Didn't get the chance."

I spoke for the first time. "You sure you weren't there the night she was killed?"

Singer's eyes blazed. "Meanin' did I kill her?" He stood up and leaned over the table. "You got beans for brains? She was my friend." He looked over at Hattie. If there had been doubt before about Hattie Carter's role as housekeeper, it was dispelled by the look on her face. It was obvious that Hattie knew about Rita and didn't like it. But Singer regained control and said to me in an even tone, "Just a friend. I wouldn't never do nothin' to her." He glanced at Hattie. "Or *with* her." Hattie sniffed and her pencilled eyebrows lifted a fraction of an inch.

"Okay," Jackson said, "we'll leave it. She ever get you tickets to things?"

Singer sat down and answered, "All a' time. That's how she paid me back for the things I did. A patient she treated regular gave her tickets to pro games. She never used 'em. Passed 'em on to me." His smile was genuine. "We were one big 'you scratch my back I'll scratch yours' club."

Jackson turned to me. "Lieutenant?"

"Just a couple things. You know an Angelina Frontada?"

The dark brown eyes never flickered. "Never heard of her."

"Can you alibi the night of Rita's murder?"

"Every minute."

"How can you be so sure, a month later?"

"I can read the papers. Knew you'd come by some day." He grinned and added, "What took you so long?"

I couldn't help liking the guy, but I had a job to do.

"Like you to stop by the precinct tomorrow and sign a statement."

Outside in the car we sat quietly while I made a few notes in my little book. "So wha'd'ya think, Randy," I said finally.

"Don't believe a word he said."

"Rita Mendiola was a virgin."

"There's more'n one way to skin a cat."

"He says he has an alibi for that night."

"We'll check it out."

"He denies knowing Mrs. Frontada. Yet *she* knew *him*. Says he killed Rita." I enjoyed the role of devil's advocate, especially with a sharp cookie like Jackson.

But then Jackson switched roles. "I believe *her*, don't you?"

"She's a kook," I said, switching roles myself.

"She had his name," Jackson reminded me, "whether she's nuts or not."

"Remembered the name from the hospital somehow, and it came through in her trance."

Jackson started the car, made a U-turn, and said, "You're just bouncin' your own doubts off me, aren't you?"

I flicked a thumbnail against my teeth, a habit I have when I'm perplexed. "I don't know. I went over there half expecting to arrest a murderer. Now I'm not so sure. If anyone in this infernal triangle stuck a knife in Rita, I'd say it was the girlfriend. Or even the wife."

Jackson nodded. "Pretty nice place he's got there. And did you see the ice on the girlfriend's finger? And the gold chain? Pretty classy for a med tech's girlfriend."

"Maybe Hattie's got her own money." But I opened my book and made a note.

"Now who's the skeptic?"

"You're right. Goes with the job."

Singer came in the next morning and wrote out a full statement. His alibi seemed airtight. He claimed to have been home all day, went out from five to seven for supper with his wife, dropped her off while he went to the drugstore for cigarettes—a five-minute drive—and stayed home the rest of the night. At least it would be airtight if his wife corroborated it, and if she told the truth.

I called Mrs. Frontada, but she refused to be interviewed unless it was absolutely necessary. She could add nothing to what her husband had already told me. I sighed and said, "Perhaps we can wait a bit then."

I got out the coroner's report again. *Virgo intacta.* No doubt about it. Singer was telling the truth about his relationship with Rita Mendiola. And if he was telling the truth about that, was he lying about everything else? And where *did* he get his money? I set the machinery in motion to investigate the bank accounts of Albert Singer and Hattie Carter.

"And while you're at it," I added, "check out the Frontadas', too."

I was up most of the night and got to the station house late the next morning. I drank a pot of black coffee and then sat staring at the cheesecake calendar on the wall. I had an ugly thought and dialed Randy Jackson on the intercom. "What do we know about the movements of Dr. and Mrs. Frontada on the night of the murder?"

"Nothin', chief," Jackson said around a mouthful of hamburger.

"Get on it, will ya?"

"I don't follow."

"You don't have to."

I cleaned out my "urgent" box and began to wonder why the station was so quiet. Then in quick succession I got reports of two homicides a block apart. I spent the afternoon sorting them out, and was about to leave the station when my intercom buzzed.

"A Dr. Frontada to see you, Lieutenant Cellini."

"Send him in."

Dr. Frontada came in, sat down without a word, and peered at me through his thick glasses.

I leaned forward on my elbows. "Your wife declined to be interviewed, said she had nothing to add." I realized my voice had an accusatory edge to it, but Frontada missed it or ignored it.

"She has change her mind."

"When can I talk to her?"

"Tonight. But first I tell you something."

"Shoot."

"She has had another spell."

"Anything new?"

"That is why I am here. And why Angelina has decide to talk to you. First she repeat same story. Then she say if police need confirmation, they look for jewelry that Rita Mendiola gave Singer in last moment to try to save her life. He take jewelry but kill her anyway."

"What kind of jewelry?"

"Gold pendant and diamond ring."

I leaned back in my swivel chair and looked out the window at the swirling snow. Was this woman actually in communication with the spirit world? Could I credit it? And if not, why was Hattie Carter wearing a gold pendant and a diamond ring? On the other hand, wouldn't there be several dozen gold pendants and thousands of diamond rings within a ten-mile radius of the station house?

"What time will you be expecting me, doctor?" I asked.

Before Frontada could answer, the door flew open and Hattie Carter burst angrily into the room, followed by a policeman holding a .38 special in his outstretched hands.

"Freeze, lady," he shouted. "I tried to stop her, Lieutenant," he added unnecessarily as Hattie turned abruptly and held her hands out so that the policeman could see she was unarmed.

"Thanks, officer," I said, "I know this lady."

"You're gonna know me a hell of a lot better if you don't call off your pigs. Y'know what they're doin' now? Gettin' into my bank account, my checking account, into . . ."

"Calm down, Miss," I said. "They're working under my orders. If you've got nothing to hide, there's nothing to worry about, is there?"

I glanced at Dr. Frontada, and Hattie realized for the first time that someone else was in the room. She turned toward him slightly and for a moment seemed almost apologetic. I watched them closely, but saw no sign of recognition pass between them. But then Frontada's eyes fixed on the gold pendant and shifted to her right hand to stare at the ring. Just as quickly, he glanced at me, then averted his gaze and looked nonchalantly out the window.

Now, that's interesting, I thought.

Frontada rose to leave. "Eight tonight, Lieutenant?"

I nodded.

When the doctor had left, I motioned Hattie to a seat. "Long as you're here, there are a couple questions I'd like to ask you."

Haughtily she sat in the chair Frontada had vacated, leaned back in it, crossed her legs, and pumped her foot up and down. Pretty bitch, I thought. Make a man do lots of things he might not do otherwise.

"How long have you known Albert Singer?"

"About a year," she answered.

"Can we skip the housekeeper bit?"

She nodded.

"Did you know Rita Mendiola?"

Her eyes remained wary but her voice was controlled. "I knew Al went over there. I never met her."

"Can you alibi the night she was killed?"

I expected her to bite my head off. The glint in her eyes told me she wanted to, but she merely said, "No."

I couldn't ask for more than that and changed the subject. "Where did you get the pendant and ring?"

"From Al."

"When?"

She thought that one over. "About a month ago."

"Where'd he get them?"

"Never asked."

"Do you know the man who just left?"

"No."

"Do you work?"

"Off and on."

"Where?"

"Here and there." Then she saw that my face was turning several shades of purple and added, "As a cocktail waitress. Or hostess if I stay on long enough to work up."

"Does the name Frontada mean anything to you?"

Almost too quickly she said, "No."

At precisely 8 p.m. I rang the bell of the Frontadas' fashionable suburban home. The doctor himself let me in and led me into the living room.

The room was furnished with heavy, dark, over-stuffed chairs and sofas upholstered in a garish red. Huge marble lamps stood on intricately carved mahogany tables. The wall-to-wall carpet was a gaudy red, just barely matching the furniture. Expensive as hell, I thought, but I couldn't live here.

Mrs. Frontada was a little woman, smaller even than her husband, and looked to be about ten years younger. Her glossy black hair was mildly bouffant with a slight upturn at the ends, framing a pretty oval face. Bright black eyes with small epicanthal folds gave her a faintly oriental look. She was dwarfed by the massive furniture.

She was not in the mood for small talk. After just

the barest of civilities she told me about her last "visitation." Her English was considerably better than her husband's.

"This was the third one, you know, Lieutenant Cellini. And just the same as before, except that Ernesto says this time Rita talked about the jewelry. He has told you about that."

"A gold pendant and a diamond ring?"

"Yes."

"Where would Rita get things like that?"

"How would I know? But in the Islands, almost all Filipinas who can afford it—and not a few men—buy gold necklaces, pendants, chains, what have you. They're a good investment now, they're pretty, and the 'in' thing. And someone may have given her the ring. She was an attractive girl, apparently. Not surprising at all."

"Did you ever know Albert Singer?" I asked.

"Not really. It's a big hospital. But the name does seem vaguely familiar. I've probably seen it on the call rotation."

I turned to Frontada. "You didn't know the woman in my office this afternoon?"

"No."

"Did you recognize the jewelry she was wearing?"

Neither of the Frontadas were in the least perturbed by my question. He answered smoothly, without looking at his wife, "No, I am never seeing it before." He gazed steadily at me, expressionless.

Cool cats, I thought as I left and climbed into my car. But there was something there, I was sure of it. If Frontada had told his wife about Hattie Carter's jewelry, why didn't she react differently? She should have said *something* to me. If Frontada *hadn't* told her, shouldn't she have been curious enough to ask what jewelry we meant?

Randolph Jackson came into my office late the next afternoon. His smile was oddly perplexed. "I've got a few things, Mike."

"Wouldn't surprise me."

"First, there's nothing on the doctor at all. His bank account shows steady deposits of about three to four thousand a month. No checks for any significant amount that look the least odd. And on the night of the murder he was totally tied up with a heart attack victim in the Coronary Care Unit. Never left except for a few minutes at a time until well after midnight." He paused, looking down at his notes.

"Go on."

"Mrs. Frontada's account is flatter'n a pancake. Almost cleaned out just a month ago. To cash."

"And before?"

"Kept a steady account of about five thousand. Nothing unusual till a year ago, then suddenly frequent checks for five hundred to a thousand dollars, made out to cash. The doctor replenished it from his account by check."

"Her activities the night of the murder?"

"She was on duty at the hospital. From three to eleven."

"Sisters of Charity?"

"Right."

"That's where the doctor was, too?"

"No, he was at Wesley."

"Were you able to check on Angelina's activities that night? I mean, did she work steady all eight hours?"

"Hard to tell for sure. In the evenings the respiratory therapists go to the wards, give treatments in the patients' rooms. Also, they're on call to the operating room, and to the postanesthesia room if a patient needs respiratory assistance after surgery. Sometimes they help the intensive care nurses when there's trouble with the respirators that doesn't require a doctor's supervision. They do keep a log. There's a gap from nine to ten-thirty when Mrs. Frontada gave no treatments and wasn't in surgery or in ICU."

"Coffee break?"

"Possible. Pretty long."

"Or just nothing doing?"

Jackson shook his head. "Unlikely. Not in that hospital."

"It's time we got back to Albert Singer."

It was dark by the time we got out to West Washington. Singer was home. Hattie Carter was gone, and Selma, Singer's wife, was there. Singer was considerably more cooperative.

"I told Selma you guys'd be back," he said. "We've talked it over and I'm gonna come clean. There's no way I'm gonna take the rap for murder when I'm clean."

Selma Singer sat dejectedly behind the dining room table, toying with the deck of cards which Singer had used just two days before. "I know about Hattie Carter, Lieutenant Cellini."

Jackson interrupted. "Did you know about Rita Mendiola, too?"

She took a deep breath. "Yeah, I knew." Her tone indicated that she hadn't liked that either. I considered telling her that she didn't have to worry about

Singer's relationship with Rita, but decided it wouldn't help much now. Besides, she was still very much included in my list of suspects and anything that would help keep her off balance would be a plus for the good guys.

"I've told her everything, Lieutenant," Singer said. "About Rita and Hattie—especially Hattie. I knew it was all gonna come out, once Hattie told me you'd landed on the jewelry." He smiled almost wistfully. "How'd you guys figure that?"

"The jewelry was from Mrs. Frontada?" I asked.

"Yeah."

"And the five grand a month ago?"

"Yeah."

"Why?"

Singer told us his side of the story. It filled in enough of the missing pieces in the puzzle that Jackson and I practically ran down the stairs of that old row house.

"Frontadas?" he shouted as he climbed in on the driver's side.

"Burn a little rubber."

A block away from the doctor's house we could see the revolving light on the ambulance. Jackson flicked on the roof lights of the squad car and threaded his way through the cars and crowd of people gathered in the street. As we burst through the door, the ambulance crew came down the stairs, their collapsible stretcher unopened, their faces impassive.

I stopped them. "Who is it?"

"The woman."

"She's dead?"

"O.D."

"Overdose of what?"

"Search me, I just work here."

Two steps at a time, I raced up the stairs and almost collided with Dr. Frontada. The little doctor was sobbing uncontrollably and shook off my hand. "Not now, Lieutenant. Give me a few minutes."

We went downstairs with him, into his study, and let him cry. Slowly he regained control, finally said, "I think it is just another spell. I do not want to hear it again. An hour later I worry. I go up and find her unconscious. Not just trance. Unconscious. I try to wake her, give her stimulant by hypo, get no response. Finally I call ambulance, but it is too late." He wiped his face with a linen handkerchief. "Lieutenant Cellini, you can tell me what is happening?"

"You don't know?" I said gently.

He shook his head. "I know something is wrong. She just say, she say over and over, after you leave last night, 'They know, Ernesto; they know,' and I keep asking her what they know? And she will not tell me."

He got up and stood by the window, watching the ambulance pulling away. "We are try to save enough money to move back to Philippines where I can get part-time work. Semiretire, you know? We have land there. Were going to build nice house, maybe like this one, only bigger windows that catch breeze."

We waited. Frontada turned around and sat down. "All right, Lieutenant."

I looked at Jackson and tapped a front tooth with my thumbnail. "I'm not sure of all the details, but this is the way I've got it figured. You're not gonna like it."

Frontada nodded. "I must know some time."

"Yes, sir. Your wife knew Albert Singer a lot better than either of them let on."

The doctor's eyes widened in fear, then filled with tears.

"They met," I continued, "at a staff meeting in the hospital. He's a respiratory therapist. Muscular, good-looking guy. A year ago they started meeting regularly, usually on nights when she was supposed to be working at the hospital. She loaned him money—lots of it—up to a thousand a month—which he never paid back, of course. Then he got tired of her, even with all that money. She was ten years older and by then he had met Hattie Carter, the woman you saw in my office the other day."

"But she is pretty, look lot younger than she is," Frontada said, his voice breaking.

"Yes, sir," I said, thinking that even now he stuck up for her. "At about the same time Singer began stopping off at Rita Mendiola's place to do odd jobs for her. She gave him tickets to pro football games, things like that. We know for a fact that he never, well, he didn't ever go to bed with her. But Angelina thought he did. One day she actually saw him coming out of her apartment building. This is hard for me to tell you, doctor."

"Go on, I must know the truth."

"Yes, sir. She must have brooded a lot about it, knew she was losing Singer, figured it was because of Rita, and finally decided to do away with what she thought was her competition."

"Mother of God!"

"She slipped away from work one night when things

quieted down a little, went over to Rita's apartment, and killed her."

"Lieutenant! She wouldn't, oh God, she wouldn't." He buried his head in his hands.

I sat for a moment, knowing I had to go on, had to get this all over with, once and for all. Frontada would never rest until he heard the story, and once he did he could start to pick up the pieces again.

"She didn't count on anyone coming that time of night. But Singer did, to finish fixing the TV. He came up the stairs just as Angelina was coming out of the apartment. He pushed her back in and saw Rita lying there with a knife in her chest. He tried to revive her. When he saw that she was dead, he struck out at Angelina.

"But Singer wasn't raised in a Sunday school, doctor. And he didn't have all that much love for Rita. Your wife convinced him he'd be better off if he didn't say anything about the murder. She promised him five thousand cash. Then she took off her ring and gold pendant and gave them to him. Together they stripped off Rita's clothes, piled them on her body, poured kerosene on it, and lit it."

"My wife?" Frontada said. "She did that?"

"That's the way I see it, sir. And of course Singer wasn't satisfied with just the jewelry and the five grand. He gave the jewelry to his girlfriend and that was his first big mistake. The second was to continue to blackmail Angelina for everything she could sneak out of the house. His lockbox at the bank is jammed with jewelry. I suspect you'll be able to identify most of it."

"And that is why she is always short of money."

Frontada was almost rational again, his eyes staring, undried tears standing on his cheeks. "But why is she suddenly. . . ?" he started to ask, then evidently saw the answer himself.

I filled in for him. "She had to get rid of Singer. He was more than just a nuisance now. And no longer her lover. She knew she could never kill again, at least not a big strong man like Singer. She hit on this occult message thing and started to have visitations from the spirit world. And it almost worked. Even after we got Singer's story, we still had absolutely no proof that he was telling the truth. If she'd kept her cool during our interrogations, it would have come down to her word against Singer's. An unemployed black man against a doctor's wife. Who'd'ya think we'd've believed? But she overplayed it with the jewelry bit. Until then Singer could bluff it out, could keep his wife from knowing about Hattie Carter. But when we found out about the pendant and the ring, it didn't take him long to realize that a murder rap was the greater of two evils."

Jackson and I stood in the cold night watching the Frontada house lights go out one by one.

"There's still one thing I don't understand, Mike," Jackson said. "The note stuffed in Rita's mouth."

I looked at Jackson and smiled. "Oh, yeah, we keep forgetting about that, don't we? Well, we weren't supposed to find that note. Rita herself tried to destroy it, knowing that if it was found it would be damning evidence against someone she really liked— maybe loved. Perhaps she'd just made the note before Angelina came in. Anyway, she remembered it, and lived long enough to tear it off the pad and stuff it in her mouth before she collapsed. But she died before she could chew it up and swallow it. And of course neither Angelina nor Singer noticed it when they were stripping her and trying to burn down the house."

"Ironic, isn't it?"

"Yeah. She tried to destroy the one clue that eventually put us on the track. Angelina Frontada saw the write-up in the paper, saw the chance to frame Albert Singer, and the plan backfired."

China Blue

DAVID GATES

David Gates has been a freelance writer since
1970, working first as a film critic for the *Cambridge Phoenix*, *Time-Out*, and *Metro Boston*. Of
his two unpublished novels, one is a mystery. Of
"China Blue," Gates says: "The story took four
or five months to percolate. It's a dry run for a
detective novel about the past inhabiting the present."

The gallery ran the length of the house, facing north
and inviting a painterly natural light, but the high
French windows that gave on the garden were curtained with some opaque stuff, making the narrow
passage dark and uterine, its further reaches receding
into shadow like cherished memories. Gooseneck
portrait lamps illuminated the shallow glass-fronted
display cases spaced along the wall at irregular intervals, and the brilliantly colored butterflies mounted
in the cases sprang forward out of the surrounding
gloom as if beating against the windows to a lighted
room. *Lepidoptera*, Buddy recalled. It was all bugs
to him, but he wasn't about to let on to the widow.

"The China Blue," she was saying, taking his arm
and steering him down the hallway, "while not so
rare today as the more threatened species of genus
Parnassius, nor as highly prized among collectors as
certain other Asian examples of day-flying Sphinx

moth, is nevertheless a valued oddity. It was only discovered to exist toward the end of the last century—an instance of that enthusiasm for the natural sciences that characterized the late Victorians. The first recorded specimen is that presented to Czar Nicholas II in 1904, by members of a Russian survey expedition returning from the Kunlun Shan, in what is now Sinkiang Province in western China; hence its romantic nickname."

She halted, drawing his attention to a bare spot on the wall. Whatever had hung there had blocked the light, leaving a dark oblong patch about eighteen inches by twenty. Buddy realized she expected some comment from him.

"Didn't take up a lot of room," he remarked, hoping he sounded as if he were pondering a clue.

She disengaged her arm from his. "You don't have much feeling for entomology, do you, Mr. Margolies?" she asked.

"I wasn't the kind of kid who pulled the wings off flies, no," he said.

"Oh, *I* was," the widow said, brightly. "I was an exceedingly curious child."

I don't doubt it, Buddy thought.

"My husband—my late husband, the Senator—encouraged me in my interests," she went on. "I suppose he felt it kept me alive to, oh, possibilities, and I daresay he was right."

"You wouldn't get any argument from me," Buddy said. He didn't travel in circles where "daresay" was common usage. "Is this the only thing missing?" he asked.

"It's meant as a signal, you understand," she said, "as a reminder of my vulnerability."

She seemed to Buddy about as vulnerable as an anvil. "Is the collection insured?" he asked.

"Of course," she said, "but I haven't reported the theft. This is a private matter."

"How so?"

"I know who took it," she said.

"Who would that be?"

"My son, Roger."

"Why?"

"Why would he do such a thing? To injure me, to revenge himself, to spite the dead."

"Didn't he get along with his father?"

"His father? Oh," she said, impatiently, "Roger is the son of my first marriage."

"Ah-*hah*," Buddy said.

She treated him to a cold look. "The collection belonged to Senator Hatch," she said. "My *second* husband."

"Anyway," Buddy said, "Roger didn't get along with his stepfather, I take it?"

"They entertained a cordial dislike for each other."

"Any particular reason?"

"Isn't it obvious?" She arched her eyebrows. "Roger was no more than a child when I divorced and remarried. He desperately resented Harvey and behaved abominably. We enrolled him in a military academy at the earliest opportunity."

"How early was that?" Buddy asked.

"Do you count psychiatry among your many disciplines, Mr. Margolies?" she inquired in return.

"I'm just trying to get a rough idea of what your son's like, Mrs. Hatch," Buddy said. "It's always a good idea to know your adversary's mind."

"Indeed," she said.

"Is he hard up for money?" Buddy asked.

"I don't imagine so," she said. "In any event, the China Blue is of little value to anyone but me."

"How come?"

"You *catch* butterflies, Mr. Margolies," she explained, with some asperity. "One doesn't build a collection through acquisition, as one might indulge a passion for contemporary art or Hummel figurines. Any fool can *buy* things, after all, with the proper advice."

Buddy chewed on that one. "However," he said, "it's apparently already occurred to you that your son might offer to return the butterfly for a price."

"I have absolutely no intention of ransoming my own property back from Roger," she said. "I don't chew my cabbage twice."

Buddy thought that one through, too. "How far are you willing to go?" he asked.

"I beg your pardon?"

"If you won't pay him for it, am I supposed to just embarrass him into giving it back, or is it all right if I lean on him a little?"

"*Lean* on him?" She looked Buddy up and down rather doubtfully. "You're not very large," she observed.

"I'm no leg-breaker, if that's what you mean."

"Pity," the widow said.

Sumner Bradford was a senior partner in the State Street law firm of Cabot, Perkins, and Peabody. Their offices occupied three upper stories in one of the skyscrapers anchoring the downtown end of the highrise spine that ran from the waterfront to Back Bay. Buddy got off the express elevator at the forty-fourth floor and wondered if he'd died and gone to heaven. Actually, it put him in mind of a unisex hairdresser's. The atrium reception area was designed around hanging plants, track lighting, wall-to-wall salmon-tinted broadloom, blond wood with wrought-iron accents, and chromed tubular furniture. All it lacked was a throbbing sound system pumping out Lionel Richie, but not even the rustle of folding money and discarded briefs penetrated to the waiting room.

He wasn't kept waiting. Buddy found himself climbing to his feet as the lawyer crossed the lobby to greet him. Sumner Bradford was in his middle sixties, quite tall, with a wind-burned face and a yachtsman's squint. He was wearing a subdued three-piece pinstripe, cut in the European manner, and had the look of a man of wide influence and untroubled serenity. Buddy took him at face value.

Bradford led Buddy down the hall to a corner office. It had a view six hundred feet straight down the side of the building to King's Chapel burying ground. "Have a seat," the lawyer said. "How did your interview with Maida go?"

"She's a fascinating study," Buddy said.

"She is, indeed." Bradford sat down and swiveled his chair toward the windows, leaning back and lacing his fingers together over his tie. "I've known Maida Livingstone Hatch more than forty years," he continued, reflectively, "and she's never ceased to fascinate me. Her husband and I were in the same class at Harvard, you know—her late husband, Harvey Hatch. He was sweet on her, even then. We all were, come to think of it." He shook his head ruefully. "And then she went and married that horse's ass,

Alden Winthrop. Well." He swung his chair back in Buddy's direction. "There was one summer Harvey and I were working in a resort hotel in upper New York state, and Maida was staying with relatives near Skaneateles. We used to double date, Harvey and me, with Maida and her cousin Polly." He smiled. "We thought we were pretty hot stuff. Followed the swing bands around the Finger Lakes. Harvey had a ten-year-old Packard with bald tires and bad springs—cut the shift lever down so it wouldn't interfere with his front-seat work." Bradford gave a short bark of a laugh.

"You and Senator Hatch go back a long way, then," Buddy said.

The lawyer chuckled. "Since God was a boy," he said. "Graduated from college together, wound up in the same outfit during the war." He leaned forward. "China-Burma-India, flying supplies over the Hump to Stilwell and Chennault. Christ, it went down to forty below, sometimes. The pilots called it The Aluminum Trail, so many planes went down." He reached for one of the many photographs on his desk and faced it toward Buddy. "That's us," he said. "Harvey's the kid on the left with the fifty-mission crush and the .45 in a shoulder holster."

Buddy leaned forward. It was a group portrait of an air crew gathered under the wing of a C-46, the men dressed in a variety of nonregulation outfits: Sherpa hats and silk aviator's scarves and flight jackets embroidered with Rita Hayworths and dragons. The fuselage of the plane was stenciled with dozens of miniature camels, like cutouts from cigarette packages.

"Those are the number of times we made it in to Kunming and back," Bradford said, indicating the camels.

Buddy nodded. He was just thirty, but the fliers looked like high school freshmen to him. "You were just kids," he said, without thinking.

The lawyer grinned at him. "We didn't know our ass from a hole in the ground," he said, "but the world was our oyster. Was it ever. Boy, the way the women looked at you in uniform." He laughed, not at all self-consciously. "It was all ours for the taking," he mused, turning the picture back around and studying it. "And we took it, those of us who lived to tell the tale."

"That's where the Senator got his start—China," Buddy said.

"A good war record never hurt a man's political chances," Bradford said, "not in Massachusetts."

"What about Alden Winthrop?"

"What about him?"

"What did he do in the war?"

"Oh, Alden was stationed here in the Navy Yard. Spent the duration close to home. Never saw action."

"So, in effect, Roger's mother dumped her first husband for a war hero," Buddy said.

The lawyer regarded him with some amusement. "You're not married, are you, Mr. Margolies?" he asked.

"Nope," Buddy said.

"Let me tell you, being married is a little like being rich: it ain't what it's cracked up to be, but it lives up to its bad press."

"I've never been rich, either," Buddy said.

"Well," the lawyer said, "I've been both."

"Tell me a little bit about Roger," Buddy suggested. "His mother seems to think he stole the China Blue."

"I wouldn't doubt it for a minute," the lawyer said. "I'd have to say Roger's been a bit of a disappointment—to his mother, to Harvey, to me, to just about everybody—maybe even to himself. Never really settled down, never stuck to anything. Moonstruck. I don't know whether to ascribe it to heredity or environment. I suppose I'd prefer to blame it on circumstance."

"You don't think much of his father, then," Buddy said.

"Alden? Nobody does, but I think the world of Maida Hatch. It's just too damn bad she had to have a boy like that, moody and unworldly and secretive."

"Is he short of cash?"

The lawyer thought a moment. "I couldn't say," he allowed, "but I shouldn't think this business has anything much to do with money, except as a means of keeping score."

"Why not?" Buddy asked.

"My guess is that Roger's trying to punish Maida for divorcing Alden."

"Is he still around?"

"Alden? I'd imagine so," the lawyer said. "I'd certainly know if he were dead." He gave Buddy a crooked smile. "Alden was a member of the Class of '41 with the rest of us, you see," he said, "although he wasn't a part of our crowd, particularly, and none of us has bothered to keep up. He dropped out of sight some time ago."

"Would you have an address on him?"

"I'm afraid I don't," the lawyer said, "but I

could make some inquiries. Why your interest in Alden? Aren't Roger's whereabouts more to the point?"

Buddy shrugged. "It's a handle," he said, getting to his feet. "Nobody's able to tell me where Roger is."

"I doubt if even Roger would be able to tell you," Bradford said, with a grimace.

"How about the insurance file?" Buddy asked. "It might be a help if I had a picture of the goods."

"I think we can manage that," the lawyer said, smiling.

"And Mrs. Hatch said something about a check, as I recall."

"By all means. Anything else?"

"My mind's a blank," Buddy said.

"Hey, lady," Buddy whispered hoarsely, slipping out from behind a life-size reproduction of a Tlingit totem carving and falling in step with Clare Churchill, "can I interest you in fencing a hot moth?" He handed her the Polaroid.

"A China Blue," she said, without breaking stride, looking at the photograph front and back. "From the Hatch collection."

"How can you tell?"

"The best specimens are currently in the Moscow Zoological Museum, for one thing," she said. "Mrs. Hatch is one of the few private American collectors to own one. And for another, her name is stamped on the back."

Buddy grinned at her. "How would I go about selling it?" he asked.

Clare shook her head. "I don't think you could,"

she said. "You certainly wouldn't be able to raise much cash on it unless the entire collection were for sale. Is it?" she asked, handing him back the photograph with an inquiring look.

"Search me," Buddy said. "Do you guys have one of these?"

"Sure," Clare said, detouring around a mockup of an Aztec ziggurat. "Since when have you been interested in the arcana of the insect world?"

"Since I endorsed the check," Buddy said. "Can I see it?"

"Right this way."

They crossed from anthropology into the natural history wing. Clare led him past long glass cases of stuffed reptiles, birds, mammals, and fish, and came at last to insects.

"The picture doesn't do it justice," Clare said, pointing out the exhibit.

"No, it doesn't," Buddy agreed, peering at the display. "That sucker is *blue*."

"Pigmentation in butterflies is primarily the reds, yellows, blacks, and whites," she told him. "True greens and blues—the iridescents—are highly unusual; our perception of blue, for example, normally being the result of refracted light."

"Is this?"

"No. This is a genuine blue, like the South American Morpheus, which was at one time used in the preparation of special inks for printing currency."

"Inks that couldn't be synthetically duplicated?"

"The French government had a monopoly on their importation, using convict labor to collect them. They come from Guiana. I assume you've heard of Devil's Island?"

"I saw the movie," Buddy said. "Can't they come up with something like it in the lab nowadays?"

"You could probably come pretty close," Clare said, "but not close enough to stand up under sophisticated spectrographic analysis. There's still a difference between organic and artificial. After all," she reminded him, "people have been trying for years to develop a satisfactory chemical substitute for chocolate without much success."

"I take the hint," Buddy said. "Let's go for a walk. I'll buy you an ice cream cone at Schrafft's."

"You must want something," Clare said.

"What I want," Buddy said, "is an ice cream cone."

Coming back through the Harvard Yard after lunch, Buddy used Clare and her faculty ID to get past the receptionist at the Alumni Office without having to lie. He consulted the Class of 1941's Fortieth Reunion Report, it being the most recent, but found nothing under Alden Winthrop's name other than the fact that he hadn't returned a questionnaire. Buddy backtracked to the Twenty-Fifth Reunion Report and got an address. It was almost twenty years out of date, but it was a start. He abandoned Clare in an advanced state of irritation and made his way across the bridge to Brighton.

The house turned out to be a small frame bungalow on the back side of Chestnut Hill, in a less-than-desirable location behind the cardinal's villa, down the hill from Boston College, isolated in the elbow of a cul-de-sac with two-family double-deckers leading in to it and out again on a dead end. The archdiocese appeared to own most of the land in back, so the house stood at the head of a sort of park, playgrounds and softball fields, and its nearest neighbor was three hundred yards to the left.

Buddy pulled up in front and went to the door. Two days' papers lay on the porch. He rang.

He waited, and had a strong sensation that movement was coming to an apprehensive halt inside. He could have been mistaken. The door opened.

"Yeah?" The guy who answered the door was in his forties, clean-shaven, with a prison haircut, dressed in chino slacks and a well-laundered denim shirt. Buddy didn't think he was Alden.

"Mr. Winthrop?"

"Never heard of him."

There was somebody else hovering just out of sight. Buddy could feel someone there, from the way the guy in the doorway was standing. "I'm looking for Roger Winthrop," he said. "He used to live here."

"Nobody here by that name, pal," the guy said, and closed the door.

Buddy went back down the steps to the car, shrugging mentally. He could feel them watching him from the house. He cranked the ignition, churned the engine, and drove off. Twenty years, he thought, what the hell. There would have been a time, probably before the war, when the neighborhood was just the ticket for a young couple starting out, but it had gone downhill. Buddy wondered if he'd interrupted the guy in the middle of whacking his wife.

He headed in to town, found a place to park near Massachusetts General, and hiked up the hill to Government Center and the JFK Building.

The women behind the counter in the Veterans Administration offices had the look, wary and impatient, that Buddy usually associated with civil servants. One was young and Irish; one was middle-aged and Latin; and the third was in-between and black. When it was his turn, he drew the Latin.

"Hi. I'm trying to track down a Navy vet, name of, uh, Alden Winthrop," he said. He fished a card out of his wallet and made a show of consulting some notes on the back. "This was during the Second World War. My dad told me I should look this guy up, but, trouble is, he's not in the phone book and the address I've got for him is out of date. Can you help me find him? I mean, can you look him up for me, see if he's still in town, see if he's even alive, for that matter? I know it's not much to go on, but I figured, what the hay, the guy was a sailor, right? So here I am, bright and early." He smiled—winsomely, he hoped.

"Service number?"

"Hunh? No."

She regarded him balefully. "Do you have his dates of service?" she asked.

"Gee, I don't know," Buddy said. " '41 to '45, I guess. That was when my dad was in. They worked in the Navy Yard, if that's any help."

"I'll see what we can do," she said. "Take a seat over there on the left. We'll call you if we have any information. Name?"

"Hertz," Buddy told her. "Dick Hertz, Jr."

He took a seat. An old guy with a bum leg shuffled over and eased into the chair next to his. "Hey, Sarge," the old guy asked him, "you got a smoke on you?"

"Sorry," Buddy said.

The old guy had a bare quarter-inch of smoldering Chesterfield stuck to his lower lip. It looked like the ashes were about to fall behind his teeth. "Tried to quit, myself," the old guy said. "More than once. Couldn't hack it. That's a joke, son." He went into a raspy spasm of coughing. It sounded to Buddy like his lungs were jumping up his throat. "I'm a Golden Shellback," the old guy said, catching his breath. "Out near Tarawa that happened, where them Marines took such a shellacking. You a Navy man?"

"Sorry about that, too," Buddy said.

"Don't make no never-mind," the old guy said. "No pain, no gain, that's what I say." He leaned over toward Buddy confidentially. "Got this off Cavite," he said, poking his bad leg, "the Philippines. Fell down a gangway. Didn't get no Purple Heart for that." He paused, looking around as if he were expecting someone. "Just a broken-down old gimp wanting somebody to talk to, that's me," he said. "You tell me if I'm bothering you."

"You're not bothering me," Buddy said.

"You're okay, kid. You're okay." He looked down at the floor and spat tobacco flakes at his shoes. "Sonsabitches," he muttered.

Forty minutes went by very slowly. Buddy let his eyes glaze over, and pretended he was riding the subway.

"Hertz?" a voice called, finally. "Mr. Hertz?"

Buddy didn't look around. He waited.

"Who's Dick Hertz, please?"

Buddy got up smiling and limped to the counter.

The VA hospital was out in Roslindale, just beyond the Arnold Arboretum, but the six-bed ward Alden Winthrop was in didn't have a view of any exotic trees, just the back end of an industrial park. Alden was in the bed nearest the door. He was napping.

303

There was a guy not much older than Buddy sitting in a straight-backed chair by the bed, watching over Alden's troubled sleep. He was a big man, about the size of the late Dan Blocker, and the chair seemed scaled for a child.

"Hello, Roger," Buddy said. He was pretty sure he'd guessed right.

The big man reared around in his seat. "Oh," he said, and turned back. "I should have known you'd be along."

"Did you, now?" Buddy asked.

"Nothing personal, fella," Roger said, not bothering to look at Buddy, "somebody like you always shows up, sooner or later."

Buddy fetched a chair and set it down next to Roger's. The two of them sat there and watched Alden. "How do you mean, somebody like me?" Buddy asked.

"Process servers, skip tracers, insurance investigators, probation officers," Roger said. "Which're you?"

"Private investigator," Buddy said.

"See?" Roger looked at his hands. "What's he supposed to have done now?"

It took Buddy a moment to understand the question. "Just routine," he said. He fished a stick of gum out of his pocket and took his time unwrapping it. "What's his trouble?" he asked, popping the gum in his mouth.

"Booze," Roger said, looking at Buddy straight on for the first time. "I thought I had him dried out for a while, even got him into a halfway house, but he fell off the wagon and now he's back in detox. Next time it'll kill him."

"Most likely," Buddy said, working the gum around in his cheek with his tongue. "How long'd you have him in the halfway house?"

"Week and a half," Roger said, "and I had to move heaven and earth to get them to take him in the first place. What happens? A couple of his old pals show up, smuggle him in a bottle, and the next thing you know, they're down in the laundry room having a party. They chased the two guys out, but they had to call an ambulance for Alden."

"Have you been nursemaiding him for a while?"

"Off and on," Roger said. "He's cagey, like most drunks, I guess. Every once in a while he throws me off the scent. Last time was a couple of months ago. I found him living out of a carton in an alley off Clarendon."

Buddy nodded. "It's a long haul," he said, "and you can't do it without him."

"My mother did," Roger said.

"Your mother did what?"

"Did without him. Cut his heart out."

"He must have been worrying that injury a long time," Buddy observed. "By now, it's just another alibi."

"Don't I know it," Roger said. He turned his attention back to Alden.

Buddy didn't think Roger's father looked in such hot shape. Compared to his classmate Sumner Bradford, for instance, sleek and sassy, Alden seemed twice his actual age. His skin was the color of glazing putty, puffy around the eyes but slack on his jowls. The flesh of his bare arms was stringy and loose, and the long body under the bedclothes was nothing but bones. Buddy estimated Alden didn't weigh more than one-thirty. He wondered if the old soak's legs would even support that much. He was startled when he saw the man was awake and studying him.

"Doesn't look like much, does it?" Alden asked in a husky voice, grinning at Buddy.

"Can't say that it does," Buddy said, smiling back.

"You a friend of my son's?" Alden asked.

"I try to keep him out of trouble," Buddy said. Roger gave him a curious look.

"You got your hands full," Alden said, closing his eyes. His lips parted slightly, and his breath whispered in his throat.

"We should talk," Buddy murmured to Roger.

"Why not?" Roger said. "Watch him while I go to the bathroom, will you?" He stood up, and Buddy moved his chair to let him by.

Alden opened his eyes as soon as Roger was out of the room. "He's got a lot to learn," Alden said, squinting at Buddy. "Maida hire you?"

"She's got a bee in her bonnet about a butterfly," Buddy told him.

Alden began to twitch and make a funny creaking sound, and Buddy looked around in some alarm for the emergency call button before he realized Alden was laughing. "She's a tough nut to crack, that one," Alden wheezed. He winked lasciviously at Buddy. "Not that it can't be done," he added.

"How so?" Buddy asked.

"Maida and I *had* to get married, if you know what I mean," Alden said. He put a bony finger to his lips. " 'S no secret."

"I bet it's news to Roger," Buddy commented.

"It's *all* news to Roger," Alden said, "the poor

sap." He made an effort to lean up onto his elbow. "You know they bought me off?" he whispered.

"Who?"

"Harvey Hatch and that prick, Skip Bradford. Tight as two ticks, those bastards from Leverett House. Paid me to get lost, ain't that a kick? A remittance man." He lay back with an exhausted smirk and his eyes fluttered closed. "They tried to get me," he said, half to himself, "but I got them first."

Buddy waited for more, but there wasn't any more. The light in the room grew cloudy as the sun started down, and supper trays clattered in the corridor. Buddy sat there in the gathering dusk and thought about disappointments, drunkenness, and death.

He gave Roger a lift home from the hospital. They rode with the windows down. It was getting cool, but the balminess of the late spring day still hovered in the air.

"I have to tell you," Buddy said to Roger, "I didn't come to the VA looking for Alden, I came looking for you. Your mother thinks you've got her property, and she wants it back."

"Sorry?" Roger said, turning from the window.

Buddy went through it again.

"It doesn't have anything to do with me," Roger said. "It's out of my hands."

"What is?"

Roger didn't answer. He was gazing out the window again.

After a while, Roger roused himself to give Buddy directions. Buddy had been out in this neck of the woods only that morning, and when they hung a left at the Chestnut Hill Reservoir, he felt vaguely uneasy. It wasn't until Roger pointed him into the dead-end terrace across from St. John's Seminary that Buddy's spirits really sank, but he was in too deep to get kosher with Roger now.

The little bungalow at the end of the street was dark.

"Wasn't this your father's house once?" Buddy asked Roger.

"It's the house I grew up in," Roger said.

"Who lives here now?"

"I do," Roger said, sounding surprised. He shifted his considerable weight in the seat to face Buddy.

Buddy kept his own counsel.

"I bought it," Roger explained. "It was for sale two years ago, and I bought it. I thought it might help me sort things out for myself, and I wanted Alden to have a place to come home to."

"Does he mean that much to you?"

"I think so," Roger said, looking doubtful. "I sometimes wonder, though, whether it's actually him I care about, or only just me."

"I don't see the harm in it," Buddy said, "I honestly don't. What difference does it make, so long as you do the right thing in the end?" The house looked the same way it had in the afternoon. The papers were still lying on the porch.

"Can you come in for a minute?" Roger asked.

Buddy pretended to be thinking about it.

"You're easy to talk to," Roger said. "I need somebody to talk to."

"I can see that," Buddy said. He pulled forward into the empty driveway. "Where's your car?" he asked.

Roger looked bashful. "I never learned to drive," he said.

"You really are the left-out kid, aren't you?"

"No," Roger said, defensively. "I get along."

Buddy followed Roger up the walk. Roger fumbled with the keys, managed the lock, and stepped inside. Buddy hung back for a moment, but it was obvious there was nobody lurking in wait. Roger turned on the lights as Buddy closed the door behind him.

"Holy smoke," Buddy said, looking around, "you've been a bachelor too long, Roger."

The living room was to the left of the entry hall, and the dining room to the right. Both of them looked as though they'd been hit by mortar fire.

"Oh, my God," Roger whispered, taking a half-dozen hesitant steps into the living room and then stopping stock-still.

Pictures had been razored out of their frames and the stuffing torn out of the furniture. Whatnots and ceramic bric-a-brac had been smashed. The stereo speakers were kicked in, the drapes pulled down, books yanked indiscriminately off the shelves, and the contents of a large desk in the corner scattered across the floor. Even the ashes had been raked out of the fireplace and the cinders ground into the rug. Shredded paper and broken glass were everywhere.

"Bambi Meets Godzilla," Buddy murmured aloud, moving forward into the room.

"You, you—*stinker*," Roger said in a choked voice.

Buddy turned quickly in his direction. Roger's fists were clenched and he was shaking with fury. "Oh, brother," Buddy muttered. There was no question in his mind that Roger could twist him like a coathanger. Buddy held his hand out in front of him and shook his head as he backed toward the doorway. "You got me wrong, Roger," he said.

"You sugared me," Roger said. "You sugared me good, and the whole time you had your eye on me, this was going on."

"Not my style, friend," Buddy said.

Roger had a wild light in his eye. Buddy decided not to say anything else. He backed into the hall. Roger stayed put. Buddy didn't know whether to stand his ground or make a run for it.

Roger's shoulders hunched, and he began to weep, silently.

"Aw, nuts," Buddy said to himself. He stepped tentatively forward into the living room again, glass fragments crunching beneath his shoes. Roger shivered and wept. Buddy put his arms awkwardly around him. It was like embracing a large, damp, and unlovely dog. Roger sagged hugely against him, heavy and male, and cried into Buddy's neck. His face, his whole body, felt feverishly hot. Buddy patted Roger between the shoulder blades. Slowly, Roger seemed to recover, adjusting his posture and taking in air in great gulps. Buddy let his hands fall away.

"I'm really sorry," Roger said.

"Jesus, Roger, there isn't anything to apologize for," Buddy said.

He led him into the dining room and righted a chair. Roger sat down. Buddy surveyed the damage. The drawers to the sideboard had been pulled out and then kicked to pieces. Silverware was thrown around the room. A glass-fronted china cabinet had been tipped over and methodically broken into splinters. The bottles on the bar tray had all been smashed, and the room reeked of alcohol and sweetened mixers. Buddy went into the kitchen.

It was worse, if anything. Cracked eggs, burst milk cartons, broken jelly jars, and pulped fruit were all over the place, mixed up with flour and rice and dry cereal. A quart jar of mayonnaise had been dropped at arm's length on top of the stove, and gelatinous blobs of goo were congealing in the burners. Buddy found a roll of paper towels, ran a couple of them under the faucet, and brought them out to Roger so he could wipe his face.

"Come on," Buddy said, "let's get out of here."

Roger nodded dumbly and followed Buddy.

They drove in to town and ate at a German restaurant on Commonwealth Ave. Buddy ordered sauerbraten; Roger had the knockwurst, bockwurst, and bauernwurst plate, with side orders of potato salad and cabbage. They were outsize helpings, and Roger wolfed his food. His eating habits left a lot to be desired, but Buddy chalked it up to grief. A boy only a mother could love, but, then, Buddy reflected, she didn't much seem to, either. He chose not to voice these thoughts.

"Are you planning to call the cops?" he asked Roger.

"Do you think I should?"

"I think you should, yes," Buddy said, "and you ought to call a cleaning service for an estimate."

"What do I tell them?"

"Who, the cops? They'll ask you what's missing, and then they'll write it off as vandals."

"*You* don't think it was vandals."

"No," Buddy admitted. "I think it was pros, and they're sending you a message, whatever the message might be, but you'd know better than I would."

"I'm not going back to that, that . . . devastation. Not tonight. I can't face it."

"I don't blame you," Buddy said.

He took Roger back to his place and made him up a bed on the couch. Roger took his shoes off and lay down in his clothes.

Buddy turned out the lights. "You okay?" he asked.

"I'm okay," Roger said, quietly. "I'm fine, thanks."

"We'll talk in the morning," Buddy said, heading for bed.

"They wouldn't have wrecked my whole house if they'd found what they were looking for," Roger said. "That's the message."

"I think you're right," Buddy said, "and it probably means they'll be back, too, to look again."

"I was always good at finding things," Roger said. "When I was little, I could always find things my mother lost, rings and keys and stuff." His breathing had grown shallower, and his voice less distinct. "Sometimes I took things myself," he went on, almost inaudible in the darkness. "I meant to give them back, but I'd hide them, and then I'd find them again and claim the reward."

Buddy stood silent, his hand on the doorjamb.

"My mother was very angry when she found out," Roger whispered. "The Boy Who Cried Wolf, she called me."

Don't press your luck, Buddy told himself.

"I took some of Harvey's things, once," Roger murmured, "but he never noticed they were missing."

Buddy pondered that a minute. "Like what?" he asked, softly.

But Roger had fallen asleep.

Buddy figured he might as well sleep on it, himself.

"Lieutenant Wagner, please."

"One moment, sir," the switchboard operator said. "Will you hold?"

Buddy held.

"Metro Division, Wagner speaking."

"Ken? Buddy Margolies."

"You're up early," Wagner said. "What can I do for you?"

"I need a favor."

"What else is new? You working on a case?"

"Looks like a bugnapping," Buddy said.

"What's the scoop?" Wagner asked.

"Man named Winthrop, first name, Alden. Age about sixty-five. Might or might not have done time anywhere in the last ten or twenty years. Can you find out for me if he has a record?"

"I'll see what I can do," Wagner said. "Can I call you back or what?"

"I don't know where I'll be," Buddy said. "How about I call you back?"

"I have to be over at the Saltonstall Building at ten-thirty. What about lunch?"

"Jake Wirth's?"

"Noon," Wagner said. "You're buying."

"No problem."

"That's what you think," Wagner said, and hung up.

Roger was still snoozing on the couch. Buddy left him a note propped up against the coffeemaker. He got in his car and drove out to the house in Brighton.

There was a cream-colored Mercedes parked in Roger's driveway, so Buddy pulled around the circle and parked on the street. The front door was on the latch. Buddy couldn't remember whether Roger had bothered to lock up the night before. He walked in.

Maida Hatch was standing in the living room amid the debris, clasping a pocketbook.

"It was a hell of a party," Buddy said. "Sorry you missed all the fun."

She turned toward him by degrees, first her face, then her shoulders and upper body, then her hips and knees, and lastly her feet. "What happened here?" she asked.

"A deed of dreadful note," Buddy said. "Macbeth says that to Mrs. Macbeth, if you take my meaning."

"You think me a monster, don't you?"

"I haven't heard much evidence to the contrary," Buddy said. "Why didn't you tell me Roger was a thief?"

"I did," she said.

"No," Buddy said, "I don't mean now. I mean when he was a kid. Things would turn up mysteriously missing, but Roger was always able to bring them to light again, for a price. A regular Artful Dodger. That's why you sent him to military school, in the end. How long did he last, by the way?"

"You're no fool, Mr. Margolies," she said, trying a smile on him.

"I've been called worse."

"I'm sure you have," the widow said.

"Roger hasn't lost his touch, from what I hear," Buddy said. "He found his father, for instance, more than once, although in Alden's case, it wasn't Roger

314

who lost him accidentally on purpose, it was your husband and his lawyer. I wouldn't mind hearing your side of the story."

"Where is Roger?"

"Turning over a new leaf, if he's got any sense," Buddy said.

"Roger never had any sense," his mother said. "Oh, damn." She fumbled in her bag for a tissue, turning her head away from him, but not before Buddy saw her eyes bright with tears. He didn't think it was an act, but he wasn't going across the room to hug her, either, as he had Roger.

"This was your house, too, once," Buddy reminded her. "Does it give you any satisfaction to see it demolished like this?"

"No," she said, quietly. Then she got mad. "What do you know about it, you little snot-nose?" she spat out, rounding on him in a fury. "You and your phony world-weary attitude and your cheap psychology, all out of books, what do you know about ruined lives and hurting people?"

"I've made some bad calls," Buddy admitted.

"I'll bet you have," she snapped.

"Who's the one getting hurt here, anyway?" Buddy snapped back, getting hot under the collar. "You're nursing a grudge that's forty years old, and your son's paying the price."

"We all pay the price," Maida said, recomposing herself into her usual glacial calm now that Buddy had lost his cool. "I paid yours," she reminded him.

Sumner Bradford walked into the room. He didn't seem at all surprised to see Buddy. "This is some Godawful mess," the lawyer said, cheerfully.

"Good help is hard to find," Buddy said.

"Not if you know the right people," Bradford replied. He turned toward the widow. "Maida?" he inquired. "If you're ready to go?"

She brushed past Buddy and went out the door and down the steps to the Mercedes. Buddy and the lawyer followed in her wake.

"She's upset," Bradford said.

"*She's* upset," Buddy said. "You told me you didn't have the slightest idea where either of the Winthrops were."

"I didn't," the lawyer said.

"I don't buy it," Buddy said. "I don't much like being used as a stalking horse, counsellor."

"I bear Roger no ill will, Mr. Margolies, I assure you," the lawyer said. "In fact, the reverse."

"He always speaks very highly of you, too," Buddy said.

"Since you're obviously in touch with Roger, Mr. Margolies," Bradford said, "I'd appreciate your giving him a message from me."

"Shoot."

"Ten cents on the dollar," the lawyer said. "He won't get a better offer." He went down the steps and walked to the car.

Buddy stood on the porch and watched them back into the street and drive away.

He went back into the house, closing the door carefully behind him. Drifting through the disheveled rooms, he had no sense of anybody's ever having really lived here. Roger had tried to camp out in his father's life, after a fashion, or a life he imagined for his father, but Alden's life had long since been wrecked and abandoned, as thoroughly as this house and its history.

Poking through the scattered detritus around the desk in the living room, Buddy came across a boy's scrapbook. The inside front cover was inscribed ROGER LIVINGSTONE WINTHROP/27 EDGEMERE TERRACE/BOSTON/MASSACHUSETTS/U.S.A./NORTH AMERICA/EARTH/THE SOLAR SYSTEM/THE GALAXY/THE UNIVERSE in the loopy script, half cursive, half block printing, of a six- or seven-year-old. Leafing through the stiff pages, Buddy found old newspaper stories about forgotten events and oddities, certificates of archery awards from day camp, a picture of a children's birthday party, a drawing of a horse, some pressed and crumbling botanical samples, and some Grape Nuts boxtops. Then the character of the souvenirs changed.

First, there was a photograph of nine young men standing on a float with a river behind them. Eight of them were holding long oars upright, with the letter H on the blades, and the ninth held a small megaphone. Buddy lifted the picture away from the page. The mucilage gave way, and he turned the picture over. Written on the back, in a different handwriting, was the legend, "A Nifty Nine," and the date, 1938. Buddy had the feeling a girl or a young woman had written that, and he suspected it was Maida Livingstone Hatch. He studied the photograph again. He couldn't recognize the Sumner Bradford of forty-odd years before, but he sensed he was there, and most likely Harvey Hatch, too; members of a freshman rowing crew. Here was Roger the secret agent at work again, trying to reinvent the past for himself.

Further along, Buddy found an article cut from an old issue of *Life*, about the Hump airlift, and then there was some material about V-J Day, but beyond this, the scrapbook was empty. When the war was over, of course, Maida had divorced Alden and married Harvey, but why had Roger collected memorabilia about a man he didn't know, and then stopped when that man became his stepfather?

Buddy flipped through the blank pages. At the back, another piece of clipped newsprint had been tucked, but not glued, and it fluttered out onto the desk. Although there was no dateline, it was recent, from the condition of the paper, and Buddy leaned over to read it.

> The People's Republic of China continues to maintain its exemption from liability in a $41.3 million default judgment involving Imperial Chinese railway bonds. A class action suit brought on behalf of the bondholders seeks repayment of principal and interest. The plaintiffs have threatened to attach two jetliners, part of China's fleet in the United States, as compensation. The U.S. Foreign Sovereign Immunities Act allows such seizures in some cases. The suit involves 5 percent Hukuang Railways Sinking Fund Gold Loan debentures, which were issued in 1911 for the construction of a railroad that still runs between Canton in the south to Peking in the north. They have been in default since the 1930s, well before the Chinese Communist government took over in 1949.

Buddy stuck the clipping in his pocket. Ten cents on the dollar, he thought to himself. And people still wonder Who Lost China?

———

Buddy crossed Washington Street and walked up Bromfield toward Tremont. Sunlight glanced off the spire of the Old South Meeting House, but the even-numbered side of Bromfield was still in shadow. Buddy went up the stairs next to Little Jack Horner's Joke Shop. There was a jeweler on the second floor, and Saul Lasky's office was on the third.

Saul was sitting at the window in his swivel chair with a pair of binoculars, watching the aerobics class in the building across the street. "Hey, kid," he said, without lowering the glasses. Tax season was just over, but Saul's desk was awash in paperwork.

"How about explaining a sinking fund debenture to me?" Buddy asked.

"Simple," Saul said, not moving from his observation post. "Here's how it works: you pony up the gimme to get something rolling, and they pay you interest on your investment every year, say, or whatever the reporting period is, and they pay you a piece of the principal at the same time, so each time they make a payment they retire some capital indebtedness, and since they're in hock to you for less, they pay you less interest. The amount of capital funding sinks. See?"

"What if they don't pay off?"

"The unpaid interest is added to the principal amount, so instead of sinking, the kitty rises, like yeast. You got a for instance?"

"Imperial Chinese railway bonds."

"Confederate money," Saul said. "In the first place, you can't sue a government. In the second place, the original deal was made with the Dowager Empress Moo Goo Gai Pan, back in the Stone Age, and the country's gone through two, maybe three revolutions in the meantime. And in the third place, the Reds say, you want to sue somebody, sue Chiang Kai-shek. I doubt if you could get a dime to the dollar."

"Funny you should say that," Buddy said.

The exercisers across the way took a break and Saul put down the binoculars. "The Peking government has been stonewalling on this, but the preliminary rulings have gone against them, and they just took on a big-time American law firm to handle the case. It doesn't mean diddly-squat, just that they've decided to contest the case in a domestic jurisdiction."

"You think it's pie in the sky?"

"I don't think there's the chance of a wet wonton in Latvia that they'll pay a nickel," Saul said. "Between the Reagan administration and the big guns at Cabot, Perkins, they'll blow the plaintiffs out of the water."

"The Chineses government hired Cabot, Perkins, Peabody?"

"Yeah."

Buddy sat there feeling deaf, dumb, and blind. "You know a Sumner Bradford?" he asked, finally.

"I know the name," Saul said. "A rainmaker. Makes clients fall out of the clear blue sky. You hire a guy like that because he has lunch with the likes of Zero Agnew or Harvey Hatch, not because he edited the *Harvard Law Review*, you know what I mean?"

"Yeah," Buddy said, "I know what you mean." He rubbed his hand over his face. "Listen, Saul," he asked, "have you ever seen one of those railroad bonds?"

"Picture in the newspaper, couple of weeks ago."

"Can you describe what they look like?"

Saul shrugged. "Like any other kind of security," he said. "It'd be about eleven inches by fourteen, heavy parchment bond, printed letterpress, with embossed seals, signatures of the principal officers, that kind of thing. It would have a decorative engraved border, black, or one of the primary colors—something tough to fake, anyway—"

"Like blue?"

"Why not?"

He turned the corner on Washington and walked down toward Stuart Street for his lunch date with Ken Wagner. It was a fair hike, but the day was fast becoming a stunner; even the Combat Zone seemed renewed by the onset of true spring. By the time he got to Jake Wirth's, he'd worked up quite an appetite.

He was early and Wagner hadn't shown up yet, so Buddy squeezed into a place at the bar between a couple of truck drivers wearing baseball caps to his left and two large men taking up what seemed like three stools on his right, and ordered an Augsburger draft. The baseball caps were discussing the upcoming Hagler-Hearns fight. The two guys on the right were chewing. They had the look of prizefighters themselves. One was black, the other one white.

"Even money," the black guy muttered out of the side of his mouth, looking straight ahead.

"I'll give you three to two on Brockton," the white guy said, washing down the remains of his tongue sandwich with half a beer.

"No bet," the black guy said.

"Faint heart ne'er won zip-ah-dee-doo-dah," the white guy said. He was practically in Buddy's lap.

Buddy knew him, although not to speak to. He'd seen him once outside Jerry Kennedy's office. Kennedy was an attorney who handled everything from personal injury to palimony, and this bruiser was a private dick. Buddy had no idea who the black man was. He shifted his position slightly to give them the once-over, but he wasn't quite casual enough.

"You trying to guess my weight?" the white guy asked him, amiably. "You want, I could stand on your face."

"I'd say about a size 48," Buddy said. "You must have boosted your clothes off the rack at one of Travis McGee's tag sales."

The guy swung toward him and grinned. "You're Buddy Margolies, right?"

"That'd be me," Buddy said.

"The life wearing you down? You look a mite peckish."

"Peckish ain't the half of it," Buddy said.

"You know what they say," the guy told him, "you can fool some of the people all of the time, and all of the people some of the time, but you can't kid a kidder."

"I don't know about that," Buddy said. "Look at Nixon."

"*You* look at Nixon," the guy said.

"We done here?" the black guy asked.

The white guy looked around at him. "You got a wild hair up your nose, or what?" he asked.

"There's no percentage letting the grass grow under your feet," the black guy said, standing up.

"No rest for the wicked," the white guy said, easing off his stool. He laid a twenty on the bar. He was wearing a pale windbreaker, worn chinos, and Puma running shoes, and he had a cannon the size of the *Andrea Doria* stuck in a spring-clip hip holster. He tugged the windbreaker down over it.

The black guy was dressed in Giorgio Armani slacks with pleated pockets, two-hundred-dollar tasseled Swiss loafers, too much gold, and a designer T-shirt that said MAKE MY DAY. He was dangling a London Fog raincoat over one arm in spite of the bright and glorious weather, and Buddy made out the shape of what might have been a sawed-off shotgun underneath.

"Good hunting," Buddy said.

The black guy offered Buddy a steady gaze that probably didn't last much over ten seconds but which seemed to go on for about a minute and a half. Buddy didn't dare break eye contact. The black man's high Asiatic cheekbones and shaved head shone like burnished teak, and looking up into his impassive face was like trying to stare down a tractor-trailer rig. He turned and walked toward the door, and Buddy found his breath. "Does he respond to voice commands?" he croaked.

"Not in my experience," the white guy said, amused. "He's got what you might call an *attitude* toward commands, voice or otherwise. I always make sure he's well-fed before I take him out of his cage."

. Buddy watched the black man make his way out. Ken Wagner was just coming in through the saloon entrance, and the two men exchanged a wary look, neither friendly nor hostile, like predators avoiding each other on a jungle path.

"Take my advice," the other guy said to Buddy as he moved off in the black man's drag coefficient, "get to them before they get to you." He sauntered out. He and Wagner affected not to notice one another as they passed in the aisle.

Wagner took the stool next to Buddy's. "What're you having?"

"Tongue sandwich," Buddy told the bartender.

"Reuben," Wagner said. "And a tall ginger ale, no ice."

Buddy ordered another beer. "What've you got?" he asked the detective.

"What I've got," Wagner said, "is that your friend did six years of a ten-to-fifteen at Walpole. He got out a year ago."

"That figures," Buddy said.

"What else I've got, and this is gratis," Wagner went on, "is that he was tight with a pair of hardcases named Tulkinghorn and Miller. B and E, assault, grand theft auto, weapons charges, you name it, and they were sprung this past month."

"I didn't imagine Alden was keeping the best company," Buddy said. "What was he in for?"

"Forgery," Wagner said. "Counterfeit securities."

Buddy went back out to the VA to talk to Alden, but Alden wasn't in his room. Buddy wandered down to the solarium, and then up to the lounge. Bill Cullen was giving away a nine-hundred-thousand-cubic-foot icebox on TV, but nobody was watching. Buddy flagged down a candy-striper in the hall.

"Mr. Winthrop? No, I haven't seen him, but I only came on at ten. Maybe you should talk to the supervisor."

Buddy angled down to the nurses' station.

"No," the supervisor told him, "I haven't seen

him. He ought to be here," she said, consulting her patient roster.

"You're sure he isn't scheduled for a sponge bath or the bus trip to the VFW?" Buddy asked.

"No," the supervisor said, flatly. "Are you a member of the family?"

"Friend," Buddy said. "Friend of the family."

"He's due for medication at noon," she said, doubtfully.

"What kind of medication?" Buddy asked.

"I'm not at liberty to discuss treatment with you," the nurse said.

"Look, lady," Buddy said, "the guy could barely stay awake yesterday, let alone get to the can under his own steam, and you can stand there and tell me he hobbled out of here without anybody noticing he was trailing a set of hospital jammies under his overcoat?" He swallowed, hard. "I'm sorry," he said. "You must get a lot of this."

That didn't cut any ice with the super. The look in her eyes would have scratched glass.

"Has his son been in to see him today?" Buddy asked. "Big fella, looks like a tackleback for the Patriots, running a little to slack?"

"I have no record of visitors," she said. "Excuse me." She walked away.

Buddy gave it up and went downstairs. He used a pay phone in the parking lot to call home, but all he got was his own answering machine. He stood a moment in thought, and then climbed into his car.

He followed the bus route, starting in Jamaica Plain and working his way in to town, looking at every cocktail lounge and checking out every package store.

It was a tedious business, but he got lucky at the Mass. Ave. intersection, in a corner outlet down the block from Boston City Hospital, where a man answering Alden's description had bought one of those flat half-liters of wine you can fit in a back pocket, along with a fistful of nips and a Megabucks ticket. There were a lot of men in this neighborhood who fit Alden's description, Buddy reflected, and by this time it was getting dark. He turned north, on a hunch, driving up past Symphony Hall and across the bridge into Cambridge.

He picked up Alden's trail again above MIT, in a black bar called Father's Five he'd been thrown out of, and then at the Hi-Lo, a dive between Central and Putnam squares, but it ran cold after eight blocks. He circled. Sitting in the car opposite Goodwill Industries, he considered his options. Alden didn't have anywhere to go, not that Buddy knew of, and here he was, steering for a crash and burn, maybe for keeps this time. There wasn't a bar in Harvard Square that would serve him, not in his condition. If he passed out in the Yard, the campus police would roust him, and if he lay down for a nap in the Common, the local cops would take him in. It was worth a shot. Buddy drove back to police headquarters on Green Street, but came up empty.

"You know," one of the detectives in the second floor told him, "you're going to have to be awful lucky to catch up with him, not if he's in as bad a shape as you say he is. He could be all the way to Lexington by now."

"Lexington's a dry town," Buddy said.

He hit the street again. He stopped at the Plough,

and even Jack's; college bars, these days, but you never knew. The bartender at Jack's had just thrown a couple of guys out.

"How old?" Buddy asked.

"I don't know," she said. "One of them was forty, maybe fifty. The other one was a real crock, three sheets to the wind, you know, not to mention skinny legs."

"There but for the Grace of God," Buddy said, leaving a five on the bar. "How long ago?"

"Half hour, forty-five minutes."

He drove back toward Harvard Square and hung a right on Trowbridge, heading for Cambridge High and Latin. He pulled up outside a Vietnamese grocery and surveyed the park in front of the public library. Any body under a bush might do. He got out of the car and crossed the street to check. He drew a blank. The spotlight hit him as he was coming out.

"Something I can help you with?" the uniformed officer asked him, getting out of the squad car with his hand at his hip.

"Maybe," Buddy said. "Let me show you some ID." He waited for the cop to nod, and then he moved slowly, keeping his free arm away from his body as he pulled out his license. "I already poked my head in at Central Square," he said, handing his ID to the patrolman. "They offered to put it on the radio."

The cop on the sidewalk spoke with the driver, and they both consulted the clipboard on the dash. "Right," the outside cop said, handing Buddy back his photostat. "Good luck." He got back in the blue-and-white.

"Wait," Buddy said. "We're talking about two guys, now, maybe three."

The cop regarded him balefully through the car window.

Buddy held out his hands supplicatingly. "I'm not joking," he said. "This guy's not on his own."

"You are," the patrolman said. They pulled away.

Buddy got back in his car and drove around the block. He found a parking place on Kirkland near the Memorial Church. Alden was a Harvard man, after all. He knew the territory. Buddy got out of the car and walked along past Francis Avenue. He took a right on Divinity past the Busch-Reisinger. There was a little institutional garden hidden in an angle of the Peabody Museum, where Buddy had spoken with Clare Churchill. A pedestrian bridge led across to the Tozzer Wing, and there was a ramp underneath. In that shadowy space was a huge stone ball dating from the pre-Columbian period, some four feet in diameter. The plaque on the pedestal read, simply, "Monumental Stone Sphere," and Buddy caressed it as he passed, for luck. The small park lay beyond, fronted on three sides by the brick façades of the zoological exhibits. It was dark in there, and the blackness was no more inviting than the bottom of a cat box. Buddy went in slowly, giving his eyes time to adjust.

He found the dead man more or less in the middle of the small garden. It was Alden, all right, and he'd been stiff some while. He stank of apricot brandy and sloe gin, from the broken bottles in his pocket. One thing or another would have gotten to him in any case, but someone had made sure. The back of his head was caved in.

Buddy went home. He took a long, hot shower before he called the police. After that, he got into bed and lay awake for what seemed a few too many lifetimes. He felt about a thousand years old, and the weight of his own mortality pressed on him like a blanket of sorrows.

The next morning he set out to find Roger. This time Buddy carried a gun, a .380 Colt compact. It wasn't his usual practice, but he was thinking of Alden with his brains bashed in.

He drove out to the house in Brighton. He made a pass around the circle and kept going without slowing down. The newspapers that had been lying askew on the porch had been taken inside. He took a couple of wrong turns before he found the service road that led in to the fence surrounding the playing fields behind Roger's house, and parked there. Buddy couldn't have said why he was being so cautious, but the night before had left him with a bad taste in his mouth and a nagging uneasiness. He approached the house from the side, on foot, not that there was much cover, and he wondered what anybody watching him would think. He stuck his hands in his pockets and strolled along with his head down, as though he were casting about for something he'd lost in the grass.

There wasn't a sign of life about the bungalow. He tried the back door, but it was locked. Buddy examined the lockset. It was a Schlage, set against a flush jamb, and Buddy forced the latch with a credit card. He was in.

He shut the door silently behind him and stood there with his ears pricked. A radio was playing, faintly, in one of the bedrooms, tuned to Easy-Listening. He heard another sound, a soft slap like a shoeshine cloth. He heard it again. He went through the pantry and into the back hall.

"This is stupid," a man's voice said. "We're getting nowhere fast."

"Hey, it's gonna work, no problem," a second man's voice replied. "I saw it on the cover of an *Argosy* magazine."

They were in the bedroom to Buddy's left.

"Now, Roger, honey," the second man's voice said, "you heard what Hal said. We can make it hurt, if that's what it takes, so why don't you tell old Fritz where you hid them, and then we'll let you have a nice rest."

Roger made no audible reply. Buddy took out his gun and moved past the bedroom on cat feet.

"Show him the color of his guts on the floor," the first voice said. "That'll bring him around quick enough."

Buddy stepped into the doorway. Roger was spread-eagled across the bedframe, face down, his wrists and ankles tied to the bedposts with torn sheets. The mattress was on the floor and the box spring had been reversed so the coils were uppermost, and there was a six-inch hunting knife wedged point-first against Roger's belly. He was keeping himself off the knife by holding his arms and legs stiff, and the effort made him quiver. The guy crouched next to the bed slapped Roger gently on the back of one cramped-up thigh with a doubled-over towel, making his body wiggle, and the knife twitched as the vibrations ran through the bed.

"Stop it," Buddy said, holding the gun out in front of him with both hands. The man at the foot of the bed spun around and made a jump for him. Buddy flinched and shot him. The round caught the guy in the lower lip and split his jaw open. His head snapped back and he went down without a whimper, all in a heap, like a marionette with the strings cut. The second guy started up out of his crouch and froze, looking up the sights of the .380 at Buddy's face. "Get him off of there," Buddy said, "or by Jesus I'll do it myself while you're picking your teeth out of your brains." His voice shook.

The guy reached under Roger for the knife, one-handed, and carefully extracted it. Then he came to his feet and cut the sheets at Roger's wrists. He moved cautiously down to the foot of the bed and cut the ankles free.

"Chuck it," Buddy said, keeping the gun steady.

The guy dropped the knife and shoved it out of reach with his toe.

Buddy moved his head slightly.

The guy backed away from the bed. He never stopped looking at the gun.

"Roger," Buddy said.

Roger lay on the inverted box spring, breathing irregularly. He had wet his pants.

"Roger," Buddy said again. "Roger, it's okay, now; it's over with." He moved to the side of the bed, and reached out to touch Roger's shoulder. He only took his eyes off the other guy for a second, but it was enough.

It was like being hit by a truck. The gun went off harmlessly and spun out of his hand, and then he was down on the floor on his back and the guy was choking him, the crook of his elbow behind Buddy's neck and his forearm pressing down on his throat.

Buddy thrashed helplessly, trying to kick the guy or punch him or just get a grip on him, but his windpipe was being closed off and purple spots were flickering in his vision. Buddy started to go under. He felt as though he were swimming, and the guy's face was changing color. Then Buddy managed to catch a breath. His limbs were numb, but the pressure on his neck was gone. A bare foot above his own face, the other guy's face was darker than boiled beets, and his tongue pushed through his lips.

"Roger," Buddy whispered from his bruised larynx. "No."

The guy's face was almost black, now, and then his neck broke, and he was suddenly cast aside; and there was Roger's face, sweaty and tear-stained, looming over him, and Roger's hands tugging at his shoulders.

"Buddy? Buddy, are you okay? Please, Buddy, say you're all right."

"I'm all right," Buddy said, hoarsely. "Let me up, Roger, for Christ's sake." He rolled over onto his elbow. "Is he dead?" he asked, glancing at the second thug.

"I'm afraid so," Roger said, sitting back on his haunches. "I didn't mean to kill him."

"I'm glad to hear that," Buddy said, "but I'm just as glad you did." His esophagus felt like he'd drunk a quart of bleach. Roger helped him to his feet, and Buddy sat on the edge of the bed and massaged his neck.

"Can I get you a glass of water?" Roger asked him.

"I'll be okay," Buddy said, "just give me a minute."

Roger sat down on the box spring next to Buddy, regarding him with concern. He really was kind of like a dog, Buddy decided, or maybe it was more on the order of being responsible for a man's life if you saved him from drowning or whatever. If that were the case, they were even.

"These . . ." Buddy began. He had to stop and clear his throat. "These guys were in jail with Alden," he told Roger. "They came up with a scheme involving some old bonds Harvey Hatch brought back with him from China as souvenirs, after the war. They weren't worth anything at the time, except as curiosities, but there was reason to believe they might be worth something now. They planned to up the ante by making fakes, and Alden went along because it was a chance to stick it to Sumner Bradford by palming off a batch of counterfeits on him, but to pull it off, they needed the originals, which is where you came in, Roger, because it was you who'd stolen them from Harvey in the first place, isn't that right?"

"Yes," Roger said, simply.

"How old were you?"

"Eight," Roger said.

"And the butterfly?"

"What butterfly?"

"The China Blue," Buddy explained. "Alden needed the China Blue to manufacture an antique ink for the forgeries that would hold up for authentication purposes."

"I didn't take the China Blue," Roger said, bewildered.

"Oh," Buddy said. He looked at the two dead men on the floor by the bed. "Well," he said, "that's that, then."

"I'm glad you're my friend, Buddy," Roger said.

Buddy looked at him. Then he patted his knee. "I'm glad you consider me your friend, Roger," he said.

They heard somebody come in the front door.

"Sit tight," Buddy whispered. He squared his shoulders and stood up slowly, checking his motor reflexes. He retrieved his gun from the corner and slipped out into the hall.

He peeked around the corner of the doorway to the living room. Sumner Bradford stood by the fireplace. He had picked out a cabinet photograph of Maida Hatch from the scattered personal effects strewn about the floor and propped it up on the mantelpiece. The frame was bent and the glass was cracked, but the young woman of twenty who looked forward out of the hopeful past still achieved an expression of erotic petulance that bridged the years. Buddy put away the gun and walked in.

"Two generations of men," the lawyer said, turning around. "Father and son, and neither one able to win her affection."

"It's a long time to carry a torch, counsellor," Buddy said, "but it isn't her fault, is it?"

"No," Bradford said, "mine, I suppose. The damage was already done."

"That's one way of looking at it," Buddy said. He felt Roger come into the room behind him.

"Hello, Roger," Bradford said.

"You killed my father," Roger said.

"No," the lawyer said.

"You caused his death, just like you ruined his life."

"Alden had a lot of practice ruining his own life," Buddy said. "Besides, he wasn't your father."

Roger stared at him.

"Harvey Hatch was your father," Buddy went on. "Your mother married Alden when she found out she was pregnant, and the heroes, here, were out of town."

"No," the lawyer said, again.

"You protected him all your life," Roger burst out. "You kept him out of trouble, you helped him get elected, you even *pimped* for him." He flushed, and hurried on. "You always did his dirty work, even when he got Maida pregnant, with *me*, and you made sure he wasn't around to face the music."

"No," the lawyer said for the third time, "that was me. I'm the one who ran away." He looked at the picture of Maida. "I'm your father, Roger," Sumner Bradford said.

"We all make mistakes," Buddy said, and turned to go. "Sorry about that, Roger," he added.

The Chinese railway bonds turned out to be worthless, of course; the courts deciding that a sovereign government was indeed immune from suit. Sumner Bradford died of a self-inflicted gunshot wound, and poor Roger was twice an orphan. The China Blue was never recovered.

ABOUT THE EDITORS

MATTHEW J. BRUCCOLI, president of Bruccoli-Clark-Layman Publishers, is the author of many books, including a recent biography of Ross Macdonald. He is a professor of English at the University of South Carolina. RICHARD LAYMAN, author of *Shadow Man*, a biography of Dashiell Hammett, is an authority on contemporary crime fiction. Together they edited *The New Black Mask*, a series of eight mystery anthologies.